ALIAS: MITZI & MACK

VICTORIA LANDIS

This book is a work of fiction and is a product of the author's imagination. Names, characters, and places are used fictitiously. Any resemblance to locales or actual persons, living or dead, is entirely coincidental.

Cover design and illustration by Victoria Landis

www.victorialandis.com

www.landisdesignresource.com

ALSO BY VICTORIA LANDIS

Blinke It Away

ISBN-13:978-1492907930
ISBN-10:1492907936

For all the *fools* who never give up, no matter how many times they're told they're crazy misfits. They are the ones who change our world.

ACKNOWLEDGMENTS

I first wrote this story in 1998. Rewrote it in 2003. Rewrote it again in 2008. This final version began in 2010. Along the way, quite a few people read the darned thing. God bless them. I hope they'll have the patience to indulge me one more time and see how their valuable feedback influenced the book.

Thank you Lori, Don, Ann B., Rene, Gill, Louise, Elizabeth, Ann Marie, Cheri, Stephanie W., Pat, Bob, Margie, and Pam.

Thank you to my amazing critique group—Ann, Gregg, Stephanie, Randy, and Richard.

Thank you to Mystery Writers of America, a most awesome organization.

A special thanks to Neil Nyren. I'm not name-dropping (I swear). Neil attends our Sleuthfest writers' conference when he can and is beyond gracious with his time. While chatting with him over a cocktail one evening, I threw my elevator pitch for this book at him, wanting his feedback on a few key components. His answers changed the book dramatically—for the better.

And always, my dearest friends, without whom I'd be nowhere—Ann, Cheryll, Jan, Margie, and Pam.

CHAPTER ONE

"I wish she would stop staring at us," Shirley Nowack whispered.

The saleswoman, with her hair tensed into a precise bun and tiny black-rimmed glasses perched mid-way along her pinched nose, peered over her lenses with an air of disdain. She sat behind a carved and gilded Louis-the-something-or-other desk.

The antique store's phone jangled.

"Popover's Proprietary," the woman said in an arrogant tone. "May I help you?" She kept her icy gaze on Shirley and Shirley's best friend, Dora Flynn.

"We're two old ladies," Shirley said. "What does she think we're going to do? Schlep out of here with a thousand-dollar chair?"

Dora glanced up from the small brass lamp she held in her hand and snickered. "You said *schlep.* I'm rubbing off on you." She returned the saleswoman's glare. "To hell with her."

Shirley winced. "Shhh. She might hear you."

The woman hung up the phone.

"Who cares?" Dora increased her volume. "*She's* here to wait on *us.* We are the customers. She is *the help*—at our beck and call. That's right, isn't it?"

The last sentence, meant for the saleswoman, made Shirley cringe.

The woman glowered.

“Maybe we should go,” Shirley said.

Dora smirked. “She’s nothing but a clerk working for minimum wage plus commission. You know, I’ll bet if I flashed a few hundreds, she’d get on all fours and bark to sell me this overpriced lamp.”

Feeling the heat of blood rushing to her face, Shirley fled to the sidewalk and took several deep breaths.

A minute later, Dora emerged from the shop, held open the door, and turned to yell into the interior. “Enjoyed the warm and welcoming atmosphere of your store.” She let go of the handle. The door closed. With a polished affectation, Dora’s hand brushed something invisible away from her clothing. "I don't want the stink of that snob's energy piggybacking me all day."

“Good heavens,” Shirley said. “That woman made me feel like I did something criminal by simply entering the place, but did you have to say the barking thing?”

“I thought she needed a comeuppance for being so rude. Took me years to stand up for myself. You can’t allow people like her to win. Remember, they can only make you feel bad if you let them.” Dora fluffed her hair and repositioned her huge knock-off Chanel sunglasses. “Don’t let them.”

Shirley eyed Dora’s home-dyed blonde tufts. Dora’s hair had an over-processed texture and hints of pink in the back. She didn’t know how to tell her.

They continued east on Pearl Avenue toward the ocean.

“The island of Sago Beach is a dream,” Shirley said, reveling in the view. “Every time I come here, it’s more beautiful. Like a fantasy place.” She gestured around her, then pointed to a planter overflowing with lavender blooms. “Pretty exotic flowers. What do you suppose these are?"

"No clue."

"Immaculate streets," Shirley said. "Even the parking meters shine like they’ve been scrubbed.”

At the metered spaces, late model BMWs, Audis, or

Mercedes shot reflected beams of sunlight into the fantasy land. Doubled parked here and there were Bentleys, Rolls Royces, and limousines with their engines running. "Do you suppose they're all actually waiting for the rich people to shop?"

"The drivers?" Dora chuckled. "Of course. You don't expect Mrs. Big Deal to wait more than thirty seconds for anything, do you?"

Shirley marveled at the royal palms lining the avenue. She craned her neck to see them rise from wide planters imbedded among the sidewalk pavers. The palms soared sixty feet into the blazing blue sky. How different they were from the anemic withered ones in West Sago Beach where she lived.

Dora shook her head. "Who are you? Fraulein Maria gaping at Captain Von Trapp's house? I've got to get you out of the retirement village more often."

"I *love* that movie." An image of Julie Andrews singing on an Austrian mountaintop danced into her mind.

"I know." Dora took her arm. "Come on."

"Well, it is just so amazing," Shirley said. "I'll bet half of America doesn't know people really live like this, not only on TV."

"Might piss them off, in this economy, if they found out now," Dora said.

Most of Pearl Avenue's buildings were original and conveyed the essence of old South Florida and the Addison Mizner age. They were stucco structures, painted in ochres and earthy terra cotta hues, and accented by dark-wood doors and iron fretwork. In a few places, new jarring angular buildings were jammed between the old and interrupted the pleasant scene. Strange spikes of metal and glass protruded from the façade of one. It looked plain wrong.

The delicate scent of a jasmine vine drew Shirley to a nearby planter box below a shop display window. She loved jasmine. Then she noticed a black-beaded evening gown on a mannequin in the display.

Dora came along beside her. "That's a gorgeous dress. I could never wear it. I'm too stumpy. But with your shape? Ooh-la-la. Stanley would love it on you."

For a flashing moment Shirley saw Stanley, her husband of forty-eight years, dressed in a tuxedo and whirling her, in the dress, on a dance floor. She sighed. "I could never afford that."

"Go in and try it on. What's the harm?"

The thought intimidated Shirley. "Why?"

"For fun. So we can see how you'd look if you were rich. You'd outclass them all." Dora grinned.

Shirley leaned down and pecked Dora on the forehead. "You can be so sweet." She admired the dress some more. "It's probably priced in the thousands."

When Dora didn't respond, Shirley turned to see her peering beyond the mannequins. "What are you staring at?"

Dora's voice raised an octave. "I think that's Catherine Von Cletan in there."

"Who?"

"The rich maven whose picture is plastered on the Sago Beach Journal society pages every week. Always in charge of some charity ball. She's richer than God. She runs this island." Dora lifted her glasses and leaned closer, nearly touching her nose to the glass.

"Runs the place? She's the mayor?" Shirley didn't recall Sago Beach's mayor being a woman.

"No." Dora rolled her eyes. "She's—oh. She's headed this way." She grasped Shirley's arm and spun her so she now faced Dora, her back to the shop door. "I don't want her to think we're staring at her. Pretend we're in a conversation."

"We *are* in a conversation." Shirley started to glance around.

"Stop," Dora said.

Shirley froze.

"Don't look. Talk to me."

"About what?"

"Shhh."

Behind her, Shirley heard the door swoosh, heels clattering on the pavers, and a loud *harrumph* as someone walked to the street. A thick, flowery perfume hit her nose, and she sneezed. She reached into her purse for a tissue.

"Her chauffeur is helping her into her Mercedes now," Dora said. "Did you *see* the diamonds?"

Shirley wiped her nose. "No." She pivoted and watched the chauffeur close the door and return to the driver's seat. "I didn't even see *her*." The black car drove away.

"She had 'em everywhere. Rings, bracelets, earrings. I didn't see a necklace, though. Guess that would have been tacky for midday, huh?" She cackled and poked her elbow into Shirley's side.

"She made a noise like she wasn't too happy," Shirley said.

"Didn't look it, either," Dora said. "Guarantee you the store didn't have anything in her size. She's pretty broad in the beam. Makes me seem skinny. And now that I feel thin by comparison, let's go to Alfred's."

"Who's Alfred? A friend of yours?"

"Don't I wish. No. It's *the* place to see and be seen now. Opened in December." Dora started walking.

"I don't want to be *seen*." Shirley stowed her tissue into a baggie in her purse and hurried to catch up.

"Silly. They won't pay any attention to us. We're nobodies. They'll be gawking at the beautiful people."

"This is the off-season. Even I know the *beautiful* people are in Europe or the Hamptons or somewhere."

"Which is the only reason we'll get in the place. You never know who might be around in the summer." Dora picked up the pace. "Isn't this fun?"

CHAPTER TWO

Fifteen minutes later, Shirley stirred sweetener into iced tea and observed the surroundings from their tapestry-upholstered booth. Alfred's encompassed three dining rooms with large archways connecting them. Dora requested a table in the center room so she could peek into the other two.

Hanging from twenty-foot ceilings, massive crystal chandeliers lent a soft glow to the windowless room, and every niche, arch, and column boasted intricate dark woodwork that gleamed from polishing. Shirley admired the details. Her eyes fell on Dora, seated to her right and leaning sideways straining to see something.

"I think that's Leo Edwards," Dora said. "But the maître d' and the waiter are blocking my view." She glanced at Shirley's tea. "Are you sure you don't want a more festive drink? Here. Try mine." She thrust her Singapore Sling at Shirley.

Shirley took a sip. "It's good."

"Want one?"

"No, thanks. I'm driving, remember?"

"Good," Dora said, "they've moved." She squinted toward the other end of the room. "I'm sure that's Leo Edwards."

"I never heard of him." Keeping track of the *who's who* delighted Dora, but Shirley wasn't interested enough to make the effort.

"He's the guy who started the Bigger, Faster Pizza chain."

"That, I've heard of. My grandkids love their pizza." Shirley followed Dora's gaze. "Where?"

"Right over there." Dora kept her hands near the table, but pointed with her right while shielding it with her left. "Second table from the fountain. In the blue."

The unshaven blond man wore a rumpled sky-blue silk shirt and looked no more than thirty. Two stunning Latina women sat with him. From their sloppy mannerisms, Shirley guessed the trio had been partying too long, on what Stanley would call a *bender.* One woman rubbed his hand and whispered in his ear. The other's hand went under the table. Shirley saw subtle movements in the woman's upper arm and gasped. Leo's eyelids closed, and his lips parted.

Shirley squinted. "Is she doing what I think she's doing? In public? That's disgusting."

"Guess he's having his dessert *before* lunch," Dora whispered. "He's married. And not to either of them. I saw a picture of his wife. She's a stacked blonde."

"How do you remember this stuff?" Shirley tsked. "I will never order another Bigger, Faster pizza." A couple exited the booth to Shirley's left. The dividing wall between booths came to her chin. She watched in fascination as it was stripped, cleaned, and reset with linens, silver, and sparkling crystal. The busboys made almost no sound, and they finished faster than she thought possible.

"I should have dressed fancier." Shirley pulled her sneakered feet closer to the seat.

"Nonsense. It's summer. You look cute in your white top and tennies."

Their handsome, twenty-something waiter brought their lunches. Crab cakes for Shirley and pasta Bolognese for Dora.

Dora gave him a big smile and patted his arm.

He winked at her and left.

Savoring her first bite, Shirley closed her eyes. "Real crab. Very fresh. It's wonderful."

"Look who's coming in," Dora said. "It's Catherine Von Cletan again. He's leading her this way."

The maître d' escorted two women who looked to be in their sixties.

"Which one is Von Cletan?"

"Fat one on the right," Dora said. "See the bracelets and rings flashing?"

"Ah." Both women had money, anyone could see that, but despite her considerable bulk, Von Cletan walked with a regal air. A woman at another table said hello to them as they passed, but they snubbed her. Shirley shook her head at the rude behavior.

"They're going to sit next to us," Dora said. "Wow. Von Cletan shouldn't wear dresses. She's got big ankles. Daikon leg."

"What's that?"

"Japanese radish. I'll explain later."

Von Cletan cast a side-glance at Dora and Shirley as she settled into her booth, her disapproval obvious. Shirley wondered if Dora noticed, then decided she hadn't.

Dora sat gaping, her eyes wide.

Being taller than Dora and seated closest to Von Cletan's booth, Shirley saw the top of Von Cletan's thinning head of hair and her companion's face.

"I can't see anything," Dora whispered. "What are they doing?"

A raspy, sophisticated voice ordered a martini. "You know how I like them, Hamri."

Hamri nodded.

The friend's softer voice asked for Bombay Sapphire and tonic.

"Can you hear them? What are they saying?" Dora seemed ready to jump out of her seat.

"They're ordering drinks," Shirley said.

"What are they having?"

"Shhh." Shirley put a finger to her lips. "Quiet down. A martini and a gin and tonic."

"Which ordered which?"

And so it went for the next thirty minutes. She ate her lunch and encouraged Dora to do the same while relaying almost every word uttered from Von Cletan's table. Shirley, tired of the pretentiousness, wanted to leave Sago Beach and go home.

At last Dora finished, and the check arrived in a brown leather folder with the Alfred's logo embossed on it in gold swirls. Shirley gasped when she glimpsed the total. "Seventy-eight dollars? For a little lunch like that?"

"We're paying for atmosphere." Dora dug her wallet from her purse and pulled out five twenties, depositing them inside the folder. "I'll treat. Hey. We could stay and have coffee."

"No. I'm ready to go."

Dora seemed disappointed, but Shirley didn't care.

"I need to use the potty. Want to come and check out the ladies' room?" Dora asked.

"No. You go ahead. I'll wait here." Repositioning herself on the cushy bench, Shirley watched Dora saunter across the dining floor.

Her *sexy* walk, Dora called it. She used it to attract men. What few men there were. Dora was sixty-eight. There were slim pickings in the dating pool of men her age. Shirley half-smiled as Dora disappeared down a hallway.

The conversation to her left began to register, and she tried to block it out. She'd heard enough complaints about Catherine Von Cletan's household staff. Then a few words pulled her in.

"What about Tony?" the nicer voice said. "You said he was most, um, accommodating."

"Roberta. It's just so . . . so . . ." Von Cletan paused. "Pathetic. That's the word."

"Now, now. I don't believe that's the word needed here," Roberta said. "After all, what else are you to do?"

"It's embarrassing." Von Cletan's rough rasp sounded

choked up. “You’re so fortunate.”

Shirley didn’t dare glance their way. She stared straight ahead and pretended to be fascinated by the small cut-glass vase of pink tulips on her table.

“I don’t know if a total lack of . . ." Roberta lowered her voice. "A total lack of sexual desire is what one would term fortunate.”

Shirley strained to hear.

“You need a better vibrator.”

“I must tell you,” Roberta said. “I have tried. I really have. I even bought a book. Diddled with myself for days to get in the mood. It didn’t work. It was beyond boring.”

Covering her face with her napkin, Shirley couldn’t help snickering.

“I’m sorry to hear that,” Von Cletan said.

“Don’t be. I don’t miss it.”

“Well, I do. And Tony is very . . . courteous. Heaven knows I pay him plenty to be courteous, but I can’t *let go.* I want to feel uninhibited. He’s too young. Too handsome. Too perfect.” Von Cletan sighed. “I’m self-conscious with him. He wouldn’t touch me if he weren’t making good money to do it. I don’t blame him. What forty-year-old man wants a sixty-four-year-old, wrinkly, overweight woman? I’m not fulfilled by the experience.” She paused. “What I wouldn’t do for an older man. One who could still deliver. He’d be wrinkly too, so he wouldn’t care that I am.”

Roberta tittered. “Good luck with that. An old man who’s single, functional in bed, *and* wants a woman his own age? I’m not sure that animal exists.”

“You’re a real balloon popper, aren’t you?” Von Cletan said. “I need another drink.”

“You look pale,” Dora said. “Are you alright?”

Startled, Shirley hadn’t noticed Dora returning until she stood beside her. Gathering her wits and her things, Shirley gazed at her friend and stood. “I’m fine. Let’s leave.”

During the walk to the car, Shirley felt such gratitude for her tall, strong, and willing husband. They still had sex. Not as often as when they were younger, but . . .

On the drive home Dora chattered, but Shirley's mind buzzed with astonishment. An older woman so desperate for a man, she'd pay for sex. She supposed situations like that had always existed, but she'd never heard of them. How could Catherine Von Cletan, or anyone for that matter, get undressed in front of a man young enough to be her child?

Maybe they didn't undress. Maybe the women wore a nightie to bed. Or a robe, and everything happened in the dark.

"That's how I'd do it," Shirley said.

"That's how you'd do what?" Dora asked.

CHAPTER THREE

Stanley Nowack scratched his head, reread the statement, and set it on the dining room table. They'd lost money again in their investment account. He tamped down his rising anxiety and took a deep breath. He didn't understand. The account rebounded a bit when the stock market did, but now the funds weren't doing as well. If this kept up, between what he and Shirley needed each month and the funds' lackluster performance, they would run out of money.

He leaned back in the chair and put his hands over his face. He and Shirley were healthy and strong. Their parents and grandparents all lived well into their nineties.

Unless he did something to change their finances, he and Shirley might spend their last years sleeping on park benches. Or sponging off their children, which was worse.

A car door slammed. He covered the report with the front section of the newspaper and picked up the sports section. Not prepared to share the bad news with Shirley, he wanted a plan of some kind first.

"Goodness, it's lovely out." Shirley came through their townhouse's jalousied front door and kissed him on the cheek.

The smell of fresh air arrived with her, mixed with her usual clean, soapy aroma. Light reflected from her straight, shiny, gray pageboy cut, and the skin crinkles around her moss-green eyes only made them prettier. Her smile cheered him, reinforcing his conviction to delay sharing the bad news until he had at least a glimmer of hope for the situation.

She touched his shoulder. "Have you been outdoors at all today? Besides your crack of dawn trip to the hardware store, I mean."

"Took me till now to fix the darn shower door." He stood and stretched. "How was Sago Beach?"

"Oh, same, same." She headed upstairs. "I'll tell you about it in a minute."

When she disappeared from view, he took the investment report to the downstairs guest room, which doubled as a home office, and filed it in a drawer.

"Where'd you go?" Shirley called. "Stanley?"

"Coming."

She had her face in the refrigerator. "What do you want for dinner?"

"Anything's fine."

She popped up and grinned at him. "Have I told you how much I appreciate you? I am so lucky. Sometimes I forget."

We'll see if you feel that way after I tell you we're going broke, he thought. He smiled at her. "Thanks. Me, too. Tell me about Sago Beach. Did Dora behave herself?"

"For the most part. Dora is Dora, you know. I wish I had her moxie."

"I'm sort of glad you don't."

She described her day, and her words flowed over him about an antique store and a rude clerk, a fancy black dress, then Dora's fascination with some fat rich woman. He nodded along, preoccupied with their finances.

His friend Henry Cushman had mentioned finding a new financial planner a month or two back. Henry seemed pleased with the man's service and advice.

While Shirley finished her day's synopsis, he decided to visit

Henry and ask about the finance guy.

"You need the car anymore?" he asked. "I want to get out for a bit."

"No." She had her back to him, chopping onions on the cutting board. "Dinner's at five-thirty."

"Roger," he said on his way out. He chuckled as he unlocked the Buick. Since retirement nine years earlier, dinnertime was always five-thirty. She didn't need to tell him.

***

The phone on the wall rang. Shirley wiped her hands on a towel and answered.

"Hey, Mom. It's me."

"Nina. Everything all right?" Shirley tucked the receiver between her shoulder and neck and, stretching the curly and tangled old cord, went to continue chopping.

"Yup. Just wanted to be sure you have the new flight information. I emailed it to Dad yesterday. We're coming in next Thursday at eleven. We'll rent a van and be at your place by twelve-thirty. The kids are really looking forward to a warm ocean."

"Sounds great, dear." They chatted for a few minutes, then hung-up.

Shirley couldn't wait to see Nina, her husband George, and their three children, although Sean—the oldest—was twenty-two and entering his senior year of college. Hardly a child.

"He grew up so fast," Shirley said, shaking her head. She pushed the onions into the hamburger mix in the frying pan, covered it, and poured a glass of iced tea. Carrying it into the living room, she found the remote wedged into the side of Stanley's brown recliner and sat on the faded floral-print sofa.

She flipped channels until she found a talk show that seemed promising. One guest left the stage, and the host introduced a woman starring in a new reality show about cougars.

That sounded dangerous. The woman glided onto the set. She was petite, platinum blonde, and in her forties. "She doesn't look strong enough to be working with big cats," Shirley muttered. "She's out of her mind."

As the host interviewed the woman, understanding dawned on Shirley. She watched agape as the woman explained how she lured in and enjoyed very much, thank you, having affairs with men in their twenties. Shirley hit the off switch.

"Goodness. What is going on out there?" Everywhere she turned, it seemed, women were seducing younger men. Where the heck had she been?

CHAPTER FOUR

Two nights later, Shirley invited Dora and her current beau, Morty Lappet, to join them for a dinner out celebrating Stanley's seventy-fourth birthday. They occupied a coveted table by the window. She tried to ignore Morty's disgusting ogling of the waitress and glanced at Dora to see if she noticed.

"For God's sake, stop staring at her boobs." Dora poked Morty in the arm.

Dora had indeed. Shirley watched their buxom brunette waitress blanch, finish pouring the house red from a thick glass carafe, and make a quick escape.

"I wasn't staring." Morty's cheeks reddened.

"You have a bit of drool you might want to have a wipe at," Shirley told him. She grinned at Dora.

"Funny." Morty raised his napkin to his lips.

"Don't let them needle you," Stanley said. "She is a beautiful girl." He turned to Shirley on his left. "But she's too young to be of any real value, not like these women here."

No wonder I love this man, Shirley thought, beaming at him. He never failed to make her feel appreciated. The familiar strains of Tommy Dorsey's version of *String of Pearls,* one of her favorites, floated from the restaurant's speakers and competed with the sounds of conversation, laughter, and silverware clattering on plates.

"What a charmer." Dora lifted her glass. "A toast to Stanley. Happy Birthday to a wonderful friend and one of the hottest men over seventy I've ever seen."

Shirley raised her wine and clinked glasses with them.

"And I'm the other one, right?" Morty asked.

"The other what?" Dora took a long sip, set the wine down, then stared at the ceiling and rubbed her bare arms.

"Never mind."

"Thank you, Dora." Stanley shook his head. "She's just making an old man feel good on his birthday, Morty. One more toast." He placed a hand on Shirley's shoulder. "To my green-eyed girl."

Her eyes met his, and she saw him again as he was in his twenties.

"What'll you have, my dear?" Stanley asked.

Brought back to the present, Shirley perused the daily specials on the laminated menu. "I might do the piccata."

"That's not on the early-bird side of the menu, only the ones over here." Morty reached across the table and jabbed a warted finger on the left page of Shirley's menu.

She peered up from the listings and caught Dora rolling her eyes. "Thank you." Although Morty knew the tab was hers tonight, the man couldn't seem to help himself. She'd saved her winnings from playing tinkle gin for the meal, and she planned to order whatever she wanted.

"I'm having lasagna." Dora put her menu down.

"Veal parmigiana for me," Stanley said.

"I've had that here," Shirley said. "It's salty. You should order chicken marsala. I heard it was excellent."

"Fine. I'll have the marsala," Stanley said.

"And I want the piccata." Shirley took a sip of wine, feeling extravagant.

Morty's incredulous expression suggested she'd gone hog-wild. She plastered a pleasant smile on her face.

The waitress returned to the table. The girl's red, white, and green plastic nametag said Ricky's Thrifty Italian on top and identified her as Jeannie in gold cursive letters. She took their orders.

Morty began to hum *I Dream of Jeannie.*

Dora sent him a scathing glare.

Shirley wished she'd dump Morty. He was thin but doughy, and Shirley avoided staring at his wobbling, fleshy double chin. His face fixed in a permanent frown, he did nothing to redeem his lack of looks by being dismal most of the time. By contrast, Stanley was tall and fit, with a defined face—broad brow, high cheekbones.

"Is that it then, folks?" Jeannie asked.

"One more thing," Dora said. "Could you ask the management to raise the temperature a bit? The vent's blowing on us."

"Yes, please," Shirley said. "I don't want my neck to get stiff." She buttoned her beige cardigan.

"Should I ask them to move us to another table?" Stanley asked.

"To where?" Shirley scanned the dining room packed with seniors in for the early-bird special. At five-thirty, a queue of customers already waited in the entry. The savory aromas of sauces and frying sausage pervaded the dining room, and her stomach responded with a growl.

"I'll ask the manager." Jeannie hustled away.

"What a business," Morty said. "We should open a restaurant. Look at this place. It's a gold mine."

"No, thanks," Stanley said. "To have to please this crowd every night?" He sat back and gestured. "I'm not looking forward to working like a dog at my age."

"That's an odd thing to say. Why would you?" Shirley cast a questioning eye his way.

Stanley grinned and shrugged.

"Okay, Grandpa," Morty said. "How about a miniature golf

course? You can't go wrong with that."

Dora chuckled. "Why don't you do it yourself, Morty?" She nudged Stanley. "Did you hear from your kids?"

"I—"

"Nina and George sent Stanley a beautiful package," Shirley said. "He can't wait to open it. And Fletcher and Janice will join us for cake later at the house."

"Are the little ones coming?" Morty asked.

"I assume so," Stanley said. "I didn't ask."

"They'll come. Fletcher wouldn't dare show up to Grandpa's birthday without them," Shirley said.

Jeannie set down a napkin-lined wicker basket full of gooey garlic rolls.

Shirley and Dora helped themselves.

"Watch it with the garlic," Morty said. "The car's going to reek on the way home."

"Hush up." Dora grabbed another roll for herself and handed one to Stanley. "Garlic is very good for you. Could add years to your life. Everybody knows this. Here." She put one on Morty's plate. "Eat some. If we all do, it won't matter."

After dinner, Stanley held Shirley's hand as they trailed Dora and Morty to the parking lot. The four of them piled into Shirley and Stanley's battered white Buick.

Morty lowered his backseat window.

"What are you doing?" Dora asked. "It's eighty-seven degrees out there. You're letting the heat in."

"The garlic. It stinks in here."

"I told you to have some. Close the window. The wind's messing up my hair."

Morty did so. "Crank the air, Stanley."

In the front passenger seat, Shirley watched monotonous, neon-lit strip malls on Manatee Boulevard flash by. The setting sun cast a pinkish glow on the withered palm trees struggling to survive their entombment in the asphalt parking lots of empty storefronts, nudie bars, and liquor stores. How many of her neighbors in Silver Sago Retirement Village had seen the paradise across the Intracoastal in Sago Beach?

CHAPTER FIVE

"Home at last," Shirley said when Stanley turned into their covered carport. She bustled ahead, unlocked the door, and turned on lights. Her brown sandals clacked against the stark white tile as she walked to the kitchen.

Dora followed her. "What're we having for dessert?"

"There's birthday cake from Plotznik's Bakery in the fridge. Why don't you get it out?" Shirley set placemats, plates, and silverware on the mahogany dining room table, then started the coffeepot.

Dora positioned the cake on a pressed-glass platter. She loved sweets, and it showed. Her shape had morphed into an apple-on-toothpicks, as Nina described it. All stomach and breasts. But her legs stayed slim, not like that Von Cletan woman's chunky ones. Dora wore skirts to show hers off. Tonight though, her emerald-green skirt paled in comparison to her top—a short-sleeve T-shirt plastered with aqua-sequined fish she'd found at the flea market.

A knock rattled the pebbled-glass jalousies on the front door.

"They're here." Shirley made it to the door as Fletcher, her son, let himself in. She hugged him. "Where're Janice and the kids?" She peered beyond the door to the driveway.

"Mom," Fletcher said. "I'm sorry. They couldn't come."

Stanley joined them. "What's the matter? One of the kids sick?"

"Yeah. Something like that." Fletcher handed his father a small box wrapped in shiny yellow paper and tied with a blue bow. "Happy seventy-fourth, Dad. Next year's the biggie."

"Thanks." Stanley placed it on the table next to Nina's present.

Shirley sensed something off-kilter and itched to probe into why his wife and children were no-shows, but wouldn't until Dora and Morty went home. She joined the others in the living room.

Fletcher shook Morty's hand and gave Dora an affectionate peck on the cheek. He sat on the sofa beside Morty and helped himself to the bowl of roasted nuts on the travertine and glass coffee table. "Cashews? Mom, you went all out."

Dora scooted in next to Fletcher. "No one should look this good." She cupped his chin in her hand. "Check this face." Turning his head until he faced his father, she sighed. "Stanley, do you see your son? Such a handsome man."

Fletcher blushed and hugged her. "I love you too, Dora."

"He's a looker, alright. Takes after his mother in that department." Stanley patted Shirley on the arm. "Thank God, the kids resemble you."

They'd done this routine a hundred times. She'd say how the children actually took after him. Tonight Shirley just nodded. What was wrong at Fletcher's house? "Maybe I should call Janice." She headed for the kitchen. "See if she needs help."

"No." Fletcher leaped to a stand. "Don't call her. She's fine. But tired. She wants to rest."

"So who's sick?"

"I suppose she is."

"You suppose? Don't you know? If she's sick, you should be home with her."

"No. She wanted me to come. Said she needed some quiet

after putting the kids to bed."

"Okay." Shirley's internal red-flags did a frantic wave. She cut a glance at Dora, who raised her eyebrows slightly. Fletcher wasn't fooling anyone. She gestured toward the food. "Time for cake and coffee, everyone."

They moved to the dining table and sang an off-key, but heartfelt, rendition of *Happy Birthday* to Stanley. He blew out the one candle on his cake.

Shirley sliced and served while Dora poured the decaf.

"I've been waiting to tell you a story." Dora put the pot on the burner and rejoined them. "It happened a few days ago when we were at the main pool by the clubhouse."

"*You* managed to not tell something for a few days?" Stanley said. "I don't believe it."

Dora balled up her napkin and threw it at him. "Quiet, birthday boy. This is a ripe one. I sat on the pool steps, splashing myself with water now and again. Edna Reilly comes along and sits beside me. She's wearing a new bathing suit, and I could tell she felt good about it. She's lost a bit of weight. She got so heavy for a time."

Shirley murmured her agreement and peeked Fletcher's way, who flinched and looked at Dora.

"I'm sorry," Fletcher said. "Remind me who Edna is."

"She's the one who wears the headbands. She substitutes for our card and mah-jongg groups. Anyway, she says to me that Betty Hackner got herself a new boyfriend. And then she winks." Dora illustrated the exaggerated wink.

"Who cares?" Morty licked icing from the tines of his fork.

"Betty's husband's been gone for two years," Stanley said. "She ought to go out, have some fun." He turned to Fletcher. "Betty's the one who always does a solo in our community show. You know, the blonde?"

Fletcher laughed. "Dad, no offense, but at your age all the ladies are some version of blonde, aren't they?"

"Not your mother."

"I'll ignore that, young man. So," Dora said, "I'm wondering why the wink. I ask Edna, why the wink? And she whispers, 'Betty's *paying* her new boyfriend.'"

"What?" Shirley put her coffee down.

"To do what?" Stanley asked. "Paying him? I don't understand."

"It wasn't clear to me, either," Dora said. "I'm thinking, does it mean she's paying for his dinners and movie tickets? Is the guy broke or what? I mean, Betty's a nice looking woman, only in her early sixties. She doesn't need to be a sugar mama."

"I agree." Shirley picked up the cake knife and a glob of chocolate fell to the table. With her left hand, she rescued the orphaned piece, ate it, and smacked her lips. "Who wants more? There's so much. Eat, please."

"I'm not finished," Dora said. "Edna winks again and nods up at the lifeguard stand. 'That's him,' she says."

"No." Shirley's hand flew to her mouth, causing bits of icing to fly from the knife. She twisted and saw chocolate splatters on the white wall behind her. "Oh, for Pete's sake."

"That's right," Dora said. "Jeff, the young guy with the muscles."

"He couldn't be more than twenty-five," Shirley said.

"Horseshit," Morty said. "I wouldn't believe a word out of Edna's mouth."

"It's ridiculous." Stanley passed his plate to Shirley. "Give me a small piece, please."

"I'm not so sure." Dora retrieved the coffeepot. She poured more for everyone as she continued. "That's what I thought, too. And why I didn't say anything. Edna says it started when Betty wanted to go to the symphony, during *the season.* She wanted a young, handsome escort just once more in her life. Jeff needs to save money to finance a move to California, so she paid him to go with her. Although he's hunky, he seems to have a brain, and he and Betty really got along. Betty told Edna he loves opera."

"It's not that bad," Stanley said. "There are lots of lonely people here. What's wrong with getting a little taste of youth again?"

"You made it sound seedy," Morty said.

"She got a *taste* alright, and more than a little." Dora sat and opened a sweetener packet. "It's become an involved relationship. She's still paying, and they're doing the horizontal boppity bump. It's like that old movie. *Harold and Maude*."

"Man, that's gross." Fletcher made a face.

"That part has to be gossip," Shirley said, aghast. Another one? "You don't believe her, do you?"

"Heck no. Edna's a notorious liar," Dora said. "But yesterday, I saw him enter Betty's apartment in the middle of the afternoon."

"What, were you on a stake-out?" Morty asked.

"No. I needed to return a casserole dish to Elinor. She's part of our mah-jongg group, Fletcher, and she lives right across from Betty. We stood there chatting when Jeff walked up to Betty's place and rang the bell. She let him in, and he didn't leave for an hour."

"You were spying," Morty said.

"Not at all, simply catching up on news. I hadn't seen Elinor in a while," Dora said. "What am I supposed to do? Not talk with a friend because her neighbor has a visitor?"

"I'm not convinced," Shirley said, not wanting to believe it. "Maybe he's giving her massages. I remember someone telling me Jeff was also a licensed massage therapist. Our village board is very picky about who they approve to work at the clubhouse."

"That's got to be it." Stanley looked relieved.

"Think about this," Dora said. "If it were a man in his sixties, dallying with a woman in her twenties, would you have a problem? Movie stars and rich businessmen do it all the time."

"If he paid her, it's prostitution," Morty said.

"It's wrong, even if nobody gets paid," Stanley said.

"I'm thinking it's not safe," Dora said. "I know if someone

that young and gorgeous so much as touched me with *that look* in his eye, you'd have to scrape me off the ceiling."

Fletcher snorted. "You crack me up."

"I hear that massage is very therapeutic." Shirley tilted her head and rubbed her neck. "My doctor's been telling me to try it for my neck and shoulder stiffness. Maybe I should call Jeff and make an appointment."

"God, Mom," Fletcher said. "Not funny."

"Won't happen in this lifetime. You stay away from him." Stanley scowled. "Can I open my presents now?"

"Please." Shirley snickered, tickled she got a rise out of her men. "Start with this gorgeous box from Nina." She pushed it down the table toward Stanley. "I'm dying to know what's in it."

Stanley opened the attached gift card. "Whenever we're blue, we then think of you. You're the heart of our crew, and the one with a clue. We'd never want you to come down with the flu."

"What the heck does that mean?" Morty asked.

"They always write their own poem inside the card." Shirley imagined Nina and her children working on the poem together. "Wasn't that clever?"

"I have no idea what it meant." Stanley grabbed a corner of the paper and began to rip.

"Don't tear it," Shirley said. "It's too beautiful. I want to save it. Peel back the tape and unfold it."

"Forget that," Fletcher said. "Go ahead and rip it."

"You kids will never understand depressions or war time," Dora said. "We were raised by people who saved every scrap of paper and string."

"Money doesn't grow on trees, you know." Handing the unwrinkled sheet of wrap to Shirley, Stanley lifted the box lid. He pushed layers of tissue aside and removed a lustrous, midnight-blue, terry bathrobe.

"Ahhh." Shirley stroked it, then noticed the pocket detail. "Goodness, it's got your monogram on it—in silver. She has the most wonderful taste."

"I want to feel." Dora reached and squeezed a sleeve with both hands. "Ooh. It's thick and cushy. It's the most beautiful robe I've ever seen."

Stanley stood and held the robe against his body. "Looks like it'll fit."

Shirley glanced into the box. "There's more. There are house slippers to match."

"Of course there are," Fletcher said, sarcasm dripping.

"Nina thinks of everything." Ignoring Fletcher, Shirley dug the slippers out and handed them to Stanley. "She's worried about you getting the flu. That's what the poem was about."

"Yes, she's thoughtful," Fletcher said. "Except it's the middle of summer. In South Florida. Nobody gets the flu in July."

"That doesn't matter," Stanley said. "Your sister knows how I freeze when your mother puts the air down."

"Why *do* you do that, Mom? Outside, the air is like an oven, and you could store sides of beef in here."

"And it's such a waste of money," Morty said.

"It's much warmer than the restaurant was," Dora said. "Now *that* was a refrigerator."

"Morty's right," Stanley said. "It's expensive and a waste." He walked to the thermostat, changed the setting, then sat again. "Now I want to see what you and Janice gave me."

Shirley stared, disbelieving. He never overruled her on the temperature. She ignored Morty's gloat.

Laying the robe and slippers in their box, Stanley put Fletcher's gift on his place mat.

"It's store-wrapped." Shirley focused on the yellow box. "Janice *must* be ill. I've never seen a present from you two that was store-wrapped."

Inside the small box sat a hinged watch case. Stanley lifted the lid.

Shirley leaned over him and gasped. A gold watch gleamed

against black velvet.

"Holy Moses." Stanley stared at it. "Is it real? I mean, really a gold watch?"

"That's a beauty." Morty rose from his seat and moved around the table. "Let me see that. Looks expensive."

"I hope you didn't overdo it." Shirley squinted at the name on the dial. "What brand is it? Pie-a-jet?"

"You pronounce it *pee-ah-zhay*," Fletcher said.

"Have you heard of that before, Stanley?" Shirley said.

"No."

"I have," Dora said. "They make a *very* good brand. First class stuff."

"Thank you." Stanley stood and hugged Fletcher. "It's beautiful. I've never had a watch anything like this."

"Well, it's about time you did," Fletcher said. "You deserve it, Dad."

Removing the trusty Timex that Shirley bought him thirty years earlier, Stanley tried on the Piaget. "Wow. Between this and the bathrobe, people are going to think we hit the lottery."

"Only if you wander the streets in your robe, dear." Shirley gathered up plates and silver and carted them to the sink, thinking Fletcher overspent. Plus her husband was in danger of joining Morty's dark side in the battle of the cheapskates versus the normal people. Was there a full moon?

Dora joined Shirley in the kitchen, carrying the remaining plates. "I'll help you clean up, then Morty and I are going. Okay, love?"

"Why so early?" Shirley asked. "I thought we'd play cards."

"I'm in the mood, you know? If I don't get him home soon, he'll fall asleep, what with the two desserts he ate and the wine at dinner. And he is no good in the morning, believe me. You understand, don't you?"

"Sure." Shirley cringed at the image. "We'll play another night."

"You're a peach, doll." Dora gave her a hug.

CHAPTER SIX

Shirley squinted at the spattered white wall. She dabbed the wet sponge again on one of the chocolate spots. "Darn it. Without my glasses, I can't tell if I got it off or made it worse." Her right knee cracked as she rose from the floor.

"Fletcher, take a look here," she said.

Fletcher walked to her and stared at the spot. "It's wet now, so it looks darker. Guess you'll have to wait till it dries before you know."

The sound of water rushing through pipes, then the creak of the wooden treads announced Stanley's return from upstairs. Shirley turned to see him heading for his recliner in the living room.

"It's getting late. I need to go. Happy birthday, Dad. Thanks for the cake, Mom." Fletcher hurried to the door.

"Just a second, buster." Shirley set the sponge on the counter.

Fletcher froze in mid-step, then did a slow pivot toward her. "Me?"

"Yes, you." She frowned at Stanley, who froze with the TV remote poised in mid-air and aimed at the television. "Aren't you going to ask your son anything?"

Stanley's eyebrows rose. "But it's my birthday."

"You know as well as I do something's up." She faced Fletcher. "What is it? Your father and I can both tell when you're dodging us. What's the matter at your house? You and Janice have a fight?"

"We'll talk about it another time." Fletcher gestured to Stanley. "It's his birthday."

"For corn's sake. He's not five. Now explain what the problem is." Shirley crossed her arms and gave him her sternest stare.

"You might as well." Stanley set the remote on the coffee table. "She'll call Janice the second you leave anyway."

Fletcher exhaled and sat at the table, looking resigned. "I wanted to wait, but okay. We're divorcing. I moved out two days ago."

Glancing at Stanley, Shirley sighed and pulled out a chair. "I knew it. Somehow I knew it was really bad." She sat, biting back the expletives she wanted to scream.

"What's her name?" Stanley left his recliner and stood in front of Fletcher and Shirley.

"This is why I didn't want to tell you," Fletcher said. "You're jumping to the wrong conclusion."

Relief flooded Shirley. There was hope.

"You didn't cheat on Janice?" Stanley asked.

"I suppose—technically," Fletcher said.

And—poof. Hope evaporated. Gone with the last wisp of smoke from the birthday candle. "Technically?" Shirley said.

"Janice and I haven't slept with each other in a year. We've been no more than roommates. She's probably found someone else, too."

"With two little kids? I doubt that," Stanley said. "This is your second divorce. And for the same reason. You cheated on Lauren also."

"With Janice," Shirley said, shaking her head.

"Will you try counseling this time?"

"There's no point," Fletcher said.

"What about Alice and Tyler?" Shirley said. "Isn't it worth trying to fix things for them?"

"Why throw away the last six years?" Stanley said.

"I have to," Fletcher said. "I'm in love with another woman."

Stanley rolled his eyes. "You're always falling in love. What's this one's name?"

"Tanya. Tanya Monroe." Fletcher stood. "Don't look at me like that. Come on, almost fifty years together? You can't tell me that either of you never once cheated." He stared at Shirley, then Stanley.

"No," Shirley said.

Stanley cleared his throat and seemed a little nonplussed.

Standing, Shirley faced Stanley. "Well?"

"No. I never cheated on you."

"You hesitated. You came close, didn't you?" Fletcher said. "See? And you're a rock of stability. If it can happen to you, it can happen to anybody. People fall out of love all the time."

His face reddening, Stanley put a hand on Shirley's shoulder. "It was nothing."

She jerked away from him. "Define nothing."

"Wait a minute. We're talking about our son the serial cheater. You and I can square things later."

"Whoa." Fletcher backed toward the door. "You know what? At forty-six, I don't need my parents in my personal business. You wanted to know. Now you do. I'm done. Happy birthday, Dad." He let himself out.

Shirley watched his car drive away, then turned to Stanley, not sure what happened.

He looked guilty.

"So square it now." Her mind raced through their history together, trying to find a time when things weren't good between them.

"Aw, honey." Stanley tried to pull her close.

She batted him away. "Who was it? And when?"

He let out a deep breath. "It's not important. It was ages ago. I haven't thought about it in years. Nothing happened."

Clamping her jaws together, she stared—hard—into his eyes.

"Fine." Stanley sat on the chair Fletcher vacated. "Remember Grace Berkus?"

An image of a hefty redhead with forty-two-double-d's flashed into Shirley's mind. "Our neighbor? That trashy woman who guzzled box wine? Married to Big Jim?"

"She flirted with me a lot."

"She threw herself at every man on our street. All the wives knew it. You actually thought about sleeping with her?" The sting of betrayal zinged her. "I can't believe it. Why?"

"At the time, you always seemed mad at me. You were going through menopause. I was lonely." He touched her hand. "But I relied on my commitment to you. I'm glad I did. No one could ever replace you."

Those difficult years came flooding back to her. She'd felt horrible and unbalanced every day, like she didn't fit in her body anymore. She'd lashed out at Stanley.

"I remember," she said. "I *was* awful to you."

Standing, he pulled her close and enveloped her in his arms.

Her able and strong husband nuzzled into her neck. It felt so good.

"It's my birthday, and it ended on a sour note," he whispered. "What do you say we go upstairs and cheer each other up? It's been a while."

She felt a sappy smile take over her face, and as he led her to the bedroom, she counted her blessings and thought of that lonely rich woman nobody loved.

CHAPTER SEVEN

"At least Fletcher can afford to support them." Dora's chubby fingers hovered above one of the ivory-colored tiles, her face a study of deep concentration.

"Play one already," Elinor Gulicky said. "I could've knit a sweater by now."

Shirley watched Elinor push her glasses up—again. The weight of the thick lenses kept them in a perpetual slide down her sharp nose. "Why don't you wear contacts?"

"I've thought about it," Elinor said. "But I hate the feeling of anything in my eyes."

Two days after Stanley's birthday and Fletcher's divorce news, Shirley sat around a gray folding card table with Dora, Edna Reilly, and Elinor in Dora's ground floor living room playing mah-jongg. The afternoon light streaming through the awning windows highlighted floating dust motes, and the aroma of baked brownies lingered.

"I hate losing another daughter-in-law," Shirley said. "I've become attached."

Dora placed her tile, then looked at Shirley. "Look at the bright side. You know what Ginny's going through."

"Who?" Shirley asked.

"You know," Edna said. "Ginny McElroy? Used to be on

Dora's bowling team. She's got that huge mole on her cheek."

"She really does need to pluck the hairs from that brown mountain," Dora said.

"Mow the lawn's more like it," Edna said. "I think she's part Lebanese or something."

"That explains her lack of wrinkles," Dora said. "I think I'd rather have smooth skin and have to eliminate the extra hair than the other way around."

"Who's going to tell her? You're the bravest," Elinor said to Dora, then turned to Shirley. "Ginny's daughter and four grandchildren had to move in when the husband dumped them."

"If you leave it to me, one of these days I'll have a glass of wine too many and go at her with the tweezers," Dora said. "Better if one of you tells her she's scaring people with that nasty thing. Subtlety isn't my strong suit, and you know it."

"Shirley, you could do it," Elinor said. "You're nice. She won't hate *you*."

"I've never met her," Shirley said. "Enough about a mole. You said I was lucky?"

"Right. The son-in-law. Said he didn't have any money." Dora shook her head. "A year later, and he's crying poverty. The daughter's got to threaten him with court action to collect the measly six hundred a month he's supposed to give her."

Shirley nodded, wondering how these three knew Ginny's private business so well, then recalled that Dora's story about Betty Hackner's young lover came from Edna. She was the queen of Silver Sago Village gossip.

"I haven't seen Ginny since May." Edna shrugged. "I hear it's not going well." The pink headband holding back her curly brown hair showcased an inch of gray roots. She wore tiny, jointed pink flamingo earrings that bobbled whenever her head moved.

"I had lunch with her awhile back," Elinor said. "The noise level in the house gave her headaches, and oh, was it messy. Four grandchildren, can you imagine at our age? She was going bonkers."

"That would be the killer for me," Edna said. "The noise. I cherish my peace and quiet."

"Well, you raised five boys. It's a wonder you didn't *accidentally* misplace one of them. I think I'd have been sorely tempted." Shirley pushed her chair back. "I'm getting more iced tea. Anybody want a refill?"

"You're still shell-shocked, Edna. I can't imagine the bedlam," Dora said.

Shirley glanced out the window, couldn't believe the scene, and burst into laughter. "Aagghh." She pointed.

Shrieks and giggles erupted. The women rushed to the window.

An ancient man inched his way across the parking lot, moving with great difficulty and leaning on a three-pronged metal cane. Wearing a brown suit jacket with matching vest, white shirt, and a dapper striped bow-tie, he exuded an air of old-world dignity as he proceeded.

However, the man wore nothing else. Naked from the waist down, he had no boxers, no socks, no shoes. The skin hung loose and baggy from his stick-like thighs.

"Old Mr. Peters got away from his nurse again." Laughing, Dora wiped at tears. "I'm sorry. I've got to sit down."

"You'd think his dingle would feel the breeze and tip him off that something's amiss," Edna said. "Poor soul."

"How old is he?" Shirley asked.

"Got to be ninety or more," Dora said. "He seemed fine until his wife died just before Christmas. Then he started doing the weirdest things. These last two months, stunts like this happen all the time, though I've never seen him without his pants before."

"Well, there's a mercy," Edna said.

"Bless his old heart. He belongs in a home," Shirley said.

"Wow. And I thought gravity did a number on women," Dora said.

Edna whistled. "Yes, indeed. Those are some stretched out, low hanging—"

"Edna, stop," Shirley said.

"That's why I wouldn't let my husband wear boxers," Dora said. "Tighty-whities kept him in shape till the day he passed. I think Mr. Peters' daughter in Sarasota arranged for him to go to an assisted-living facility near her."

"You mean his apartment's going to be available?" Elinor asked. "I'd love to move to a ground floor unit."

"Spoken like a true ex-New Yorker," Shirley said.

"I'll mention it to his nurse, to pass along to the daughter," Dora said. "It would be much better for you."

"There, but for the grace of God." Shirley's mirth subsided, and the awful idea that she and Stanley might someday be in a similar condition frightened her. What if Stanley went first? Would Nina and Fletcher try to micro-manage her, make decisions for her? Move her back to New Jersey? Nina would for sure. Her daughter was a compulsive detail person—and bossy about it. She shuddered at the thought and gestured to the door. "Come on, girls. We need to help him."

"Here comes the nurse," Elinor said.

A middle-aged woman in a blue uniform ran to Mr. Peters, put her arm around him, and turned him the other way. She sent a pleasant wave to the women peering through Dora's glass, half-smiled, and led the man home.

"Too late," Dora said. "We've been busted."

"She looks like a nice woman," Shirley said. "I hope she's sweet with him. Where were we, ladies?"

"Yep, show's over," Edna said. "I believe it was up to me. And are you ever going to serve those brownies, Dora?"

CHAPTER EIGHT

A few days later, after breakfast, Stanley fished the investment file out of the drawer and brought it to the table. He sat beside Shirley and waited for her to glance up from the newspaper.

Her eyes stared into his. "I know that look. What's the matter?"

"I've made some horrible choices, it seems." He frowned. "And I'm so sorry."

"What *kind* of choices?" Her voice had an edge of suspicion.

"Nothing bad. Well, that's not true. It's bad, but . . . Let me start over." He wiped his brow. He felt like such a failure, it made him sick. "It's about our finances. I miscalculated and made some awful decisions. Things haven't worked the way I planned. We're running out of money."

Her face was pure confusion.

"We are spending too much," he said.

She tilted her head. "*We* spend too much? You're kidding."

"I mean, it's costing us way more to live than I figured nine years ago. Every year gets more expensive. Our investments rose again when the stock market rebounded, but the type of funds we have didn't go anywhere near their pre-recession levels. I should have switched them to something else, but I didn't know to. It's my fault."

"How bad is this situation?"

"If we want to maintain our lifestyle, such as it is, we'll have to start dipping into the principal, not just take the interest anymore. Every year, it'll dwindle. We'll have less and less to live on. If we live another ten years, knock wood, with a lot of luck it may work out okay." He rapped his knuckles on the table. "But what if it's another twenty for one or both of us? Or what if one of us needs hospitalization or continuous care? We'll be wiped out."

"This is terrible. How long have you known?"

"Not long. At first I thought it was a matter of time until the funds did better. I don't think we can afford to wait and see if that happens. We need to get jobs. If we can bring in enough to cover our expenses every month, we may not have to sell the townhouse."

Her eyes grew huge. "I am not selling my home." She stared at the front windows. "A job? Doing what? Who would hire us at our ages?"

"It's making me ill thinking how I messed things up. I'm so sorry." He reached for her.

She avoided him and walked into the kitchen.

"I'm sure you've noticed senior citizens working at Happy Mart," he said.

She whipped around to face him. "Everyone we know shops there. I am *not* going to wait on my friends in a tacky purple smock while they pity me behind my back. They already know we're tight on cash, but that would be humiliating."

"You won't have to. I applied there two days ago. The manager said I could start as a greeter after Nina's visit. I'm sure you'll find something better." He sighed. Her reaction was about what he'd expected. "There's hope."

Silence followed, and he winced at the glare she sent his way. She crossed her arms.

"I went to see Henry Cushman," Stanley said. "A while ago,

he told me about his new financial guy, Alexander Weiss. Alexander put him in slightly more aggressive investments, and Henry's pleased with the results." He gauged her mood—the anger persisted. "I met with Alexander. He thinks he should place most of what we've got left into the same fund as Henry. If we lived off our job earnings, then we could get back faster and not have to work more than a few years. I think."

"What about Fletcher?" Shirley said. "He's a disaster with women, but with money, he's good. Why don't you have him look it over?"

"No," Stanley said. "You know I don't want the kids privy to our private finances." Having Fletcher and Nina learn their dad screwed things up was more than he could take.

"I'm not too thrilled having them know our private business either, but this is a serious situation. Can't you swallow your pride a little?"

That hurt. "It isn't my pride. At this point, it's academic. The damage is done. Say I let Fletcher review things. He'll say what's gone is gone, and we need to take more aggressive steps with what's left. Same as Alexander Weiss told me. Fletcher would tell Nina. You know he would. Then we have the kids nagging us all the time, asking about it. How dare we go to a movie? How dare we go out to dinner? Nina would drive us nuts and want to know where every blasted cent is going. You know I adore her, but she's a control freak. I'm telling you it will drive a stake right through our relationship with the kids."

She nodded. "You're right. She would obsess over it."

"They both would."

"This isn't fair," Shirley said. "We did everything right. Scrimped and saved. Drove every car we had until it rusted apart." She threw her hands in the air. "Why us? We might as well have spent as much as we could on vacations and fun, actual *fun*, and we would have wound up in the same place we are now." Her face took on a faraway look. "I so, *so* wanted to go to Paris one day. Since I was a kid. Remember? We talked about it all the time when we got married." Her mouth set in a determined frown. "Then the children came, and we stopped talking about it. My dream . . . faded away."

"I've always wanted to see Italy. We talked about that, too. It's not only us. Lots of people are stuck in this mess."

"I don't care," she shouted. "We're in this situation, and we don't deserve it." She sat across the table and shook her head. "Never, in a million years, would I have believed it if someone told me twenty years ago that this is where we'd wind up."

CHAPTER NINE

Fletcher felt high with euphoria. Tanya lay naked on her back beside him, her breasts joggling as her chest heaved for air. His heart continued to hammer.

She opened her eyes and smiled. "That was epic. You're amazing." She stroked his cheek.

Her seductive body stunned him. He couldn't comprehend how much he craved her. Every time they made love, his desire intensified. They were three months into their affair, and he still *could not get enough.*

"Say something," she whispered.

He grinned. "I . . . I can't believe you're real. And that you want me."

"Want you?" She propped herself up on one elbow. "I can't help myself."

Fletcher watched her gorgeous breasts fall into place, her long blonde hair cascading around them, then studied her narrow waist curving to her hip.

"Yoo-hoo." She giggled. "Over here."

Her big golden-brown eyes stared into his. He saw endless days of happiness in them. Finally, this was the connection he'd always imagined. It had to be.

"You are hot. Like—all I want to do is stay in bed with

you—hot. You're spoiling me."

"The gray hairs and wrinkles don't scare you?" He'd considered dying his hair.

She leaned in and kissed his chest. "Stop asking me that. I told you, I've always been totally into older men." She returned to lying on her back and closed her eyes. "I can't understand how your wife didn't want to have sex anymore. It's not because you've lost your mojo, baby, 'cause you've got it. I know, maybe she's really gay, but wanted to have some kids, and didn't know how to tell you."

"I don't think Janice is gay." When he first took up with Janice, he was married to Lauren, his first wife. The same thing happened. Lauren, after a few years, never seemed to be in the mood. Their lives revolved around Katie, their daughter, now ten. He loved them, but felt alone then.

A raven-haired beguiling temptress introduced herself as Janice LaDianetto at a party given by his and Lauren's neighbors. Lauren said she had a headache and left the party early, insisting Fletcher stay. He did. Janice and he, overwhelmed by lust and tequila, found their way to her car. Before her, he'd had a few quick, meant-nothing affairs, but he fell hard for Janice.

"Well, whatever her deal is," Tanya said, "she's a fool." She sat, stretched, grabbed an oversized white T-shirt from the floor, and slipped it on. "Did you decide where you're taking me Saturday night? You said you wanted to do something special." She turned to face him.

"I think I mentioned my sister's in town with her family?" He hoped Tanya liked his plan.

She looked apprehensive. "Yeah."

"I told my parents I'm bringing you to dinner at their house Saturday night. It's time to meet them and my kids. They're going to love you." He stood and pulled on his boxers.

Her face fell. "I don't know."

"It'll be great. I want you to go. Please?"

Her lips formed a full pout. "But that's not special. You

made me think we'd go somewhere fancy and expensive."

Even unhappy, she was sexy. He scrambled for an edge. "Tell you what. You come meet my family, and afterward I'll take you to the Scorpion Club on South Beach. We'll stay out all night dancing if you want."

"You can get us into the Scorpion?" Her eyes grew huge. "You've been holding out on me, dude." A sly smile crept onto her face.

"Got to keep some things a surprise." He hated nightclubbing. "A friend of mine knows the owner."

"Yeah? What else haven't you told me?" She walked to him, placed her hands on the waistband of his boxers, and pulled them down.

"No." He gave her a gentle push. "We'll be late for work. I'll make the coffee."

"I don't care." She kissed him on the lips, then kept moving south.

"Shit." His body didn't care about work either, it seemed.

CHAPTER TEN

"He's bringing her here tonight?" Nina sounded incredulous.

Shirley nodded. "I hate the idea, too. But he insisted. Said he wouldn't show up at all unless he could bring Tanya." She peeked around the corner of the kitchen to see who might overhear them in the living room. George, Nina's husband, sat on the sofa with his feet on the coffee table, his eyelids drooping. Video game sounds wafted from the spare bedroom.

"George looks exhausted." Shirley leaned against the counter.

"He'll get over it." Nina sat at the tiny dinette table. "Finish about the bimbo."

"She's his soul mate." Shirley shuddered. "What does that mean, anyway? Every time he falls in love, he swears he's found his soul mate." She opened the refrigerator and grabbed the mayonnaise. "Don't forget about the macaroni."

Nina checked her watch, then looked at the boiling pasta on the stove. "One more minute. If the impact of his actions weren't so tragic, it'd be hilarious. How the heck did Fletch come from this family? You, Dad, and me, none of us are so easily led astray." She walked to the sink, positioned the stainless colander, and donned oven mitts.

"My Uncle Patrick. Grandmom's brother?" Shirley said.

"He was the only one on either side of the family who couldn't keep his particular in his pants. If you'll forgive my bluntness."

Nina snickered as she turned off the burner, lifted the pot, and drained the noodles.

Steam fogged the area, and Shirley stepped back.

"Have you spoken to Janice?" Nina asked.

"I called her. Said she wasn't ready to talk about it yet."

Throwing the mitts into a drawer, Nina smiled. "At least she's willing to let us have the kids tonight. Some women would have been bitchy about it."

"Janice is a thoughtful girl. Just the same, I warned your father and Sean when they left here to pick up Tyler and Alice not to say anything to Janice about Tanya coming tonight."

"Mom. Janice is not thoughtful. She was the other woman, also. Lauren was devastated. If you ask me, Janice got what she deserved."

Shirley poured more iced tea into their glasses on the counter. "I know you never liked Janice because of that. But I'm more practical. I have to get along with my ex-daughters-in-law if I want to see my grandchildren." She carried the teas to the dinette and sat. "The noodles have to cool before we can add the mayo. Have a seat."

"Think he'll marry this one?" Nina sat, frowning.

"Lord, I pray not. Two alimony payments and support for three children? He can't afford to get married again." What if he has to live with us, Shirley thought, panicking.

"I think he's doing better than you know," Nina said.

"I sure hope you're right. Your father and I can't afford to take him in." She realized, after they were out, how her words betrayed her.

"What? Are you and Dad hurting?" Nina's brows narrowed. "Are you in trouble?"

"No." Shirley forced a smile. "Of course not. I meant we don't *want* him to live with us. We have such incompatible lifestyles. I misspoke."

"Uh-huh." Nina took a sip of her tea. "What's Tanya like? She another brunette?"

"She's an *angel.*" Shirley imitated Fletcher's inflection from a phone call she had with him earlier. "She's *perfect.* I'm going to *love* her." She waved her hand, then sighed. "She's twenty-four and a blonde."

"*Twenty–four?*" Nina's eyes widened. "Is he nuts? His oldest nephew's almost twenty-two. Your son is a fool being led around by his peck—his *particular.*"

"Aren't you exaggerating a bit? Fletcher is a good man. He's got a problem, though."

"Can we have a snack? We're hungry."

Nina's teenagers, Mary Ann and Charles, rounded the corner and entered the kitchen.

"Dad's sleeping again," Mary Ann said. She gave Shirley a brief hug and stroked her hair. "Grandma, you have the prettiest hair."

Feeling a rush of emotion, Shirley blinked back tears. "Honey, you can have anything you want." She stood and enfolded her in her arms, enjoying the baby powder scent Mary Ann favored.

Charles rolled his eyes. "Suck up."

Shirley laughed. "Get over here and hug me."

The thirteen-year-old boy did, and Shirley squeezed the two of them as hard as she could. "Goodness, I miss seeing you kids."

She fixed a plate of cheese and crackers and sent them back to their video game. She sighed again, watching them walk away.

"You'd give them anything, wouldn't you?" Nina asked.

Shirley nodded. "Probably."

"What happened to the woman who raised me? Who wouldn't cut me slack if my life depended on it?"

"That's different." Shirley chuckled. "My job is to spoil them rotten, then hand them back. It's your problem." She lowered her voice. "George has done little but sleep since you got here on Thursday. Do you think he's okay?"

Nina shrugged. "He's been working a lot of night hours. Got a few clients looking at some expensive restaurant spaces, and they expect to be wined and dined in those neighborhoods in prime time. At night. We're not complaining. After the last few years, any business in commercial real estate is wonderful. Let him work his ass off."

CHAPTER ELEVEN

Fletcher heard dishes clinking, television noises, and conversational tones from inside as he and Tanya approached his parents' door. "Ready?"

She nodded.

He knocked, then opened it. The townhouse was abuzz with activity. Nina and his mother were busy in the kitchen, and George, Sean, and his father were talking in the living room. His youngest children, five-year-old Tyler and three-year-old Alice, played with blocks on the floor.

Tyler glanced up. "Daddy," he yelled. He dropped his blocks and ran to him.

Alice followed, making small shrieking sounds.

Fletcher picked Tyler up and swung him around. "My man." He kissed him on the cheek, then bent and swept Alice up with the other arm and kissed her. "Hey, sweet girl. Got a kiss for Daddy?"

Alice pecked him, then wriggled. "I want down."

He set her on her feet, and she went back to her project.

"Where's Katie?" he asked Tyler.

"She didn't want to play with us. She's with the big kids."

"I see." He set Tyler down. "This is Tanya. Tanya, my son, Tyler."

Tanya smiled at him. "Hey there, little fella."

Tyler looked confused, then ran to Alice and the blocks.

"I don't think they like me," Tanya whispered.

He put his arm around her. "They're young. They'll like you when they get to know you." He steered her further into the living room where his father, George, and Sean sat gape-mouthed, staring at Tanya. All three stood up. Exactly the reaction he'd hoped for. He felt like a winner.

"Everybody," Fletcher said, "this is Tanya. Tanya, my dad, my sister's husband George, and my nephew, Sean."

Tanya flashed a brilliant smile. "So nice to finally meet you." One by one, she shook their hands.

"Um. Yes," Stanley said.

George and Sean both muttered something.

Fletcher turned Tanya toward the kitchen. "Now to meet my mom."

As they walked away, he heard Sean say, "Holy crap."

It made Fletcher's whole week, maybe his whole year.

***

"Mom, did you see them come in?" Nina, her hands in the sink rinsing romaine leaves, nudged her shoulder into Shirley's.

"Yes, I did," Shirley said. "But I hardly caught of glimpse of her." She set the knife on the cutting board. "I suppose we should be polite and go out there." She headed for the living room and almost walked into Fletcher as he and Tanya entered the kitchen.

"Oh. Sorry." Shirley backed up a step.

Fletcher hugged her. "Mom, this is Tanya." He beamed at his girlfriend.

Tanya smiled. "Hi, Mrs. Nowack. Very nice to meet you." She extended a hand.

Shirley stared at Tanya's hand. The girl had black fingernails with tiny pink polka dots on them. She shook the hand, then assessed the rest of her. About five-six, tanned, short upper torso on top of long thin legs, long blonde hair with bangs, and a perfect complexion. She wore a denim miniskirt and an unbuttoned white dress shirt over a yellow T-shirt. It was hard not to stare at her enormous breasts straining the fabric of the tee. No wonder her son seemed a dribbling idiot.

"I'm Nina, Fletch's sister." Nina joined them. "What? No hug for me?"

Fletcher nodded. "Hey, Stretch."

Nina wrapped her arms around him, rocked him sideways, then pushed away. "You don't look too damaged."

Tanya seemed puzzled. "Fletch and *stretch*?"

"From when we were little. Nina was the tallest in the neighborhood for years. And it rhymes, so—you know kids."

Nina placed a hand on Shirley's arm. "Mom, say hello to Tanya."

Shirley shook off her daze. "Hello." She looked at Nina, who wore a frozen smile.

"You two look busy with the cooking. Is there anything I can do to help?" Tanya said.

"No, we can—"

"Yes," Nina said. "Absolutely. Fletch, go hang with the men. We'll call you if we need you." She ushered Tanya to the dinette table. "Sit. You can cut vegetables while we get acquainted."

Giving her daughter a warning glance, Shirley set another cutting board, a paring knife, and two cucumbers on the table. Nina could be intimidating, and Shirley wanted things to be pleasant. The girl might wind up as part of the family. What if this one also wanted children? Shirley caught herself before she made a tsk sound.

When Tanya settled in her chair, Nina brought a paper bag full of corn and sat across from Tanya.

"I was going to shuck those," Shirley said.

"You relax," Nina said. "Drink your tea."

Shirley leaned against the counter and picked up her glass.

Tanya examined the knife, then began to cut a cucumber.

"Make the slices thin, please," Nina said. "Now, tell us all about yourself and how you and Fletch met."

***

Fletcher grinned as he passed through the living room on his way to say hello to Katie, MaryAnn, and Charles. He sensed a new respect from George and Sean. Before this, George always made him feel inferior. Now, George's envy showed. He and Nina were approaching their twenty-sixth anniversary. George oozed with the boredom of so many years with one woman. Fletcher could almost feel it—a vapor cloud buzzing with the electricity of insurrection wafting around him. Maybe he should warn Nina, he thought as he entered the spare room. Then again, maybe not. Nina-the-perfect wouldn't believe him.

"Hey, Uncle Fletch," Mary Ann said.

Charles looked away from his video game, then paused it. "Hi."

"Daddy," Katie said. "It's about time." She dropped her controller and stood to hug him. "Mom says you need to call her."

He hugged her and leaned to kiss Mary Ann on the cheek. "I will call your mother," he said to Katie. He turned to Mary Ann. "How are you? Anything new in acting camp?"

Mary Ann rolled her eyes. "I'm not going this year. I'm fifteen."

"Right." Fletcher exhaled. "Katie, my love, I hope you're teaching your cousins a thing or two."

"Actually," Charles said, "she is. She's freaking ten, and I swear she's better at this level than I am." He pointed to the frozen image on the TV screen.

"I'll leave you to it, then. Carry on." Fletcher chuckled as he headed toward the living room.

His father and George, talking in low voices, stopped when he came through the doorway. Sean wasn't there anymore.

"Where's Sean?" Fletcher asked.

Stanley grinned and pointed. "Like a magnet. Kitchen."

Fletcher hurried around the corner.

Sean stood, leaning against the refrigerator, fussing with the label on his beer bottle. He glanced at Fletcher, and his face reddened.

Tanya smiled. "Honey, your family is so nice."

Shirley and Nina both sported stiff smiles. Nina started nodding. That was a bad sign.

His eyes settled on Tanya's chest. The vision of her naked came to mind, and the all too familiar stirring began. He made his eyes meet hers. He cleared his throat. "You know, it occurred to me perhaps I should show you around the Silver Sago Village grounds while there's still light." He held his hand out to Tanya. He wanted her away from Nina, and he wanted to get her alone.

"But," Tanya looked at Nina. "I'm not—"

"Don't be silly." Nina popped from her seat and removed the knife from Tanya's hand. "Go with Fletch. He's right. You should see how nice they keep the village."

"Well, if you're sure." Tanya rose and wiped her hands on a towel. "I'm all yours, sweetie." She stood by Fletcher. "See you in a bit, then."

"Bye," Nina said, waving like a flight attendant.

Fletcher turned Tanya toward the door. "Back in a few minutes, Dad," he called to Stanley.

"Don't forget to show her the resurfaced shuffleboard courts," Shirley said.

***

Shirley sighed. Sean's face was pure lust.

"Go wash out your eyeballs," Nina said, snapping her

fingers in front of him.

He put his beer on the counter and escaped from the kitchen.

"Seems the men are putty in her hands," Shirley said.

"Show her the shuffleboard courts? Honestly, Mother," Nina said.

"What?" Shirley said, confused. "They just redid them. They're the nicest in West Sago Beach. All the teams who come here say so."

"That may be true, but Tanya will never see them. Didn't you notice the lurid gleam in your son's eyes? He can't see past his *particular*."

"Oh." Shirley felt a blush blooming on her cheeks. "Goodness. You don't think he's going to . . . Oh, my." Could Fletcher really expect to have sex with Tanya right then? Where? She shuddered, deciding she didn't want to know.

"Judging from the urgent way he raced her out of here—yes, I *do* think he's about to. She's got him acting like a crazed sex-addict. The lust was palpable."

"Lord, help me."

"I *know*—I can sense it—she's using him, and I hate her for it."

"Please be on your best behavior during dinner. Fletcher wants you to approve of Tanya. Can't you pretend to, even if you don't?" She wondered how they would manage to be polite through the meal.

Pointing at Tanya's abandoned task, Nina snorted.

The mangled cucumber Tanya tried to slice was a mass of goo on the cutting board. "She doesn't seem to have much talent in the kitchen," Shirley said, "does she?"

Nina exploded with laughter. "Stop. You're killing me." Using her thumb and forefinger, she picked up what was left of the cucumber and threw it into the garbage disposal. "I've never seen anyone turn it into mush like that. Her talent definitely lies in another room."

“Nina Marie,” Shirley said. “Behave.”
"Please don't make me."

CHAPTER TWELVE

"Why, Miss Scarlett, you act upon me like a tonic." Thirty minutes later, Fletcher bowed and opened the townhouse door for Tanya.

She crinkled her nose. "Huh?"

"*Gone With the Wind*?" Seeing no recognition on her face, he gave up. "Nothing." He kissed her cheek. "After you."

He followed her in. George and Stanley were at opposite ends of the dining table. Sean stood nearby with the extensions leaned against him.

"Ready?" Stanley said. "Pull."

The table separated in the middle, and Sean placed two three-foot extensions in the gap.

They pushed the table together. Stanley brushed his hands on his khakis. "Shirley? All yours. We men folk did the hard work." He winked at Tanya.

"Where have you two been?" George said. "Sort of hot out for a walk, isn't it?"

Having an afternooner in the pool house George could only *wish* for. "We managed to find shade." He steered Tanya into the living room, where they sat on the sofa.

Footsteps pounded down the stairs, and Nina came into view. She smiled at them. "*There* you two are. Did you enjoy yourselves?"

People who didn't know Nina well wouldn't have picked up on her slight sarcastic inflection, but Fletcher did. She always saw right through him. He smiled back. "We did. A leisurely *stroll* on a summer afternoon kicks my mood into high gear. I recommend you and George try it sometime."

"We do our share of strolling. Though not being attention seekers, we prefer to *stroll* without making big fuss about it," Nina said.

"What are you talking about?" George said. "We never walk anywhere."

Fletcher snorted with laughter.

"Go back to sleep." Nina retreated to the kitchen.

A minute later, Shirley came from setting the table, waved to Fletcher and Tanya, and walked past them into the hall. "Attention all children. Wash your hands. Dinner is served." She hustled back to the kitchen.

"Last time everybody was here, we had Bigger, Faster Pizza," Katie said, rounding the corner. "Can we do that again?"

"Absolutely not." Shirley shot Fletcher a menacing look. "Do not let your children eat there."

"Why?" Fletcher cocked his head sideways. "They love that pizza."

Carrying a bowl of macaroni salad, his mother stopped and whispered to him. "The owner is a disgusting pervert. You *don't* want to know how I know."

He and Tanya exchanged puzzled glances. He shrugged.

Everyone helped carry and place food, then found seats.

As Fletcher pulled out a chair for Tanya, Nina approached.

"No, no." Nina took Tanya's arm. "I saved a place for you between me and Mom." She grinned at Fletcher. "You see her every day. We want to continue getting acquainted."

He watched with trepidation while Nina sat Tanya down. He checked his watch.

"Daddy, I get to sit next to you." Tyler beamed at him.

"I'm really happy about that." He hugged Tyler, then sat, trying to hone in on what the women said at the other end of the table.

"I get to sit on his right," Katie said. "That's more important than the left, isn't it, Daddy?"

Mary Ann, across from Fletcher, nudged Charles on her left. "Jeez, how'd we miss fighting about that all our lives? I didn't know right or left side mattered."

"Neither did I," George, Stanley, and Sean said.

Charles laughed. "Now we have to fight about it. I don't want to look back on my childhood with regrets."

"Won't make a difference," Mary Ann said. "Sean's always sucked up all the air in the room, anyway."

"Don't hate me because I'm beautiful." Sean did a faux hair toss.

Fletcher leaned toward Katie and whispered, "You're in the best seat. But we'll let Tyler think he is."

Smiling, she stabbed a forkful of her macaroni salad.

Stanley and George began talking sports, Sean and Mary Ann bantered, and tiny Alice hummed in her booster chair, happy sitting next to her grandma.

Nina asked Tanya a question, but with the other conversations happening, Fletcher couldn't discern the words. He strained to hear, catching only odd syllables, but overheard Mary Ann just fine.

"Her boobs are fake, Sean. Stop drooling," Mary Ann whispered.

Fletcher looked up. Sean's gaze flashed from Tanya's chest to his plate.

When Mary Ann saw Fletcher staring at her, her eyebrows rose, and she sent him an apologetic shrug. "Well, they *are*. Any fool could see that."

"Least she *has* some, Miss Pancake Chest," Charles said.

"Excuse me," George said to Stanley. In a stern whisper, he said to the teens, "Find something else to talk about."

Maybe bringing Tanya wasn't the best idea. Fletcher checked his watch again. It was six-thirty. George admonished his kids, but Fletcher saw him leering at Tanya, too. How soon could he whisk her out of there?

"Have you tried to speak to Janice?" Stanley asked Fletcher.

"Not a good time for this, Dad." Fletcher gestured toward Tanya.

Stanley made a face. "Your mother and Nina have her full attention. She can't hear us at this end of the table." He lowered his voice. "When we picked up Tyler and Alice, Janice's eyes were red. I think she was crying."

"I tried yesterday. She said tell it to her lawyer," Fletcher said. "You and I can discuss it when we're alone."

George nodded.

Fletcher wanted to punch him. None of it was any of his business. George passed judgment on whatever Fletcher did. He didn't appreciate George's condescending attitude.

He glanced at Tanya. She returned Sean's smile. A jolt of jealousy hit Fletcher.

"You wouldn't have a chance with her, you know." Mary Ann spoke again, her voice even quieter.

"Trust me. I could get her," Sean whispered back.

"Nope. She's only after guys with money, like Uncle Fletch. *Trust me.*"

"Uncle Fletch isn't rich. She probably thinks he is because he drives a nice car. But that *is* why men like to make lots of money, dorkus-brain," Sean said. "They want the perks that come with it. The babes, the cars, the boat. I'll have it all. If you're nice to me, maybe I'll let you work on my yacht."

"You're a moron."

***

Shirley waved good-bye to Fletcher and Tanya and closed the door. "That was quite a dinner." She entered the kitchen.

Mary Ann plopped herself on one of the dinette chairs. "Oh. My. God. What a freaking tease. Poor Uncle Fletch. Her boobs look like if you stuck a pin in them, they'd fly all over the room, like a balloon. Sean's going to go blind."

"That's not polite," Nina said.

"She's right. Don't scold her for telling the truth," Shirley said. "Tanya is nothing but trouble with a capital T. She's got Fletcher so blindsided he doesn't know what he's doing. Poor Janice is what I'm thinking." She stooped and opened a drawer, searching for a container lid.

"Janice got what was coming to her. Karma," Nina said. "Mary Ann, would you go spend some time with the little ones? Grandpa's going to take them home soon, and you won't get another chance to see them on this trip, I don't think."

"Fine." Mary Ann jumped up. "But if there's another wedding for Uncle Fletch, I'm not going." She left the room.

"There won't be a wedding," Nina said in a quiet tone. "Never. Not to that blow-up doll come to life. She's got the same brain power as a sex toy, too."

Shirley stopped searching and turned. "How do you know he won't marry her?"

"You heard Tanya accept my invitation to go shopping together tomorrow?"

"I thought it was a bit much. You're not good at faking niceties. You're really going?"

"Um-hmm. And I've become skilled at faking all sorts of things."

"Mercy. Don't tell me anymore. There are some things a mother doesn't need to know." Peeking around the corner into the living room, Shirley saw George on the sofa with his eyes closed. Stanley sat in his recliner with his hand on his stomach watching television. The six cousins were in the spare room with the video games.

"By the way, George is asleep again," Shirley said. "Isn't it odd? He woke up and seemed pepped up and perky through dinner."

Frowning, Nina shook her head. "Young blonde bombshells have that effect on him. And concerning the bimbo, not only will there not be a wedding, I predict she'll be gone from his life pretty darn quick."

"What are you going to do, lose her at the mall and hope she can't find her way back?"

"No, but that's a great plan B. Thanks." Nina poured a glass of cabernet from the open bottle on the counter, then took a sip. "Plan A is to let Tanya in on a few *facts* about Fletch."

"What facts?" Shirley tried imagining anything that would sway the girl. "We found out during dinner she knew Fletcher was married when she took up with him. What other facts could possibly scare her?"

"I'm not planning to scare her," Nina said, smiling. "I plan to lure her away."

Shirley raised her eyebrows. "Nina Marie. Is that what they call *swinging both ways*?"

Nina laughed. "You're a hoot. Relax. I'm not interested in women, even if it's for the noble purpose of rescuing my brother. Don't fret another minute, Mom. I've totally got it handled. The tramp's as good as gone."

"Well, don't go overboard. Your tendency to direct all the traffic could backfire if your brother finds out."

"I never overdo it. And I'm in the right. On the side of good against evil—simply protecting my family. No more of these cheap bimbos."

Turning toward the sink, Shirley threw up a silent prayer. Once Nina decided to interfere, there was no arguing with her.

CHAPTER THIRTEEN

With Nina's help, Tanya struggled out of an emerald-green silk sheath dress.

"I told you it would be too tight in the boobs," Tanya said.

"It's such an elegant dress," Nina said. "I thought it was worth a try." She re-hung the garment on the padded hanger and handed the next one to Tanya. "We're down to the last one. Hope this is it. You've got to present the perfect image at that dinner Fletch is taking you to next Saturday. There'll be lots of important people there."

"You mean like celebrities?" Tanya slipped the V-neck black dress over her head. "I dunno. These are all kinda, you know, old? I usually wear things that are sexy."

Nina zipped it for her and stood back, seeing Tanya's front in the mirror. "Wow. If you reveal any more than this, those aged rich coots at the dinner will have heart attacks on the spot."

"It's sort of boring. There's no sequins or crystals." She turned to face Nina.

The girl looked amazing. The dress showed just enough cleavage and nipped in tight to her tiny waist. Life sucked. She couldn't have looked that good on her skinniest day in her twenties. "You have to buy this one."

"But it hides so much of my breasts. I'm still making

payments on these things. I want to show them off."

"If you ask me, you're showing plenty." Nina gathered the rejects and hung them on a hook outside the dressing room door. "Have some mercy on my poor brother. Fletch isn't going to be able to stand up all night as it is."

Tanya flashed a naughty smile, clearly delighted. "Ya think?"

Nina nodded. Someday, Fletch would forgive her for this—if he ever found out she'd done it. "Can I ask you a personal question?"

"Sure."

"Why did you have them done so large?"

Turning for Nina to unzip her, Tanya didn't answer.

"I'm sorry. It's none of my business," Nina said.

"It's okay. Back in high school, I was flat. Scary flat. The boys were nice to me, but they weren't interested, you know? A few years later, I'd grown some, but I wanted to be noticed. So, as soon as I saved enough for the down payment, I did it. I'm not sorry, either. It worked. Men love me now." She did a once-over of Nina's chest. "You should have yours done."

Nina glanced at her B-cups.

"It's a lot more fun. It would keep that husband of yours from wandering."

The comment hit closer to home than Tanya knew. Nina winced. George had wandered, and more than once. Could the trollop tell? Maybe gold diggers were gold diggers because they had a keen sense about these things. A *stray-dar*?

Tanya handed the winning dress to Nina and pulled on her jeans. "I mean, no offense or anything, 'cause you're really pretty for your age and all, but I'm telling you—guys get stupid around these. You can have anything you want. It's a kind of power trip." She grabbed her purse and opened the dressing room door. "This is awesome. I've never shopped at Saks before."

"I'm glad we found something." Nina followed her out, and they walked to the register.

Digging through her purse, Tanya produced a black credit card and handed it to the cashier. "Fletch gave me my own card. How cool is that?"

My brother is an idiot, Nina thought. "Has Fletch told you anything about this annual dinner?"

"A bunch of old farts, like you said."

"There's one *old fart* you need to be extra nice to."

"Who?"

"Joseph R. Blenning." Fletcher had told her all the man and the dinner. Then Nina did some research on her father's computer.

"Who's he?"

"Only the founder and CEO of BlennTech. They are the largest conglomerate of alternate energy companies in the world. They're into solar, wind, hydro, natural gas, and bio-fuels. He's worth billions. And it's summer. The off-season. This must be a huge deal he's in Sago Beach for. Fletcher would love to work for them. If Blenning likes you, that would help Fletcher, don't you think?"

"I guess." Tanya took the bagged dress from the cashier.

They left the store and headed into the mall.

"Are you hungry?" Nina asked. "I'll treat for pizza."

Later, sitting in the food court where preserved palms soared under an expansive skylight, Nina watched Tanya push aside the croutons in her salad with her fork.

"This CEO guy," Tanya said. "What was his name again?"

"Joseph Blenning." Nina wiped her mouth with a paper napkin. "I love the sauce on this. I wish we had Bigger, Faster Pizza locations in New Jersey."

"Your mother said he's a perv."

"Blenning? I doubt my mother's aware he exists."

"No. The pizza guy." Tanya's face went blank. "Tell me Blenning's whole name again?"

"Joseph R. Blenning." Nina considered writing it down for her.

Tanya seemed to be committing it to memory. "He's a *billionaire?* With a B?"

"That's what I heard," Nina said. "I suppose you could look it up on the Forbes website. They list the richest people every year." She imagined the gears grinding in Tanya's head and managed not to smile. Then she aimed for the jugular. "I feel so bad for the man, though. His wife lost her battle with cancer last year. I hear he's a mere shadow without her." A sexy young slut was exactly what he needed. "You see? It's just like they say. Money *isn't* everything." Blennings' adult children would no doubt argue that point. Better Tanya fight with them over money than have her ruin Fletch's life, though.

"Hmmm." Tanya took a bite of pizza and stared into the distance.

"Anyway, it sure would help Fletch to land a job at Blenning. He could use it."

Pausing in mid-chew, Tanya set her slice down. "What do you mean?"

"About what?"

"How Fletch needs help. What for?"

"In the money department, of course." Nina kept her tone nonchalant as Tanya's eyes widened. "Leaving Janice devastated his finances. He must love you very much."

"Huh?"

"You're a lucky girl."

"He said he didn't love Janice anymore. And I don't get why it's devastating."

"They had a pre-nup. Janice doesn't have to give him anything in the divorce."

"Give *him* anything?" Tanya looked alarmed.

Nina sipped her diet soda and locked into Tanya's eyes. "The money's hers. Janice is from a wealthy family. Didn't he tell you? Oh. I guess he knew you wouldn't care one way or the other, seeing as how you love him so. Fletch makes decent money, don't worry. But he's used to a lot of luxuries in his life.

He'll have to make some adjustments. Probably have to sell his Beamer M6 convertible. I think he mentioned checking out a Camry." Nina patted Tanya's arm. "But he's got you now. *He's* happy, and *you're* happy, and I suppose, in the great scheme of things, that *is* what matters most. Isn't it?"

Tanya coughed, then spit her food into her napkin.

Pretending not to notice, Nina folded her empty paper plate in half and composed a wistful expression. "Fletch is mom's favorite. Always has been. It hurts a little to acknowledge it, but I'm forty-eight. I've got three kids and know how it is. Mom explained years ago, if anything should happen to Dad, it's Fletch she wants to live with."

Half expecting lighting to strike at her through the glass ceiling for the horrible lies and the level of bullshit she spread, Nina persevered for the cause. "And it makes sense, now, doesn't it really? Since he's down here? She'll need to be close to her friends. Fletch agreed right away, bless him. Dad's seventy-four. Did you know that? Looks good for his age, I think."

She gauged Tanya's reaction. The girl looked like she'd been walloped by a wave of ice water. Stunned.

"Still, Dad's father died of a heart attack at sixty." Dear God, I'm relentless, Nina thought, enjoying it. "Dad could go at any time. I'm so glad my family had the opportunity to visit this summer. Fletch told me you thought about nursing school at one point. You'd be ever so helpful with Mom as she ages."

She patted Tanya's hand again. "My little brother is such a sweet man. Like I said, you are one lucky girl." Slam. And dunk.

CHAPTER FOURTEEN

Stanley adjusted the ties on his purple smock and stood back to see himself in the mirror. "Shirley," he yelled.

"I'm right here." She appeared in the bedroom doorway. "Don't shout."

Stanley turned to her. "What do you think?"

"You'll charm the bloomers off the old ladies and make them forget what they came shopping for."

"Thank you." He studied her. "Have you thought about where you might look?"

"For a job?" She frowned. "No. I refuse to apply at Happy Mart. Other than them, I can't imagine who would hire me. I haven't had a job since I worked the concession stand in the movie theater in high school."

The thought of prodding her further occurred to him, then he squelched it. It would be better to bring it up again in a few days. "I'm sure you'll find the perfect thing for you."

She gave him a sour look and left the room.

***

Twenty minutes later, Stanley pulled into the expansive Happy Mart lot, searched for section J, and parked in the shade of a gumbo limbo tree. Employees couldn't take the close-in spots. He hiked to the entrance.

"Let me guess. You're Stanley Nowack." The greeter at the door, also wearing a purple smock, held out a hand. "I'm Tim Danber. They said to watch for you."

Stanley shook his hand. "So. What do I do now?"

"Just a sec." Tim hurried to the Customer Service counter and spoke with a middle-aged woman with thick glasses.

Tim seemed to be about Stanley's age, maybe a little younger. He stood a head shorter than Stanley, was bald, and a touch overweight. Stanley turned to focus on the six people in the customer service line. They ranged from twenty to ninety, as far as he could tell.

"This is Sarah," Tim said.

Stanley pivoted to see Tim and a young obese woman in a purple polo shirt staring at him.

"Hello," he said.

She nodded, looking bored.

"She'll do greeter duty while I show you around," Tim said. "We'll be back soon, Sarah."

Stanley followed Tim through the men's department to the back of the store where a set of double doors labeled *Employees Only* opened when Tim swiped his ID card into a scanner.

"You need a card to enter the stock room?" Stanley said.

"Lots more than stock back here. Apparently there's lots of folks who'd love to mess with Happy Mart."

Once past the doors, Tim led him to the left, down a hall, then past a glass-walled conference room with a huge wood table. Next to it was a large kitchen, all stainless and sparkling clean.

"What do they need this for?" Stanley never imagined anything so fancy hidden from the public's view.

"They have a lot of corporate meetings and parties at our store. It's the largest in South Florida. Here we go." Tim gestured to an area with several round tables and chairs, an employee bulletin board with OSHA postings, notices about birthdays, and inspirational quotes. "This is our break room."

Two men sat at one table, eating. They glanced up.

Stanley recognized one of them as the manager who hired him, Mr. Wheaton.

Wheaton stood, wiped his hands on a napkin, and held out his hand. "Good to see you again, Stanley. Welcome to our team."

"Thanks." Stanley shook his hand.

"If you poke your head into that office right there," Wheaton said, "you'll see Barbara. She has your nametag and will get your employee ID card ready."

His head already swirling with the new names and faces, Stanley found the young and shapely Barbara. It would be easy to remember her.

Tim showed him how to clock in and assigned him a locker. "Happy Mart prefers you keep your wallet, keys, and cell phone locked up during your shift. There were a couple times when employees had things stolen from them while helping customers."

Stanley let his surprise show.

Tim chuckled. "Yeah, I know. Hard to believe. But our low prices can attract some, uh, interesting types to the store."

"I don't have a cell phone." Stanley emptied his pockets and placed his things in the locker. He held up a roll of wintergreen mints. "Can I keep my Lifesavers?

***

After an hour of shadowing Tim, Stanley had the front door duty to himself. He smiled at everyone entering the store. Some smiled back, others scowled. He handed stickers to the people in the returns line and helped young mothers place their toddlers in the shopping cart seat. When he needed to push carts to cars and load purchases into trunks, he signaled to the sullen Sarah to play greeter. Tim told him he'd do the to-the-car service mostly for elderly women. What Tim didn't tell him was the old ladies were so demonstrative. They touched his arm, patted his hand, and one kissed him on the cheek once her frail husband was out of sight in the passenger seat.

He began to use his left hand more, in gestures and lifting, in hopes they'd notice the fat gold wedding band on his finger, but it didn't make any difference.

During a lull, he took a bathroom break and, on his way back to his greeting station, heard a familiar voice.

"Stanley? Is that you?" Dora said.

He looked to his left.

She stood holding a package of men's multi-color bikini underwear up to Morty, who, when he saw Stanley, reddened and batted the package away.

"Are you working here now?" Morty asked. "What the hell for?"

Stanley pretended he didn't see the underwear. He whipped up a lie. "I'm driving Shirley nuts being home all the time. I figured if I got a job, I'd be out of her hair, and I could use the money to play golf more often."

Morty shrugged. "Whatever."

"You'd think she'd have told me." Dora sounded indignant.

"Probably didn't think it was any big deal," Stanley said. "I know I don't. Don't be insulted. I doubt she told anyone, even the kids."

"Uh-huh," Dora said.

"Gotta get up front," Stanley said. "We'll see you tomorrow night for cards as usual, right?" He hurried to his station to find an attractive sixtyish woman waiting for help with her purchases.

Tim came to check on him once an hour, and on the fourth visit, Stanley had to ask.

"What's with the women?"

Tim looked confused. "What do you mean?"

"All the older women. They act like they've never seen a man before." Stanley fished a roll of dollar bills from his pants pocket. "And they keep insisting I take a tip. A dollar or two. Won't let me say no."

"Oh." Tim's mouth formed an oval. "You're not supposed to take tips. My fault. I should have told you. I forgot because it almost never happens here."

Stanley pointed at the money in his hand. "Happens every time."

Shaking his head, Tim laughed. "I imagine with your looks, it would." He held out an open palm. "Here. If it's okay with you, I'll put it in the employee coffee and snacks fund."

"Sure." Stanley didn't know what to make of the *with your looks* comment.

As if he'd read Stanley's mind, Tim said, "Barbara in the office said you look like Harrison Ford."

"Hmmm. Well." Shirley always said he was handsome, but Stanley chalked that up to her being a great wife who loved him. She was *supposed* to say those things.

***

Glad to be home, Stanley came through the front door.

"Dora called." Shirley had her hands in the sink, her back to him.

"There's a shocker. Guess everybody in the village now knows I work at Happy Mart."

"She said you were working for extra golf money. That was good thinking."

"Best I could do at short notice."

She faced him. "How was it?"

"Very busy." Stanley untied and pulled off his smock, and dropped it on a dining room chair on his way to the kitchen. He kissed her on the cheek.

"What do you smell like?" Her nose crinkled up. "Fast food? Did you stop and eat at The Burger Flip again?"

"No. The little restaurant near the front of the store doesn't change its fry oil enough. That's what Tim said, anyway. The smell kind of got to me after a while."

"Who's Tim?"

Stanley explained and recapped the day for her, leaving out how the women fussed over him. He wandered into the living room, turned on the television, and sat in his recliner.

"By the way," he said, "Morty wears bikini underwear."

"What?"

He laughed when he heard the disbelief, or disgust, in her voice.

CHAPTER FIFTEEN

Catherine Von Cletan paced the marble floor of her study. She glanced at her cell phone on the desk, grabbed it, and dialed her daughter's number.

"We're nearly there, Mother," Maddy said.

"It's about time. The airport's only a few miles away. What on earth took so long?"

"Normal traffic. It's five-thirty. Rush hour. See you in a few."

The connection went dead. Catherine checked her make-up and hair in the gilded mirror on the wall, then walked to her mansion's grand entry hall. The contractor and a helper were tidying up from the day's work.

"Almost done, Mrs. Von Cletan," the contractor said.

She ignored him. "Lucinda?"

Her maid came scurrying from the living room with a dusting cloth in one hand. "Yes, Mrs. Von Cletan?"

"My Muffin is almost here. I want to wait in front."

Lucinda stuffed the cloth into a uniform pocket, hustled to the entry, and opened the massive wood door.

Catherine stepped onto the veranda. At the end of the winding driveway, she scanned the road for her black S600 Mercedes. Another minute passed, then she saw it. The automatic iron gates opened, and it approached, turning to enter the front portico.

Hector, her chauffeur, emerged from the car, and moved to the rear passenger door, but it opened before he reached the handle. Maddy emerged wearing jeans and a navy boat-neck T-shirt. She'd straightened and cut her normally wavy blonde hair. Her locks were even with her shoulders.

"Muffin," Catherine shrieked. She threw her arms wide and waited. "Darling."

Maddy smiled. "Hello, Mother." She walked up the steps and hugged Catherine. She turned to the driver. "Thanks, Hector."

"It is always my pleasure, Miss Madelaine," Hector said in a thick Cuban accent.

"Bring Muffy's bags up to her suite," Catherine called backward to Hector. She assessed her only child as she led her into the house. "You look thin. Lucinda? Unpack Muffin's bags as soon as Hector delivers them."

"Hi," Maddy said to Lucinda, "I'm—"

"Shhh." Catherine waved the maid away. "Why are you so thin?"

"I'm the same weight as when I left." Maddy scanned the area. "What are you having done *now*?"

"I told you." Catherine gestured around the grand hall. "I redid the entry and a few of the downstairs rooms. It took longer than necessary. I had to fire the old contractor and hire a new one. I'm stuck here for the summer. I don't dare leave it to the tradesmen alone again."

Hearing his cue, the man waved from the crème marfil marble staircase. He peeled blue tape from the rich dark Brazilian rosewood railing.

"Hello," Maddy said to him. "It looks wonderful."

"Thank you," the man said.

Catherine scoffed and shook her head. "What's wrong with you," she whispered. Her Muffin had always been such a softie with the help. "Come. We'll go into my study. You probably need a drink."

"More than you know," Maddy said.

Catherine led the way, then closed the door behind them. "Scotch? Or whiskey?"

"If you have a decent wine, I'd prefer that. I'll open it." Maddy looked in a drawer in the built-in bar and removed a corkscrew. "Unless you want to call a servant to do it."

"Don't be coarse. It doesn't suit you, no matter how you think it will shock me."

Maddy chose a bottle of Rothschild Pauillac and opened it while Catherine poured herself two fingers of Macallan scotch. The twenty-one-year-old bottle. She'd bought a case during the frustrating reign of the last contractor.

"Really, Mother, your concern about my returning early isn't necessary." Maddy walked to the embroidered ivory silk settee, sat, and placed her goblet on the coffee table.

"That's a matter of opinion." Catherine sat in her wing chair and took a long sip, shuddering as the scotch left a smoky burn in her throat. She set the Baccarat cut glass tumbler on the table beside her. "Now. Explain to me why you broke off your engagement to Steven and left him high and dry in Paris."

Maddy stared at her. "Steven cheated on me."

Catherine almost choked. "That's it? He cheated on you? Dear girl, don't you know anything about men?" She sat straighter and leaned in, staring at Maddy. "*All* men cheat, darling. It's no reason to call off the perfect marriage. Why do you act so naïve?"

"And I didn't leave him high and dry. Well, maybe high. Not dry. When I walked in on them, the French girl was giving him a blowjob. Took them a minute to realize I was in the room." Maddy rubbed her empty left ring finger.

"An unfortunate circumstance." Catherine noticed Maddy's perfect manicure, then did a subtle check on her eyebrows and facial quality. "I'm heartened to see you're keeping yourself in good form." She'd heard neglecting personal grooming was the surest sign of depression. Her daughter was simply reacting to wounded pride then, not a monstrous heartbreak. "Given a certain amount of time for all parties to regain face, I'm sure he'll agree to the engagement again. He's crazy about you." The union could be salvaged.

"I wouldn't marry him if he begged me on his knees." Maddy sipped her wine.

"His family owns copper and magnesium mines. He's been reared to take over when his father retires. It's such a good match for the families. Equal wealth. Equal power. Just *look* at the two of you. You're both beautiful young adults who know how to behave in public. Proper upbringings. Not like those spoiled exhibitionist Hilton heirs. Think about what your children would look like. Gorgeous. What more could you want?"

"How about, oh, *love*?"

"My God, what a pedestrian thought." Catherine stopped to gather her wits. How could she get through to her? "Darling, nobody of any substance *ever* marries for love. Such a quaint notion."

"The Duke and Duchess of Windsor?" Maddy asked.

"Aside from being almost a century ago, that marriage nonetheless was a financial disaster for all involved. You've proved my point." She lifted her drink and studied the light refracted by the fine cuts of the leaded crystal, then took another big swallow.

"Lots of rich people marry for love. Things have changed since you were young."

"Not the smart ones. We've talked about this. Your father did, too, before he passed. Being born into families like ours isn't easy. There are obligations and responsibilities. We don't have the freedom to be in love with whom we marry. Ensuring that the next generation continues the tradition is of the utmost importance. Your father and I managed."

"Daddy had a mistress for the last fifteen years of his life," Maddy said. "You knew it. I knew it. The servants knew it. She came to his funeral, for God's sake. That never bothered you?"

It had bothered her. The memory of seeing Whitney Sears, her husband John's lover, at the service came back. She bristled at the thought of having had to be polite to the woman. John was discreet beyond belief. Few people knew of the affair. Catherine and John had never pretended a great love, but they respected each other, and for some reason she still didn't understand, she was jealous of John's obvious love for Whitney. She sighed.

"Mother?"

Catherine stirred from her recollection. "No. I understood it." I *endured* it, she thought. Lying to the next generation seemed to be a tradition, too. "Your father was wonderful to me. Never said an unkind word. Always proud of you. And me."

"I'm tired." Maddy drained the remainder of her wine and placed the glass on the bar's Brazilian azul bahia granite counter. "I'd like to get settled."

"We'll continue this discussion later."

"No. We won't. I'm not getting married." Maddy's face took on the same stubborn defiance she'd displayed since toddlerhood.

Catherine sighed. "I do dread when you get like this."

"Then you may as well know that I'm not doing East Hampton this summer."

Catherine brightened. "Your friends will be upset, but you'll stay here to keep me company?"

"In a way." Maddy walked to the door and opened it. "It's about time I used my degree. I found a position in West Sago Beach. I start next week. A friend told me about a new condominium near my work. I plan to buy one." She left the room.

Dumbfounded, Catherine poured more scotch and sat on the settee. The girl always had a fierce independent streak. She didn't want a debut when she was eighteen, but Catherine and John insisted. Muffin did as she was told and pulled it off to great praise. Then Catherine found the charred remains of the lovely debut photo album on the front lawn. The mark of a truly self-controlled young woman. Protest, but only so there'd be no embarrassment to the family.

They named her Madelaine Von Cletan. After graduating Harvard, she announced she would now be known as Madelaine Forsyth, Forsyth being Catherine's maiden name. They were only to use Maddy as a nickname then, not Muffin or Muffy. Catherine ignored that request, but honored the last name choice. John had enjoyed his daughter's determination to do things her own way, telling Catherine privately that sooner or later, the girl would reclaim the Von Cletan moniker. In a strange way, Catherine felt pride in her daughter's rebellion with discretion. So like her father.

Attempting to stand, she lost her balance and fell back onto the settee. The plump down cushions made a *poof* sound. She glanced at her empty glass and knew she'd had enough. Closing her eyes, the image of a young man she once dated appeared. Danny. Danny Millington. At seventeen, she met him at a mixer dance between her all-girls boarding school and the all-boys school in the next town.

She'd fallen for him by the third date. He was cute, charming, and funny. The dear boy confessed he loved her, too. Then she found out he was a scholarship student from a middle-class family in New Jersey. Knowing her parents would never approve, she broke up with him. She cried for weeks. That was nineteen-sixty-three.

Catherine wondered now what happened to Danny. Had he found true love? If he did, was he still married to the woman? What was it like to be *in love* with the man you married?

CHAPTER SIXTEEN

Stanley had brought the Sunday paper in before he left for work. Shirley muttered to herself as she tried to read the drier parts. Despite being double-bagged, there were entire sections so soaked she threw them away. Outside, the rain poured and showed no sign of stopping.

Being the new man on the schedule, Stanley had to take the shifts nobody wanted, including their sacred Sunday mornings. Shirley was not happy with Happy Mart. On the good side, the management didn't want the older employees working late at night.

To her chagrin, the want ads survived the deluge. She set them aside to begin her job search later. She became immersed in an article about a man in Delray Beach who'd married for the eighth time. His new wife was a mail-order bride from the Ukraine who looked thirty years younger than him. She was in mid-tsk when the phone jangled on the kitchen wall, startling her.

She hustled to it. "Hello?"

"Mom. It's me."

Shirley detected a quiver in Fletcher's voice. "Are you okay? You don't sound good."

"I'm awful. Tanya kicked me out. I can't believe it. I'm sitting with my things in the car outside her apartment in the middle of a damned monsoon." His voice cracked and his words came between rasps.

She knew he was fighting back tears.

"Can I stay with you and Dad for a few days until this blows over?"

"Goodness. You sound terrible."

"I am terrible."

"Of course you're welcome here, but wouldn't you rather go to a hotel? Have some privacy to sort out your feelings?"

"I don't need to sort anything. I don't want to be alone right now."

"Fine. Come on over. My mah-jongg group meets here in a few hours, though. We're having a special session to decide who will play for the village team in the county finals. Prepare for some nosy questions."

"Thanks. I'll drop my stuff off and go to a movie or something while they're there."

She heard the click on the other end and hung up the phone. She stared at Nina's framed picture on the buffet. "Nina honey, if you were here I'd hug you so hard, you'd faint. I don't know what you said to Tanya, but thank you."

Twenty minutes later, she saw his BMW M6 pull into a guest space in front of the townhouse. An umbrella popped from the driver's side, then Fletcher emerged. He leaned into the rear of the car and retrieved two suitcases. He looked flummoxed as to how to carry both with the umbrella. He set one suitcase down and trudged forward with the other.

Shirley opened the door.

"Hi." He placed the bag on the entry tile, then returned for the other.

"You're drenched." Shirley shut the door when he entered with the second bag.

"Fits my mood." Fletcher met her eyes.

His were bloodshot and glassy.

"Why don't you bring your things upstairs and take a hot

shower? It'll make you feel better. The girls won't be here until one."

Fletcher hugged her. "Thanks, Mom." He headed for the stairs, then turned around. "Where's Dad?"

"Happy Mart." They hadn't told the kids that Stanley worked there, and this didn't seem to be the time to do it.

"You didn't tell him anything, did you?"

"Not yet."

"Please don't. I'll tell him. He'll get a great deal of satisfaction from this, I'm sure."

"That's not fair."

"Yes, it is. I can't face the lecture and *I told you so* at the moment." He went upstairs.

Shirley's heart lurched. Tanya was a disaster waiting to happen. Everyone but Fletcher saw that. He'd always fallen hard for his love interests, even in high school. Pretty women manipulated him, and he failed to see it. Stanley had tried to explain about certain types of women, but Fletcher never understood and fell more often than not for that exact type. Lauren, Fletcher's first wife, was the lone exception. Despite Stanley's best intentions, his admonitions only served to put distance between the father and son.

She went to the kitchen and busied herself slicing fruit, then making onion dip to go with chips for her guests.

Hearing footsteps on the stairs, she put her task aside and rinsed her hands. "Would you like a drink?" she called.

He rounded the corner to the kitchen. "I'd love to get shit-faced, but I don't think that's what you meant."

"Iced tea or soda?" Shirley thought he looked in somewhat better spirits.

"Iced tea." He sat at the dinette. "Thanks."

She put a glass in front of him, then sat with her own. "Want to give me some idea of what happened?"

He stared into the ceiling, then at her. "It's the damnedest thing. Last night, we went to a party. Tanya looked amazing.

She wore the dress she and Nina picked out together, and it was a killer. *Every* eye in the place, even the women's, was on Tanya. I felt so proud. This incredible beauty was with *me.* We laughed. We danced. She mingled with the old codgers and made them smile. Then, on the way home, she seemed pissed at me. I asked her if I'd done something to upset her, and she wouldn't answer. She wouldn't let me touch her."

He took a deep breath, as if steeling himself not to break down. "This morning, I woke before her. Got up, made the coffee, fetched the paper. I was in the middle of the sports section when she appeared in the kitchen in her robe. I thought I'd find out what the problem was."

Shirley waited while he stared at the wall.

"She said," Fletcher said, "'this isn't working. Get your stuff and move out. Now.'"

"My gosh. Why so sudden?" Shirley said.

He shook his head. "I have no effing idea. Excuse the French, Mom. I can't for the life of me figure out what got into her head. I began to ask questions, and she got angry and started yelling. She called me a liar and a phony."

"Not to seem indelicate, but did you do anything last night that she might have thought was flirting? With another woman, I mean? Maybe Tanya's got a horrible jealous streak you didn't know about."

"No. Nothing like that. There wasn't another woman who could come close to competing with her. I was a perfect gentleman."

Shirley puzzled over his story. What *had* Nina told Tanya? She would have to find out.

"The only thing I can think of is—maybe she's scared."

"Of what?" Had Fletcher threatened her? Or maybe Janice? That didn't seem likely.

"The incredible depth of our relationship. It's a powerful love. Not everyone is lucky enough to find it. It can be frightening, knowing you've found your true soul mate."

"I can imagine," Shirley said, fighting off the urge to gag. "I'm puzzled, though. Please don't take this wrong, but didn't you tell me the same thing about Janice? You swore you'd be together forever."

"I misjudged that one." His mouth screwed up on one side. "I can compare how I feel now, to back then, and there is no comparison. This is the real thing."

"Did Tanya tell you she felt the same way? That the two of you are soul mates?" Shirley felt silly verbalizing the dopey phrase.

"She's the one who recognized it first. *Who I was.* The first time she saw me, she said." He sighed. "It's all too much for her to take in. She's young. It's too real. I have to give her time."

Pretending to digest the information, Shirley rubbed his arm. "It hurts me to see you hurting like this. True love finds a path, if it's meant to be." She smiled at him, willing him to cheer up. "Things will work out the way they're supposed to, don't you think?"

Fletcher nodded. "Yes. They will." He stood. "Thanks, Mom. I'm going to vamoose now before Dora and the gang descend. What time will it be safe to come back?"

CHAPTER SEVENTEEN

Shirley slipped into the front seat of the Buick.

Stanley closed her door, walked around, and sat behind the wheel. "Did Fletcher find a psychiatrist yet?"

"I don't think so," Shirley said. "It's only been a week since she dumped him."

"Ding blame it." Stanley started the engine. "He promised me he'd find one six weeks ago, when he left Janice. He's got a problem. He really believes that little blondie is his destiny? His *soul mate*?"

"He knows you don't approve."

They rounded the corner and headed for Dora's building.

He snorted. "Neither do you."

"Yes, but I think he knows that I'll love him no matter where he winds up." She didn't want to share the harsh opinion Fletcher held about Stanley at the moment.

"What are you saying? Fletcher thinks I don't love him anymore because he's acting like a moony teenager?"

She heard the frustration in his voice and chose her words with care. "He knows you love him. My guess is he interprets your lectures as judging him. He thinks he can't do anything right in your eyes."

"I don't lecture."

Shirley gave him a stern sideways glance and kept it on him until he looked at her.

He muttered a few words she didn't catch.

They stopped in front of Dora's where Dora and Morty stood in the shade of a mango tree. Morty made a show of checking his watch several times. If only an overripe mango would drop and burst apart on his head. Shirley opened her door.

"We were getting worried," Morty said. "Thought maybe something happened to you."

"They're only five minutes late," Dora said.

"Might miss the early-bird now," Morty said.

Stanley rolled down his window. "Get in the car."

Shirley left the front seat. "We're going Flintstones-style. Sit up here with Stanley, Morty." She studied his clothes. He wore brown polyester pants and an orange flowered shirt with a huge pointed collar. She raised her eyebrows at Dora.

"I know. I know. Don't go there." Dora climbed into the back.

Morty took the front, and Shirley sat with Dora.

"If we are too late for the early-bird," Morty said, "how about Bigger, Faster Pizza? I think it's free toppings night."

"No!" Dora and Shirley said in unison, then laughed.

"I invited Agnes to come with us," Shirley said. "We're picking her up next."

"The skinny old one?" Morty said.

"We're *all* old." Stanley put the car in gear. "Or haven't you noticed?"

"Yeah, but that crone is just plain strange," Morty said. "Spouting creepy new-age mumbo jumbo at everyone."

"I think she's fun," Shirley said. "That new-age stuff might be the secret to her health. Maybe if we listened, we could learn a thing or two. She's in her late eighties, you know."

"And she's a very successful artist," Dora said. "Edna told me Agnes sells her paintings in three galleries out west."

"Whoopee. Edna the expert again. Agnes is probably one of those crazies who splashes paint at a canvas and calls it art," Morty said.

"No," Shirley said. "I've seen her work. It's beautiful. She makes good money, too. The last time we went out together, she picked up the tab for the whole table." She winked at Dora, who smiled.

"Huh," Morty said. "I've always liked art."

***

Fletcher trudged down the stairs wearing a coffee-stained cotton robe over his boxers, sat at the kitchen counter, placed his cell phone in front of him, and checked for the umpteenth time that it was on. Maybe he should leave another message. No. He checked the time. It was five-thirty in the afternoon.

He'd called Tanya multiple times every day since Sunday. He left friendly voice mails, understanding voice mails, and in the last two days—desperate voice mails.

Why wouldn't she call him back? He never guessed she could be so stubborn. If only he knew what he'd done, he could fix it, and they would get back on course.

He pressed redial. Tanya's voice mail picked up again. He ended the call and laid his head on the counter. Where could she be at that time on a Saturday? Nobody went out that early. Except his parents and their friends.

She was on his mind every moment. He couldn't function at work during the past week. He longed to stroke the silky-soft inside of her thighs, see her smile, hear her laugh. The empty aching started again. Visions of making love to her haunted him. Taunted him. He traced circles with his forefinger over the almond patterned laminate while Tanya did salacious things to him in his imagination.

His phone rang.

He popped up and grabbed it, not checking the incoming

number first. "Tanya?"

"Sorry, man. It's Vinny."

"Hi," Fletcher mumbled.

"What's up? We still going to shoot some pool? I'm bringing Bridget, my new girlfriend. She wants to meet you and Tanya."

"I can't go."

"What're ya sick?"

"No. Had a bad week. A really bad week. Tanya broke up with me. Kicked me out."

"Shit. What for?"

"Damned if I know. It's a temporary thing, I'm sure."

"Women. Especially hot women like Tanya. Who the hell can figure them out? You should have told me."

"I haven't told anybody. I'll look like an idiot. Once we get it ironed out, I'm sure we'll laugh about it."

"I won't tell a soul. Meet us for a drink. It'd be good to get your mind off her. Where are you staying? We'll come get you."

"Nah. I'll drive."

"Okay. Meet us at Dave's Pool and Brew at nine."

Fletcher hung up and sighed. Vinny was right. He needed to get out.

The cell jangled again. "Hello," he said, feeling lifeless.

"Fletcher."

"Tanya?" His heart leaped with relief.

"Yeah. It's me. Why do you keep calling me?" She sounded angry.

"You just called me." Fletcher kept his voice calm, willing her to respond with warmth.

"You know what I mean. You left, like, a million messages this week. Twelve today. Twelve. All saying the same pathetic crap. It's over. Get. It. Through. Your. Head."

"I don't even know what I did. Why are you so upset? If we could talk about it, I know I could help you understand the fears you have about us."

"No."

"Honey, I've thought it through. I *know* you're afraid. So am I." He walked into the living room and paced.

"I'm not afraid. I just don't want you. Ever."

"But . . .we—we were so happy." Tears formed in his eyes, and he wiped them away with his bathrobe sleeve.

"You were happy."

"You said we were soul mates, and you love me. Deep in our souls, we know this is right."

"Jesus. Stop. I made a mistake. I don't love you. Right now, I'm pretty sure I don't even *like* you."

"I'm coming over. It'll be different if we see each other. Baby, please."

"No." Her voice was iron. "Do not come over. We're done. Go back to Janice. You said she wants you, so go. And stop calling me."

The phone went dead.

"Shit." Fletcher threw the phone on the sofa. "God damned shit." He slid to the floor and his tears flowed.

By seven-thirty, he got his emotions under control. He needed to leave the house before his parents and their friends returned from their night out.

He intended to head for Dave's Pool and Brew early, have a burger and a beer, and watch a ball game. But when he got behind the wheel, the car seemed to steer itself to Tanya's. He cruised by her apartment building, trying to see into her third story window.

A jarring loud honk made him check his rearview mirror, and an enormous white SUV looked like it was about to eat his car. He sped up, drove around the block, and parked at a strip mall.

He bought a newspaper at a drugstore in the plaza, then walked to Tanya's building. Across the street, he found an empty bus stop bench and opened the paper. He thought if he could seem to casually catch her on her way in or out, they could have the face-to-face conversation he knew would change her mind. He had a clear view of the building's front door and garage exit.

At eight-twenty-five, a black limousine pulled into the entrance. The driver opened the back passenger door, and an older man stepped out and entered the building. Fletcher felt a mild curiosity because while he lived there, he never saw any high-end cars, much less a limo. It wasn't that kind of place.

A red Toyota entered and parked behind the limo. Two women, dressed for a night on the town, burst from the lobby, and laughing, got into the Toyota. Both were brunettes. The car backed up, then drove away.

A few minutes later, the light went off in Tanya's window. He stared at the entry door. His jaw dropped when he recognized Tanya, wearing a low-cut black sequined gown. It looked expensive. She looked expensive. She'd done her hair swirled into a chignon, and jewelry glittered around her neck. Her hand was on the arm of the old man who entered the building a few minutes earlier. She smiled and chatted with him as the driver helped her into the limo.

Fletcher stood, dropping the newspaper on the ground. "No." His voice croaked. He tried again. "Tanya." He couldn't muster a yell—as if the muscles in his throat forgot how. He took a few steps toward the street in a daze, still not comprehending.

The limousine left the driveway and proceeded north.

His larynx finally kicked into gear. "No," he screamed. He ran into the street after them. "No, Tanya, no." The initials on the limo's vanity plate were JRB.

A car swerved past him as he ran, and he went back to the curb. JRB. He knew those initials. From the party exactly a week before. Where he and Tanya met Joseph R. Blenning. J.R. Blenning, the billionaire. That night she froze Fletcher out and the next morning tossed him out. The old buzzard must have made his move on her right under Fletcher's nose, and he never suspected a thing. Feeling nauseous, he braced himself on a light pole and caught his breath. The feeling intensified, and he sunk to his knees into the grassy swale, vomited, and collapsed.

The cool damp grass felt good on his sweaty cheek. He had no intention of ever moving from that spot. Tanya went to the highest bidder. He'd been fooled by love. Used. Again. "Why me?" he yelled. For a few minutes he let his tears drip, feeling worthless, when he felt a sharp sting on his ankle. Then another on his face.

"Go ahead and bite me, stupid mosquitoes." He didn't have the energy to swat at them. He felt another further up his leg. Then another and another. A barrage of stings on his face, arms, legs, and chest made him leap to his feet. In the lamplight, his saw an army of fire ants swarming over his clothes and sneakers.

"Shit," he screamed, wiping his face and slapping his body. He untied and kicked off his sneakers, then stripped to his boxers. The red ants covered his body. He felt one crawling onto his cheek. A series of stings on his neck and up on the other side of his face hit him. He swiped and swatted until he couldn't see or feel any more of the tiny monsters.

Grabbing his clothes and shoes, he held them away from his body as he ran back to his BMW. Cars honked at him.

"Pervert," someone in a truck yelled. More people shouted obscenities out their windows when they passed.

The stinging magnified, and he checked his arms. The bites began to swell into big red welts. He opened his car door and sat on the driver's seat with his feet on the asphalt. Examining every inch of his clothing, inside and out, helped keep his mind off the pain. When he finished, he dressed and went into the same drugstore where he'd bought the newspaper.

The girl behind the counter stared open-mouthed at Fletcher when he entered. He ignored her and found the aisle with the antihistamines.

A woman reading a box label glanced up. "Gross." She pinched her nose with her fingers and hurried away.

He found what he needed, then placed a bottle of Benadryl,

a large box of oatmeal bath, and calamine lotion on the register counter. The girl sniffed and recoiled. As soon as she swiped the Benadryl's bar code, he grabbed it, tore open the safety packaging, and took a swig. The girl looked scared.

"I'm not a crazy street nut. Just got bit by some ants." He handed her a twenty. "Keep the change." As he carried his purchases to the door, he caught of whiff of himself and realized he smelled like puke.

His parents' Buick was in the carport when he parked in front of the townhouse. Through the window, he saw the dining room chandelier lit, and Dora, Morty, and his parents playing cards at the table. He pounded his fist on the dashboard. It was almost ten. His parents usually went to bed at nine-thirty.

The idea of driving around some more came to him, but his skin crawled. He'd go insane with the itching if he didn't treat the bites soon.

His phone rang. "What?" he screamed into it.

"Whoa. Nice. Real nice," Vinny said. "Where are you? You were supposed to meet us here at nine."

"I'm not coming."

"Man, you gotta get out. Don't stay cooped up and isolated. There's a good-looking woman sitting all by her lonesome at the bar. Could distract you from your troubles."

"Shut up. Not interested. Not coming. I'll call you tomorrow." Fletcher switched it off.

All heads turned as he walked in the door. His mother's expression went from a smile to horror. Shock registered on the others' faces.

"What happened to you?" Stanley asked.

"I don't want to talk about it." Fletcher charged up the stairs.

"But your face," Shirley called. "You look . . . you look . . . grotesque."

Fletcher locked the bathroom door and shed his shirt and jeans. He started the water in the tub and poured half the box of oatmeal into it. The label promised a soothing experience. "I don't think so."

Examining himself in the mirror, he understood everyone's disgust. Red bumps covered his swollen face, neck, and chest. There had to be dozens of bites. Dried, caked vomit clung to his cheeks, ears, and part of his neck. He picked a small clump from one eyebrow and flung it into the trash.

Depressed, he peeled off his boxers, then lowered his body into the tub. Replaying the night's events, he decided he'd been lucky. The way he flailed like a mad man back to his car in his underwear, someone might have called him in as a mental patient on the loose. He sunk to his chin, wet the washcloth, and cleaned his face.

How had he let Tanya take over his brain? His entire life? He felt helpless when he met her, like he'd lost control over his common sense. She consumed him. He threw away his marriage for her. Why, from the get go, did everyone else assume she used him? How did they spot what he didn't?

CHAPTER EIGHTEEN

"Fletcher seemed a bit, um . . . different tonight," Dora said.

Shirley made herself look at her cards.

"Bet it's got something to do with that girl. It's just like the song." Morty slurped his beer. "Come on. You know the one." He drummed his fingers on the table. "*When a man loves a woman.* That's it. *Can't keep his mind on nothing else.*"

"Sure," Stanley said. "We'll go with that." He played an ace of spades that took the trick. "I believe I have the rest, also." He laid his last two cards on the table.

Dora wrote on a pad of paper and nodded. "I'm afraid he's right, Shirley. The boys have won again. Unless you have something amazing hiding in your hand."

"Nope." Shirley showed her cards. "No such luck. How much did they win on that one?" As Dora scribbled figures, she fought the urge to go upstairs and demand an explanation.

"We owe them a dollar and forty cents." Dora stretched. "I need to quit. It's late."

"I'm tired, too." Shirley reached for the mason jar of change. She poured out coins and sorted them. "Here, you tinkle-gin champions." She pushed two quarters and two dimes toward Morty and the same toward Stanley. "Don't go crazy and spend it all in one place."

Stanley scooped the change into his hand. "No, ma'am. This here's for my Tahiti vacation."

"You'd better start playing a lot more cards." Morty lifted his beer and finished it. "I've got a theory about your son."

Shirley twisted the lid onto the coin jar while cursing Morty in her head. She thought they'd changed the subject.

"Okay, I'll bite," Stanley said. "What's your theory?"

"On television, they have these commercials now," Morty said, "about a male condition called Low T."

Feeling a blush come on, Shirley waved him off. "I think we know they've put a name to the normal process of life, like it's a disease all of a sudden. It's not for mixed company."

"Hang with me," Morty said. "My guess is your son is cursed, or blessed—depending on how you look at it, with the opposite—*high* testosterone. He's got too much. Has a tough time thinking with his brain if a pretty woman's around. Like a teenager. He should get it checked out."

It was a strange argument, but Shirley had to admit it would make sense. She exchanged puzzled looks with Stanley.

"I'm going to the mall tomorrow," Dora said. "Want to come with?"

Shirley turned to her, relieved at having the subject changed again. "I can't. I'm going job hunting." She'd decided to come out of the economic shame closet, but only a step or two.

"You, too?" Dora's eyes widened. "Whatever for?"

"Times are tough for everybody," Morty said.

"A little extra money would be nice, of course." Shirley picked up and carried a few plates to the kitchen. "I think I'm bored. All I do is play cards and mah-jongg."

"Well, thanks a lot," Dora said.

Shirley smiled at her. "For heaven's sake, don't take it personally. You know I love spending time with you. But I see Stanley meeting new people. He has new stories to tell. It sounds like fun." She thought she convinced them and made a mental note to list salesmanship at the top of her skills list.

"What's wrong with the people you already know?" Dora reached for her purse on the floor, then stood.

"Not a thing." Shirley hugged her. "You will always be my best friend. I promise."

"In that case, do you want me to keep you company when you go?"

The last thing she needed was Dora's lack of a filter. "As much fun as that would be, I want to do this alone. I hope you understand."

Dora nodded.

"Let's go." Morty opened the front door. "My seventy cents is burning a hole in my pocket. I want to put it away before I spend it on something frivolous." He stepped into the night.

Shrugging, Stanley followed him.

"I never really know when he's kidding," Shirley said to Dora.

"I'm not sure he is." Dora lowered her voice. "Call me as soon as you find out why Fletcher came home looking so beat up."

"I may never find out."

Dora and Morty went out the door. Stanley put his arm around Shirley. They watched the other couple disappear, walking away in the night.

"I'm very proud of you, honey." Stanley kissed her.

"Oh? For what?"

"The way you handled the job hunting issue in front of our friends. You made it sound exactly the way I want them to see it. More of an *I need to do more* thing than the necessity it is. They don't need to know the straits we're in."

"It worked when you told Fletcher and Nina about your Happy Mart job, so I figured it would be better not to try and hide the fact I'll be working, too."

They walked inside the townhouse. Stanley closed the door. "Now." He pointed at the ceiling. "What in Sam hill do you suppose happened to him?"

CHAPTER NINETEEN

Since Stanley broke the bad financial news, Shirley checked the want ads daily. No job seemed to be anything she wanted to do or could do. Then she remembered her recent trip into Sago Beach with Dora. The shops were busy, luxury cars abounded, and the restaurant had been almost full on a mid-summer day.

The solution eased in and hugged her like an overpriced designer T-shirt. She tossed the want ads into the recycling. Want to make money? she reasoned, then go to where the money is.

Now, dressed in a black A-line skirt and a plain button-down white blouse, she leaned toward the bathroom mirror and applied eyeliner.

"Gotta go," Stanley called.

"Coming." She would drop him at Happy Mart, then take the car into Sago Beach. In spite of the fact she told Stanley she wasn't the least bit nervous, she felt rising anxiety. She grabbed her purse off the bed and went downstairs.

"You look beautiful." Stanley beamed at her from the entry. "How could anyone refuse you a job?"

She smiled and headed for the door. "C'mon, Romeo. Your harem awaits."

"What?" His eyes widened.

She winked, then went outside. He locked up and got into the Buick's passenger seat.

"What did that mean?" he asked.

"Did you think I wouldn't find out you're the toast of the elderly women at Happy Mart?" She burst out laughing. "Edna, Dora, and Agnes all saw you being fawned over by your groupies. I get full reports."

He reddened. "It's not my fault. I don't do anything to encourage them." He held up his left hand. "In fact, I wave my ring around constantly." He sighed. "It doesn't seem to make a difference, though." Lifting her chin and turning her toward him, he stared into her eyes. "You know I would never do anything to hurt you. I'm a perfect gentleman with those crazy old bats."

She melted and felt tears form. "I know. I was only teasing."

***

After she dropped him at Happy Mart, Shirley realized her nervousness had calmed. Stanley and she were in precarious financial shape, but they had each other. They were a solid team. That was a lot more than a lot of other people had, including—she imagined—some wealthy ones.

She parked her car in a lot behind a two-story complex facing Pearl Avenue. It was June thirtieth. The *season* was three months away. Every October through March, the snowbirds flocked to South Florida to occupy their second homes or condos, jamming restaurants, movie theaters, and doctors' offices. The wealthy perched in Sago Beach and Palm Beach, attended lavish charity events and parties, and spent their money. Shirley hoped her timing was good. Maybe the shops needed to time to train new people for October.

Pearl Avenue buzzed with activity. People strolled the streets, and expensive cars with chauffeurs dispatched important-looking people. Her resolve dissolved. Just like the last time she and Dora came, Shirley felt overwhelmed and out of place. An ordinary cabbage plunked into a display of fancy Belgian endive. She sat on a bench to regroup.

She wanted to go home, but chased that impulse away. Taking several deep breaths first, she stood. She was at the west end of the street and decided to work her way to the east end, then cross the street and explore the opposite side.

The nearest store was a clothing boutique. Its name, Hamish Pfeffer, glittered in gold on the window and on the multi-paned French door. She re-tucked her blouse into her skirt, smoothed it a bit, and entered.

A stern-faced lady with gray hair and three chins approached her. Shirley wondered if the woman was the sister of the awful clerk at the hoity-toity antique place she and Dora had visited earlier in the summer.

"May I help you," the woman said.

The inflection the woman used made Shirley think *what do you want* was the true question. She steeled herself. "Yes. I'm looking for employment. Do you know if there are any openings?"

With an open sneer, the woman did an up and down check on Shirley, taking time to stare at her shoes, then her purse. "No," she said. "We are not hiring." She turned and headed toward a counter full of leather goods.

"Thank you." Shirley left the store, more than a little flustered. "Why did I *thank* her?" She needed to be more, just a bit more, like Dora. "You don't thank people for being nasty."

She continued down the avenue, stopping in at stores selling luggage, jewelry, and flowers. None of them gave her a serious look. Her feet began to ache.

In a fine stationary store, the young woman behind the desk smiled at her.

"My mom does the hiring," she said. "Just a sec."

Shirley examined the array of papers, exquisite monograms,

and fancy options. She'd no idea such elaborate invitations were available, much less used. She picked up a sample of a wedding invite. The tiny sticker on the back said they were forty dollars apiece. That couldn't be right.

"My daughter said you were inquiring about a job?" a sophisticated voice said.

Shirley pivoted, still holding the sample. "Yes. Hello."

The mother, a fortyish woman in a beige suit, did the obligatory personal scan on Shirley and frowned. "Hmmm. No. I don't think so."

Shirley's heart sank. She'd made the mistake of having a smidge of hope in that store. She replaced the sample and skulked outside, feeling inferior, useless, and blinking back tears.

With an ever-increasing cloud of despair engulfing her, she crossed the street and tried four more places. All gave curt dismissals. She walked another block, saw a bench in the shade of a poinciana tree and sat. The rejection was too much. She began to sob. She'd been a fool to think anyone in snooty Sago Beach would have any use for the likes of her. Tears flowed, and she lowered her head into her hands.

"Saints alive," an effeminate male voice said. "Darling, what's the matter?"

She lifted her head to see a man with wavy brown hair squatting in front of her. He had kind eyes.

"Are you lost?"

That hit her as funny, and she laughed through her tears. She reached into her purse and found a tissue. "No. I'm not lost."

"Lance?" Another man, this one with jet-black spiked hair, came from the shop behind her. "What is it? Is there a problem?"

"I don't know," Lance said. "This lovely lady is terribly kerfuffled about something, but she hasn't told me what."

That made Shirley laugh even harder. She wiped her eyes with her tissue. "Thank you. I needed that."

The other man stood beside Lance and tsked, shaking his head. "Now you've gone and smeared your eyeliner straight to your ear."

Lance spread his arms. "It's hot as the devil's barbecue out here. Come inside and have a cold drink, then you can tell us what on earth has you so troubled." He gestured to her, tsking like his friend had. "A pretty lady like you."

Nodding, Shirley stood and followed them into the shop. On the awning and the door, the signage said *Paulina's Peignoirs*. Inside, the air conditioning made her realize how overheated she'd become. She recognized the store's sultry scent as Shalimar. The high ceiling was tented with pink silk and festooned with huge fuchsia tassels. Round tiered tables draped in pink stripes and plaids displayed panties, bras, bustiers, and teddies. Side racks along the walls held robes, nighties, and shelves of perfumes and personal products. There were several women milling about the tables.

"This way." Lance took her arm and led her to the back, where a hallway opened to a stock room and an office. He pointed to a sofa in the office. "Have a seat."

"Water?" The black-haired man offered her a frosty bottle from a mini-fridge.

"Thank you." She accepted the bottle and sat. "Thank you so much." Another wave of emotion hit her and tears flowed again. She wiped at them. "I'm sorry. I don't know why I'm such a mess."

Lance took a chair next to her, and the black-haired man sat behind the desk. They looked at each other, then they both stared at her.

Shirley drank some water and regained control. She liked these young men and figured she'd level with them. "I need a job. My husband and I are going broke, and I *have* to get a job. I've gone into every store on Pearl Avenue asking for one, and they all looked at me like I was Typhoid Mary. I'm sorry I broke down in front. I just . . . fell apart. Thank you so much for your kindness. If I may take a few more minutes to gather my wits, I'll get out of your way."

The two men exchanged knowing glances again.

"Job hunting here? On Pearl Avenue? With those shoes and that purse?" Lance rolled his eyes. "You're lucky they didn't call security."

Shirley looked at her shoes. "What's wrong with them? I polished them. They're fairly new. No holes or scuffs."

"No, no, no, no, no," Lance said. "Oh, dear God, no. Dearie, those look like you bought them at a Pay-Less."

"And the purse?" The black-haired man sighed. "Let me guess. Wanda's Discount Palace?"

Her dander rising, Shirley placed the water on a side table. "Thank you for the analysis, but this is what I can afford." She stood. "Now, if you're finished mocking me, I'll leave."

They both looked shocked.

"I'm sorry," Lance said. "We didn't mean it that way. We were trying to help. Please sit."

"Please," the black-haired man said.

She studied him, then sat.

"My name is Paul Benedetto." The black-haired man leaned forward with an outstretched hand. "I'm the *Paulina* from Paulina's Peignoirs."

She shook his hand. "Shirley Nowack."

"Lance Tillman." Lance shook her hand, too. "Let's start over."

"You're Paulina?" Shirley said. "And you both sell lingerie? To women?"

"Yes. We're partners," Lance said. "In the business and in life."

"I see."

Paul smiled at her. "We don't actually do the selling. Our clientele, as much as they profess to love us, would rather have women wait on them. Less embarrassing. We understand."

"We do have another location." Lance looked sheepish.

"In Fort Lauderdale. We sell at that one."

"The clientele there is a bit different," Paul said.

"I'll say. There are a lot of drag clubs there. The *girls* love our store. Have you ever sold retail?" Lance asked.

Shirley laughed. "In nineteen-fifty-nine. I worked at the snack counter in a movie theater."

Lance's eyebrows rose. He scratched his head. "Would you excuse us for a moment?" He gestured to Paul, and they left the office.

She sipped her water and, after a few minutes, felt silly sitting there for no apparent reason. It was time to face facts, go home, and beg for a job where people wouldn't look down on her. She stood and tossed the empty bottle in the trash.

Paul and Lance appeared in the doorway.

"I've taken enough of your time," Shirley said. "I can't tell you how much I appreciate your helping me."

"We've discussed the matter," Lance said. "We want to know if you'd consider working for us."

"In Fort Lauderdale? Heavens, no. My husband and I share a car. But bless your hearts for wanting to help."

"No. Here," Paul said. "One of our saleswomen eloped last week. Said she'd come back. Nobody's heard from her. Busy season's coming, you know."

"I thought I wasn't good enough for this town."

"Now don't react all snippety again," Lance said, "but you would need to wear better clothes and shoes."

As fast as her hopes rose, they crashed. "I can't afford to buy them."

"We talked about it. We'll help you—pay for a couple outfits," Paul said. "Lance will take you shopping. It's his hobby, doing clothing reworks. You are a beautiful woman. He'll have you looking like you belong here in no time."

"Why?" Shirley said. "You could hire someone who already had the proper things. Why would you do this?"

"We like you." Lance smiled.

"You remind me of my grandmother," Paul said.

"And I *love* a project," Lance said.

CHAPTER TWENTY

Home alone on the next Saturday morning, Fletcher sat at the kitchen counter sipping coffee, perusing the real estate ads. He wanted to find an apartment. While living with his parents gave him time to rethink and prioritize, their lifestyle and his didn't match. The early dinners and bedtimes, the washer and vacuum running at six in the morning, and the questions about where he went and with whom drove him bananas. He could tell his father's nerves were on edge, too. He picked up his pen and circled another building he thought he'd check out that afternoon.

A loud knock rattled the jalousies. He set down his mug and opened the door.

"Hi." An ancient skinny woman wearing enormous dark sunglasses, pink T-shirt, blue jean shorts, and high-top black sneakers stood on the stoop. "I'm Agnes Graber, friend of your mom's. You must be Fletcher."

He knew who Agnes was. He'd heard Shirley's friends talk about the *weird* art lady. In the flesh, she lived up to the description.

"Hello," he said. "Yes, I'm Fletcher. I'm afraid you've missed seeing my parents. They won't be home for a few hours."

She produced a square glass casserole dish from a

voluminous army-green canvas satchel at her feet and thrust it at him. "Here. This is your mother's. Betty sent it over."

He took it. "Thank you."

She didn't make a motion to leave.

"Is there anything else?" he asked.

"Sure, now that you mention it." She lifted her bag and pushed past him into the living room. She removed her sunglasses, looked startled, and turned in a circle. "I forgot how *white* it is in here. Almost blinding." The sunglasses went back on.

Fletcher nodded. "Yes. Their decorating style is early American bland white box. You get used to it."

"I'd like to talk to you."

"Me? About what?" He couldn't imagine.

"I hear lots of gossip about you when I play games with the chickees." She sat at the counter in front of Fletcher's coffee and set her bag on the floor. "That's what I call those cuckoo ladies—birdies, chickees. Nice enough, most of the time, but they waste too much energy finding out everyone else's business. Except your mother. I respect her."

Fletcher took the stool next to her and slid his mug and the pile of papers over. "Mom would appreciate that, I'm sure. So. What are the *chickees* saying about me?"

Agnes pushed her glasses down her nose and stared at him. Her short, curly, fuzzy white hair stood out in all directions, like a halo.

"Would you like some coffee? I could make another pot."

"Never touch the stuff. Stop darting around and look into my eyes."

He did and saw pale-blue irises swimming in yellowish whites. Her lids, wrinkled and freckled, stayed wide open, and he wondered how she didn't blink for so long. She wore no make-up, and the few lashes she had were bleach-white. Then he noticed her pupils enlarging, and it seemed like she'd honed in on him. He felt exposed somehow.

"There you are." Her voice became softer. "Good." She broke the gaze and took his hand in hers. "When's your birthday?

"February eleventh." Her fingers rubbed the top of his knuckles, then she let go.

She smiled. "I knew it. I'm an eleven, too. I'll be eighty-eight come November eleventh."

"Wow. Congratulations. I hope I'm in such good shape at that age. What does being an eleven mean?"

"Hope's got nothing to do with it. Don't worry about the number thing. Not yet."

Confused, he pondered again why she came to see him. He didn't dare be rude to his mother's friend. "You said you wanted to talk to me?"

"You have issues," she said.

"I beg your pardon?"

"You can't keep your dick in your pants."

Fletcher shook his head in disbelief. "What the hell? Even if it's true, what business is it of yours?"

"You can stuff your indignation. I'm here to help. You want me to help or not?"

"I don't know. What are you, an amateur counselor or something? Did my father ask you to do this?"

"Nobody asked me to do squat. They don't know I'm here."

He laughed and relaxed. "You're a real kick in the ass, aren't you? I'll bet you don't own a single lace doily."

She winked. "I hate prissy crap. I'm an artist. I sell a few oils to some galleries in Sedona."

"Arizona? Why way out west?"

"My art sells well there."

"Then why don't you live in Arizona?"

She rolled her eyes. "It's a desert. Who wants to live in an oven? Look at me. Don't you think I'm wrinkled enough? Moisture in the air is best for the skin."

"Hard to argue with that."

"When I'm not painting, I try to help people find a better path when I can, and when I believe they might be open to thinking another way."

"I'm not sure what that means." How many ways were there to think? "Your brain just thinks what it thinks."

"Not so. You attract everything that happens to you. You, and you alone, are responsible for the good and the bad in your life."

"That's pretty cosmic." He thought maybe he should ask her to leave.

"You think I'm full of new-age shit, don't you?"

Fletcher felt his face redden because that was exactly what he was thinking. "Hold on a second. Why do you know so much about me, anyway? The old ladies' gossip?"

"Wake up. You're too smart to practice willful blindness. It'll catch up with you and destroy your life. This is a retirement village. Guess what the number one topic, twenty-four seven, is around here?"

"Shuffleboard? Movies at the clubhouse? Who had their hip replaced?" Dora retelling the scandalous rumor on Stanley's birthday came back. "Oh. Other people's business."

"Children and grandchildren first. We hear it all. Marriages, babies, affairs, divorces. Whose kid bought a lake house, which grandkid got the lead in the play. Huge one-upmanship going on. Now, back to your story."

Fletcher blanched. The whole time he'd stayed in Silver Sago Village, he hadn't thought about who knew what. He let his forehead crash onto the counter. "You mean every nosy bitty and fart in this place knows what happened to me?" He doubled his resolve to find a place that afternoon.

"Watch who you're calling names, pal. If it makes you feel any better, most of them forgot you already. You're only noteworthy until someone has bigger news. Lucky for you, I have an excellent memory."

"Whee. I don't feel lucky."

"Well, you are because I'm here to help. Lauren left you because you cheated. You cheated because you didn't feel you were good enough for her. Lauren, I hear, is top notch stuff all around. You had as many affairs . . . it was three, right? As many as it took for Lauren to give up on you. You drove her away. On purpose. Before she could reject you, the *real* you, for the faults you figured she'd uncover."

"Wrong."

"Let it seep in. You do things you know will end a relationship, then chase the next girl who doesn't know you so well. You show her the charming façade. Therefore, you control everything and you can't get hurt. As a bonus, you got to be *right.* Lauren left you. You were willing to work on it."

"I was."

"Horse hockey. You were shtupping the next one while you said it." She slid off the stool, dug a paperback book from her satchel, and handed it to him. "Here. Read this. I'll call you in a week and see how you're progressing."

He looked at the book. A photo of a rainbow and an older woman's face were on the cover. "Looks like a book for women."

"Build a bridge and get over it. What's your number?" Agnes had an iPhone in her palm, poised to enter the digits.

"You have a cell phone?"

She gave him a puzzled look. "Do you think I'm too old to use it?"

"No. It's just my parents." He threw his hands up. "I gave them one last year. I pay the service on it. They refuse to use it. It's probably in a drawer with a dead battery."

"Gotta embrace the new. It's the way to feel alive."

He gave her his number, not because he believed what she'd theorized, but because she was a drastic change from most old folks. More like someone his own age.

"Gotta go." Agnes grabbed her satchel. "Let me know

what you think of the book."

He saw her to the door and followed her outside. A woman wearing a headband stood on the sidewalk staring their way. A look of recognition lit up her face.

"Agnes," the woman said, "I *thought* that was your Jeep parked there."

"Hello, Edna." Agnes leaned into Fletcher and whispered while she waved to Edna. "Never tell her anything. Biggest gossip in the village."

Edna craned her neck in an apparent attempt to see into the townhouse's open front door. "Is Shirley home?"

Fletcher shook his head. "No. Sorry."

"Well, what were you doing there, then?" Edna asked.

Turning her back to Edna, Agnes made a face. "Nosy bitch. You go in. I'll deflect and distract."

"Thank you." He pivoted and headed inside.

"That's a fancy headband, Edna. Is it new?" Agnes' voice and footsteps receded behind him. "Did you see that the Walkers got another car?"

CHAPTER TWENTY-ONE

"I can't believe this is it." Catherine gestured toward the garage. "Hector could have transported your things for you. You wouldn't have had so many trips."

Maddy loaded her last suitcase into her white SL550 and closed the trunk. "Showing up with a chauffeur toting my luggage is not how I want my new neighbors to see me."

"Darn that designer," Catherine said. "I asked her to take her time with your new place."

Maddy laughed. "I paid her extra to hurry up the basics. The rest I'll finish while I'm there. You've had almost a month to accept this. And I'm only moving five miles away."

"But to live off the island," Catherine said. "It's just so . . ." The proper words wouldn't come. Tacky and lower class did. How to express her dismay without alienating Muffin?

Throwing her purse onto the passenger seat, Maddy shook her head. "You've told me many times how you feel. This is something I want to do. My entire life has been spent in an insane world of privilege. I want to know what it's like for people to accept me not for who my family is and how much money we have, but because they like *me*." She approached her.

Catherine felt tears welling.

"Don't cry, Mother." Maddy hugged her. "We'll talk every

day and have plenty of dinners together. I promise." She stood back. "Remember your promise to me?"

Catherine sniffed. "I hoped you'd forgotten."

"No way. Thirty pounds by Christmas. I'm worried about you. Follow that diet Dr. Zimmerman put you on." She climbed into her car and turned the key.

Waving as she watched Maddy's car head toward the street, Catherine decided she needed a drink. She'd gained more since her Muffin returned from France. She felt huge and uncomfortable. Maddy thought Catherine ate because of loneliness, that she needed male company. Her daughter didn't know the half of it. Catherine's libido was in hyper-drive. She'd named her vibrator Daily Dan. But it was a vicious cycle. She felt too awful to flirt or date, which depressed her and made her eat more.

She walked inside, past the bustle in the catering-sized kitchen. That evening, she would host a political fundraiser for a former senator, now running for governor. She closed the door of her study and poured a shot of Scotch. She'd have the one drink, then a nap, a bath, and prepare for the evening.

From time to time, men made advances to her. Usually, they were younger and after what she suspected—her money. Like the gorgeous Tony, several months earlier.

Actually, Tony was honest about what he wanted. At their first dinner, he laid it out. He'd sleep with her for money. A lot of it. For the chance to experience a man like him, she paid it and gave him generous bonuses. He pretended her shape didn't bother him, but she could tell. She didn't need any more degradation.

She took a deep breath. This time, she would stick to the diet.

***

Nina reviewed her figures. She stared out the window from the desk in her kitchen and sighed. The maple tree they'd planted when they first bought the house now towered over the roof. Its leaves glowed yellowish-green in the sunlight. Charles and his friends, in the middle of a basketball game on the driveway, whooped when someone sunk a basket.

She calculated again. The mileage didn't make sense. George told her he'd gone to a client's office the day before, Saturday, in Long Branch. Since their trip to Florida, she'd gotten the feeling he was not telling her the truth about something. She prayed it wasn't another affair. But red flags were red flags, and she began to track his mileage again.

When he had returned and gone upstairs, she'd slipped into the garage and checked the odometer. Only four miles. If he went where he claimed, there should be at least fifteen miles more. Wherever he'd gone, it was closer than he wanted her to know. Why?

It was the third time in a week and a half. "God damn it all to hell." She threw the pen against the wall.

"Mom?" Mary Ann came from the den doorway. "What's the matter?"

Nina shuffled the papers into a pile and turned them upside-down. She faced Mary Ann and smiled. "Nothing, dear. Couldn't get my checkbook to balance. I shouldn't have cursed."

"Want me to ground you?"

"If it means staying in my room with no television or phone calls, or having to make dinner? Yes, please. What will you serve tonight?"

"Ha ha." A small backpack was slung over one shoulder. "I cleaned my room. Can I go to April's house?"

"Sure. Be back by six." Nina watched her daughter exit through the garage. The girl did an exaggerated walk, swaying her hips as she passed Charles and his friends. One of the boys stood still and stared until Charles threw the basketball into his back.

Nina rolled her eyes. Back to George. She'd follow him

whenever she could. But how?

***

Fletcher parked in a guest space at The Chancellor Palms condominium. Getting out of his car, he glanced up at the fifteen-story tower. It was contemporary, but not too stark. The agent told him it was only a year old.

He went inside, gave his name at the lobby concierge desk, received a guest pass, and was told Rick Santos, his realtor, was upstairs. So far, he liked what he saw. Everything looked upscale and clean.

When the elevator opened on the twelfth floor, he walked to twelve-sixteen. It wasn't an end unit as he'd hoped. The apartment to the left was the corner unit, number twelve-eighteen. A briefcase held the door to twelve-sixteen open. He knocked, then entered.

"Rick?" he said.

"Fletcher, come in." Rick, a husky short man wearing khakis and a plaid dress shirt, came into the entry hall. He spread his arms and looked around. "What did I tell you? Quite a place, huh?"

It had high ceilings, Palladian windows, and upscale molding details. Fletcher walked into the living room. There was a view of the Sago City Center, a booming shopping and office complex, with the Intracoastral Waterway beyond it, then Sago Beach Island. The aqua-blue Atlantic shimmered in the distance.

"Not bad." Fletcher smiled. "The owner still wants to do a lease with an option to buy?"

Rick nodded. "They'd prefer to sell right away, but yes, they'll rent to you first."

"Show me the rest." The kitchen was dark cherry cabinets and black granite with stainless appliances, the dining room had framed beveled mirrors, the three spacious bedrooms each had their own bathroom, and a powder room faced the entry hall.

Fletcher loved it. "It's exactly what I need. How soon can I move in?"

After he signed the paperwork, he went to the hall and waited while Rick locked up. The elevator dinged, and he saw a tall young blonde walking his way. As she got closer, he tried not to stare. She was beautiful. Stunning. But not like Tanya at all. This one was classy. Understated elegance. Old-fashioned movie-star glamour. Lauren Bacall class. Princess Grace class. He slapped himself mentally, reminding his brain he'd sworn off the young ones.

She smiled as she passed. "Hello."

Rick grinned. "Hello."

She stopped at twelve-eighteen's door, fumbled in her purse, and came up with keys. She looked back at them. "Are you my new neighbors?"

Rick pointed to Fletcher. "He is."

God had a horrible sense of humor, playing very evil tricks on Fletcher. He nodded. "I am." He walked to her with his hand outstretched. "I'm Fletcher Nowack. I'll move in next week."

She shook his hand and smiled, revealing perfect white teeth. "Maddy Forsyth. Very nice to meet you."

An electrical quiver shot through him, and he thought the same shock registered in her eyes.

She disengaged her hand from his and opened her door. "Well. Guess I'll be seeing you."

"I guess." He retreated to his door, where Rick stood wide eyed.

"Man, you got the luck." Rick elbowed Fletcher. "You should buy a lottery ticket for tonight."

CHAPTER TWENTY-TWO

Working at Happy Mart exposed Stanley to a segment of life he didn't much care for. Every day it became harder and harder to smile through the trials of his shift.

He had to be in early that day. Happy Mart started its annual Christmas in July Blowout sale at eight in the morning. Still yawning, he kissed Shirley goodbye when she dropped him off at seven.

"Good luck today," she said.

He waved, then entered at the employee's side door using his ID card. He'd told Shirley some of what went on at the store, but not the worst of it.

As Stanley clocked in, Tim entered and poured a cup of coffee. A dozen other employees milled about.

"This'll be your first big sale day," Tim said. "Brace yourself. It'll be good training for the day after Thanksgiving."

Stanley helped himself to coffee. He checked to see who was nearby, then whispered, "This is a depressing job, you know that?"

Tim chuckled. "Don't let the nutty ones get to you. Try to think about our regulars who always say hello, like we matter. That's what I do."

When they went to unlock the front doors at eight, a long

line had formed. Customers streamed in, and the Customer Service counter line got lengthy in a hurry. As the wait dragged on, patience eroded and tempers flared.

"Jesus, lady," a testy male voice said. "Get back where you were."

Stanley turned to see an elfin, elderly woman shuffle further to the front of the line. He groaned.

She wore a blue-veiled pillbox hat, a moth-eaten gray sweater over her pink-checked housecoat, and black orthopedic shoes. He and Tim had already escorted her to her original place in line twice. Stanley walked to her.

"Ma'am, you need to stay where you were in line," Stanley said, keeping his voice low and gentle. "The people in front of you don't appreciate your cutting in."

Her rheumy eyes looked up into his. "All I want to do is return my marmalade. I bought the wrong kind by mistake."

"Yes, I know. You told me. If you can't wait your turn, maybe you could come back in a few days, when the lines aren't so long."

"It's only a small jar."

"That doesn't matter."

She stroked his arm. "You're such a handsome man."

He jerked his arm away. "How about coming back later in the week?"

"No. I want my money now."

When Stanley left her in the place he knew she'd started at, the woman behind her gave him an exaggerated eye-roll.

He looked for Tim and found him embroiled in a verbal tug-of-war for the remaining chair in the waiting area about thirty feet away.

"But I got here first," a young woman with a huge baby bump said. She moaned with her hand on her belly as she lowered herself into the chair. "You have a cane, lean on it."

The old man she spoke to looked as though he would hit her with it. "You kids today. You're all brats. All of you." He glanced past Tim to Stanley. "Isn't there anything you can do? I have to wait for my wife. She's in the line, over there." He pointed toward the end of the line. "I might pass out."

"Wanna take odds it's marmalade lady?" Tim whispered.

Stanley scanned the people who occupied the other six seats. In a loud but non-threatening voice, he said, "Would any of you be willing to give up your seat for this man? Please?"

Silence ensued. If it were a cartoon, crickets would chirp. A woman checked her manicure. Another texted on her cell. A man reading *Sports Illustrated* never looked up.

"Tim, make sure he doesn't fall," Stanley said. "I'll be right back." He hurried to the break room, borrowed a chair, and hustled to the front with it.

While Tim helped the man to sit, the old guy made a juvenile face at the pregnant woman.

She sneered at him.

Later, coming from the break room after wolfing down the lunch Shirley packed for him, Stanley saw with dismay the line was no shorter and the faces in it no more pleasant. Tim and the other greeter on duty, Marjorie, looked resigned and weary.

He signaled to Tim that he'd returned, and Tim sent Marjorie scampering like a rabbit to her break.

"Next year," Tim said, "remind me to schedule my vacation during the July Blowout."

"Me, too." Stanley walked to the end of returns line.

"What the fuck is taking so long?" a harsh female voice said.

He turned to see who spoke. A thirtyish bleached-white blonde, wearing a low-cut leopard-print spandex top, black spandex pants, and tons of jewelry snapped her fingers at him. A cute boy of about four hung onto her leg. Stanley had a difficult time not staring at the rose tattoo on her left breast.

"I'm sorry, ma'am," Stanley said. "We've got six people working the Customer Service counter. They're going as fast as they can."

She scowled.

Stanley shrugged and took a few steps back, counting the people in line.

"I'm hungry, Mommy," the boy said. "You said we could eat."

"Ain't gonna happen soon, Kenny. So shut-up about it."

"But I'm *really* hungry."

Stanley lost count and started over.

"It ain't my fault these idiots can't figure out how to run this place," the mom said. "It's their fault. The morons who work here."

That comment ticked Stanley off. If he weren't a gentleman, and she weren't a . . . he stopped mid-thought. She wasn't a lady. He wanted to punch her.

With a look of determination, the boy marched to Stanley and kicked him hard in the shin.

"Owww," Stanley yelped.

"Stupid," the boy shouted. "I'm hungry."

Stanley bent over to catch his breath and counted to ten, then twenty. He limped to the break room, ripping his smock off on the way. His shift ended at two. It was ten till. He found Wheaton and handed him the smock. "I appreciate your hiring me, but I quit."

Wheaton looked shocked. "Why? You're doing so well, and you're popular with the customers."

Wincing, Stanley lifted his pant leg to reveal a three-inch bruise with blood seeping from it. "The customers have turned ugly."

"We need to fill out a report. Have a seat." Wheaton dialed his phone. "Barbara? We have a—"

"That's okay. I'm sure it's not serious. Just hurts like the devil at the moment." Stanley took his wallet and keys from his locker. "*You* should be out front dealing with the jackals." He stepped with care past Wheaton, through the crowded aisles, and found Tim.

They exchanged numbers. On his way out, Stanley turned

back and yelled at the Customer Service employees, "Save yourselves."

***

"The little shit was wearing cowboy boots." Stanley grimaced as Shirley examined his shin. Sitting in the kitchen with his leg on another chair and his pant leg pushed up, it surprised him how much the bruised area had spread. "The whole world's going down the toilet, you know that?"

Shirley wiped the crusted blood with careful strokes of the washcloth, then studied it. "It doesn't look like it needs stitches."

"Maybe I shouldn't have quit," he said.

"You'll find something else."

"Who's going to hire me?"

"You don't know until you get out there, do you? Whatever it is, it's got to be better than Happy Mart." She squeezed some antibiotic cream from a tube, then covered the center bloodied part with a bandage.

"That's true. I'd like to stay in touch with Tim, though. Would you mind if we invited him to one of our potlucks? He's a great guy. I think he's lonely since his wife passed a few years ago."

She laughed. "Fresh male blood? The girls will love it. Ask him, please."

"Maybe I should warn him."

"Don't you dare."

CHAPTER TWENTY-THREE

Sitting on the bed, Shirley tucked her stockinged feet into her new shoes. She touched the fine leather and admired the way they made her feet look smaller.

Stanley appeared in the bathroom doorway, brushing his teeth, a little foam escaping his lips. He gave her a thumbs-up, then went back to the sink.

She checked that she had her essentials in the proper purse. The one that matched the shoes. She chuckled thinking of her shopping trip with Lance. He was like a kid with a new puppy, training her eyes to be more discerning. Giving her hugs when she made good choices.

"I don't see what the difference is," Stanley said.

"In what?" She twisted to see him walk to his dresser and take a shirt from the drawer.

"The clothes. The shoes. Don't take this the wrong way. You look beautiful in them, but you looked beautiful before. I don't get what the big deal is."

"I didn't either." She stood and inspected herself in the mirror. "I'm beginning to. Tell you one thing I didn't expect—the expensive shoes? Much more comfortable. I used to think one hundred dollars for a pair of shoes was crazy expensive. Who ever dreamed you could spend over a thousand on a pair?"

Stanley blanched and looked about to keel over. "How much did those—the ones you're wearing—cost?"

"I can't remember." She saw his growing horror. "No. No. Lance didn't spend anywhere near that, honey. Maybe two hundred? They were having a great sale." She glanced at her watch. "We'd better go. I've got to be at Paulina's in twenty minutes."

They locked up and climbed into the Buick.

While Stanley drove, Shirley thought about her new employers. On her first day, Paul spent the whole shift with her, teaching her about the garments and personal products and what different customers expected in the way of service. The customers ranged from snotty as hell to extremely kind. The challenge was sizing them up as they entered the store, so she'd know how to approach them.

The boys, as she called Paul and Lance, seemed to adopt her as their honorary grandmother. She turned out to have a knack for sales. Lance looked like he'd burst with pride when she made her first sale, over five hundred dollars, on her own. It surprised her when one woman tipped her a fifty for her help. The older customers were starting to ask for her.

They passed over the Intracoastal. "Now when you meet them, be nice," Shirley said.

He glanced at her. "You didn't need to say that."

"You forget how many times I've been in the room when you and your friends make gay jokes. Little asides about effeminate tendencies. But I know you're not a homophobe."

Stanley parked behind the building, and they entered through the back door.

"There she is." Lance popped his head out the office. "My girl." He came into the hall and hugged Shirley, then eyed Stanley. "Is this who I think it is?"

Shirley smiled and moved aside. "Lance, this is my husband, Stanley. He's been wanting to meet you and Paul."

"Hi." Stanley put his hand out. "Nice to meet you."

Paul came from the shop and joined them. "Did I hear right? Is this our Stanley?" He winked at Shirley, then shook Stanley's hand. "Paul Benedetto. We *love* Shirley. We're so happy she chose our store to break down in front of."

Stanley's eyebrows shot up. "What?"

Shirley cleared her throat. "I didn't tell him that part." She turned to him. "It wasn't a big deal. I got a bit overheated that day, is all. I'll tell you about it at home."

"Well." Stanley looked awkward. "I wanted to thank you for giving Shirley a chance and for all the new clothes and things. We'll pay you back."

Lance tsked. "No need."

Stanley grimaced.

"Stanley's job hunting this morning," Shirley said. "He quit his job at Happy Mart yesterday."

"Uh-huh." Lance's hand went to his mouth. "Can't blame you there."

"It was bad." Stanley moved to the door. "I'll be back at five, honey. Sell a lot of underwear." He left.

"Oh, my stars and bars," Lance said. "He's quite the hunk, isn't he?"

Paul slapped him playfully in the back of his head. "No need? Of course there's a need. That's a macho guy. Doesn't want to take any handouts. I like him, Shirley."

"Me, too." She laughed. "He can be stubborn, though."

Rubbing his head, Lance stared at the closed door. "Your children must be *gorgeous*."

***

There were three other saleswomen. Vera, the assistant manager, Jessie, and Angela. Shirley had worked with them all, but preferred to work with Vera. A striking brunette with a model's figure, Vera had an uncanny ability when it came to matching the customer's personality. She was deferential with the aloof snobs and a warm, welcoming friend to the others.

Late that morning, a black Rolls Royce pulled into the striped no-parking zone in front. A uniformed driver made his way around the car and opened the rear passenger door. A pair of long lean legs stepped out with a graceful flair. Attached to the legs was a red-haired woman who looked to be in her thirties. She wore an expression of disdain.

"Vera?" Shirley walked to her at the register counter. "This one looks like she'll need you, not me."

Vera glanced up and her face paled. "You're right. Go tell Paul that Baroness Wittenberg is here." She snatched a breath mint from a tin under the counter, smoothed her hair, and with a regal air of her own, walked toward the front.

Shirley hurried to the office.

With his bare feet on the desk and a phone earpiece in his right ear, Paul stared at a sheaf of papers in his hand. He looked up when she knocked and gave her a *just a sec* finger.

She went to the desk, grabbed a pen, and scribbled on a scrap of paper, *Baroness Witten-something is here!*

"I'll call you back." He tore the earpiece away, swung his feet off the desk, and bent to put his shoes on. "Thanks, Shirley."

She headed to the hall.

"Wait."

She stopped and turned.

"Do not talk to her. In fact, wait for me." He came from behind the desk. "She's prickly. Nothing personal, but don't even look at her if you can help it." He led the way to the shop. "Thank God Vera's here today."

She followed him out. Vera and the Baroness stood talking by the VIP room door. The VIP room was a key-locked lounge and dressing area reserved for the richest or most famous clients. They'd shown it to Shirley, but it hadn't been used on any of her shifts to date. Vera unlocked the VIP door.

Shirley felt a nudge on her shoulder.

"New customer by the robes," Paul whispered.

She nodded, spotting the woman and heading her way.

***

The Baroness stayed for two hours. Paul served her champagne and assorted fruits, nuts, and candies. Between other shoppers, Shirley helped by running for the items Vera felt the Baroness might consider, then re-hanging or folding the rejects. By the time the Baroness left with a few thousand dollars' worth of lingerie and skin care products, it was past lunchtime.

Shirley finished neatening things and went to eat. She enjoyed taking her bag lunch outdoors, to get some fresh, albeit hot, air. A big oak tree in the parking lot behind the building cast its shade over a bench by Paulina's back door. Paul put the bench there for that purpose. The employees were not to loiter on Pearl Avenue on their breaks.

All she could think about while munching her turkey sandwich was how Dora would devour the story of a real baroness in the store. The boys emphasized discretion about their customers, but Shirley figured she could change the baroness' name and tell Dora everything. To be even safer, maybe she'd tell her the woman was a duchess.

Vera peeked from the back door. "Shirley? There's a woman here who only wants you to wait on her. A friend of yours, she said. She's, um, quite unusual."

"Be right there." She gathered her things, went inside, and freshened up. Which of her friends could afford to shop at Paulina's?

Coming from the hall, she recognized the halo of white hair. Agnes stood at one of the skirted tables, rummaging through silk panties. She wore long blue jeans instead of her usual shorts, a pink polo shirt, and jeweled sandals in lieu of the normal high-top sneakers.

Shirley blew a sigh of relief. She approached Agnes. "What

a wonderful surprise."

Turning with a black thong stretched between her bony hands, Agnes smiled. "This is a classy place you're working at." She jiggled the thong. "What do you think of this?"

Not sure how Agnes meant the question, she played it neutral. "Thongs are okay, I guess. For the right person."

"How about for me?"

"To wear?"

Agnes looked at her as if she'd sprouted cauliflower from her head. "No, for a sling shot." She put the thong down and elbowed Shirley. "Got a hot date. Well, maybe not hot, but he's breathing."

Shirley giggled. "Who's the guy?"

"Don't tell any of your chickee friends. I don't want them knowing any more of my business. I've had two dates with Jerome Simms. He lives in your neighborhood."

"Jerry? I know him. His wife passed four months ago." Shirley figured him to be in his early eighties.

"I call him Jerome. He's antsy for me. Took me to dinner and invented several dumb reasons why I needed to come back to his place. I didn't go for it. I'm making him wait and suffer. Anticipation and all that."

Don't wait too long, Shirley thought, he might be nearing his expiration date. "Dallying with a younger man?"

Another deadpan stare from Agnes. "At my age, there isn't anything *but* younger men. I have to compete against you sweet young things in the village. Jerome, however, said he's had his eye on me for a long time, and that his wife stopped wanting sex years ago. I know he's ready for some action."

A shiver ran through Shirley at the vision that conjured. "You think a thong is the right thing?"

"I don't know. What do you recommend?"

"How about a negligee?"

"Too demure. I'm going for the jugular. I'll take the thong and one of those push-up bras, too."

"All right." Shirley kept her tone even. She realized she could be in Agnes' situation in fifteen years, which triggered a mental note to switch to a better wrinkle cream.

CHAPTER TWENTY-FOUR

Stanley wasn't in a good mood when he pulled into Paulina's lot a little after five. The back door opened, and Shirley, waving to someone behind her, came out.

Once in the car, she leaned in and kissed his cheek. "Any luck?"

"I guess you could call it that." He steered out of the lot and onto Pearl Avenue, ignoring the surprised pedestrians' stares when the Buick passed by. Bite me and my jalopy, he thought.

Shirley nodded, then turned to watch out her window.

They rode in silence to the Village. It was times like these he appreciated his relationship most. Shirley knew when to prod, and when he needed to unwind.

When he parked at the townhouse, she went on ahead and up to the bedroom.

Stanley took a can of Bud Light to his recliner, leaned back, popped the top, and turned on the television, his eyelids losing the stay-open battle.

"Baked chicken for dinner okay with you?" Shirley asked.

He opened his eyes. "Must have dozed off. Sure. Chicken's great."

She'd changed into tan shorts and a blue T-shirt. She walked to the end table, shook his empty beer can, then carried it away.

Clattering and clinking sounds came from the kitchen. Stanley flipped his recliner to upright, stretched his arms, and stood. He ambled to the counter and sat on a stool.

In the middle of opening a package of chicken, Shirley turned and smiled at him. "Feeling better?"

"Yes. Just needed to get my head in a different place," he said.

"Ready to tell me about your job hunt?"

"Spent most of the day frustrated as hell. The good news is, I did get one. The bad news is—it's at The Burger Flip. Don't yell at me."

She closed her mouth and gestured for him to continue.

"I started at Electronics Heaven this morning. They weren't hiring. Then I went to the Sports Section. Got a no there. On to Golf Central. That was a no. Went to the hardware store, the pool supply store, and an ice cream parlor." He clasped his hands together and cracked his knuckles.

"That's going to give you arthritis," Shirley said.

"Baloney. Old wives' tale." He ignored her frown. "Toys Galore needed someone, so I filled out an application and the *manager* interviewed me right there." He snorted. "You should have seen this kid. Couldn't have been more than twenty-one. He said he'd be in touch, but I could tell there was no way I'd get that job."

"How do you know?"

"The person needed extensive knowledge of video games. I said I could learn, and he gave me a strange look, like he doubted that could ever happen."

"I'm sorry."

"By three, I realized I skipped lunch, and—I repeat—don't yell at me, I went to The Burger Flip. While there, I thought, why not? I asked to see the manager, and lo and behold, it's an older guy, maybe in his sixties. His name is Walt Jenkins. Turns out he's the owner of that franchise and several others in the area. I explained my situation to him, and he said he'd give me a chance. I start tomorrow. Gotta be there at nine."

She stared at him. "Congratulations on the job. What did you eat at three o'clock?"

He laughed. "Not enough to ruin dinner."

"Are you sure you want to work in a fast-food place?"

"I'm sure I don't. But what choice do I have? At one point during the day, I did think about going back to electrical work."

"You weren't licensed in Florida. Not to mention how sick of it you were when you retired."

"You don't need your own license as long as you work for a licensed company. What stops me is two things. Construction is down, and hoards of younger guys are hunting for electrical jobs, so why would they take a geezer? And, climbing into hot attics in South Florida is a huge problem. I don't know if, physically, I could handle it. It was bad enough in Jersey."

CHAPTER TWENTY-FIVE

A few days later, Dora, sitting in Shirley's kitchen, set her mug on the counter. "A duchess, huh? From what country?"

"Heavens, I don't know. Funny. I didn't even think to ask." Straining to remember if Paul or Vera mentioned it, Shirley peered into Dora's cup, retrieved the coffee pot, and poured refills. "She was a beautiful young thing, though. A bit on the skinny side." She returned to her stool and sat. "And what an attitude she had. Paul told me to avoid looking at her." She studied Dora's face. Her blue eye shadow had settled into the creases of her eyelids. "I really thought you'd be more excited."

Dora snorted. "I'll bet she was an imposter. Some rich royal wannabe. There just aren't that many duchesses, you know."

"No. I didn't."

"Dukes and duchesses are in line for the throne. Right after the King's or Queen's kids. Now, if she said she was a countess or a baroness, her story would be more believable. Poor ignorant thing probably didn't bother to do her homework before acting out her little façade."

Shirley grimaced and took a deep breath. "All right. Fine. She *was* a baroness. I made up the duchess part because Paul and Lance told me not to divulge the names of our clientele. How in the world do you know about royal rankings?"

"I love that stuff. Several countries still have royal figureheads. And my romance novels are full of royalty. Wanton princesses, evil dukes, inept kings. See? If you read those instead of your awful crime mysteries, you would have known, too."

"That's not all I read. I like historicals also."

Dora's hand patted her lips as she faked an exaggerated yawn.

The sound of heavy footsteps came from the stairs, and Shirley turned to see Stanley descend, then hustle to the door with a strange look on his face.

"What's the matter?" Shirley asked.

"Nothing." Stanley smiled. "I, uh, I told Henry Cushman I'd uh, go hit some balls with him, and I forgot. Now I'm late. Be back soon." He opened the screen door and let it bang shut behind him.

Shirley and Dora stared at each other.

"It's like he forgot something important," Dora said. "Hmmm. Not your anniversary. That's in May. And it's not your birthday, either. What do you suppose . . ."

Shaking her head, Shirley said, "No idea. But it's pretty obvious he isn't going to the driving range." She grabbed the dishtowel and rubbed at a dried spot of coffee on the counter. It was rare to see Stanley flustered. Could it have anything to do with The Burger Flip job? "Maybe he lost it?" She gasped, then covered her mouth.

"Lost what?" Dora's eyes bored into her. "Something's up. Why don't you tell me what's wrong with you two?"

"I can't." Looking away, Shirley watched as the Buick left the carport.

"What could be so bad that you can't tell your best friend? I know you're having money trouble. Anything else going on?"

"How did you know that?" Shirley thought they'd been so effective with their *we're just tired of retirement* excuse.

A sagacious frown appeared on Dora's face. "Stanley got a

job at Happy Mart. Now he's serving burgers and fries? You're working for the first time since high school. Maybe the others believe you're bored, but you can't fool me."

Shirley's pulse raced. Her body tensed with the flush of instant shame. "Yes, we're running a little short. The recession knocked us for a loop. Please don't tell anyone else. We haven't even told the kids. Because we're working now, they think we've gone middle-age crazy—albeit two decades late. We told them we were going out of our minds with the inanity of retirement. They seemed to buy it."

"I won't. I haven't. What's the big deal, though? You think you're the only ones who lost money in the past few years?"

"Did you?"

"Well, yes, but my investments rebounded."

"Try to imagine that you won't have enough to live on when you'll need it most."

Dora seemed to take that in. Her face reddened. "I see what you mean. It doesn't make sense, but I'd be embarrassed." She put her hand on Shirley's arm. "How bad is it?"

"We only need to work for a few years, to make up the loss, then we'll be fine."

"I can lend you some."

The whole conversation made Shirley cringe. It wasn't Dora's fault, and she was a good friend for offering, but Shirley felt like crying. She batted back the tears. "Please don't. I'm feeling humiliated enough as it is. Stanley would have a heart failure if he knew you'd figured it out. He feels it's all his fault. Please just pretend you have no idea. Go along with our plan. Okay?"

Dora's eyes looked glassy. "You got it, doll. Whatever you say."

***

Around five, Shirley set up the ironing board in the living room and turned on the television. She sprayed starch on the white blouse she planned to wear to work the next day, lifted the iron, and went to work on the wrinkles. The television became background noise as her conversation with Dora kept re-circulating in her mind.

Were she and Stanley the only ones they knew with this problem? Life in Silver Sago Village hadn't changed. Everyone seemed to be doing the same things as before the recession. Same number of dinners out. Same number of excursion busses to casinos. Was no one else's life affected? Or were there others, but like she and her husband, too mortified to admit it? It *was* like admitting to ineptness. To failure. To screwing up royally. So demeaning. But why?

She envisioned Edna sitting by the pool, whispering to the other women, asking *have you heard about the Nowacks? Don't tell anyone, but . . .* Shirley groaned.

The door opened, and she glanced to see Stanley coming in. His face pale, he stared at her, then at the floor.

Something was wrong. She set the iron down and walked toward him. She braced herself. "What is it?"

Stanley brushed past her, sunk into the sofa, and buried his head in his hands.

"Stanley, you're scaring me." She sat beside him, not knowing whether to touch him or not.

A tremor racked his body. He looked at her with tears in his eyes. "I don't know how . . . I feel so sick about it."

Shirley's hands began to shake. "Just tell me what happened." She held her breath.

"Our money's gone." He let out a low-pitched wail. "That son of a bitch took it all."

The words sunk in. Panic struck. Her heart raced. She felt instantly weak. "What?"

He straightened, touched her hands, and took a deep breath. "I'm so angry it's hard to speak." His words were slow and deliberate. "The investment guy Henry sent me to? Alexander Weiss? This morning Henry had an appointment with him. When he got to Alexander's office, it was cleaned out. No one there. No computers. No desks. No plants. No people. Everything gone."

"Oh, my God."

"Henry called him, and the phone was disconnected. The voice mail on Weiss's cell phone was full. He went to the business next door and asked if they knew anything. They said one morning last week, they arrived at work and saw the place was empty. That's all they knew."

Shirley felt like the blood in her body had drained out. "No. It can't be. He must have moved to another office."

Stanley shook his head. "Henry called the police. They put him in touch with a federal agency called fin . . . fin something. They handle investment fraud. It looks like Weiss never really invested anybody's money. Instead, he took it with him out of the country. They think maybe he's in the Caribbean." He laid his head on the sofa back and closed his eyes. A tear ran down his cheek.

"You didn't give him all of our money."

"No. But he's got three-quarters of it."

She stared at her knees, feeling hopeless. "What are we going to do?"

He didn't say any more, but she hadn't expected an answer. Voices from the television drifted into her consciousness. She'd been so absorbed she'd forgotten it was on. She stood. Testing her legs first, not trusting them, she walked to the TV and shut it off. She perched on the arm of Stanley's big lounger.

"We have to sell our house." Stanley stood and wiped his face with the back of his hand. "We'll pray for a miracle." He put his hand in his pocket and pulled out a stack of lottery tickets. "Maybe we'll win the lottery. I really don't know what the hell we're going to do."

***

Two hours later, Shirley stared at the cold pizza on her plate. She'd warmed up leftover slices in the fridge and barely remembered doing it. She felt disconnected from everything, as though she were in a fog. Stanley, sitting across from her, seemed to be going through the same thing.

They hadn't spoken in those two hours, so Stanley's voice startled her.

"I think . . ." he said. "I think what we need to do now . . . is go to work tomorrow as normal. The money we make plus our social security will cover our monthly bills for now. We have a couple thousand in our savings. If we have unexpected expenses or repairs beyond that, we'll have to take it from our Vanguard account. There's about twenty thousand in there. On my next day off, I'll check out rentals. See what we can afford after we sell this place."

"I don't want to sell my home." Shirley surprised herself with her gruff tone.

"You think I do?"

"I want to wait. See what happens. Maybe they'll recover the money. Then we'll be sorry we sold so fast."

"Don't worry. Nothing's selling fast. In fact, it'll be a miracle if it sells, period."

"We are not listing this house. Not yet." Shirley glared at him. "I refuse."

CHAPTER TWENTY-SIX

"No, no, no. I think the new ecru lace line needs to be featured there," Paul said.

Shirley glanced his way. Paul and Vera stood a foot apart, both staring at the black and pink bra display taking shape near the front door. Vera looked like she was having trouble maintaining her composure. Shirley went back to her work.

"Shirley?" Paul called. "What do you think?"

Shirley didn't turn. "For heaven's sake, I'm the last one to ask." She reached into the box by her feet and grabbed another pale-blue satin padded hanger. From the portable chrome rack on her right, she transferred a midnight-blue silk nightie from its wire hanger onto the padded one. The two blues enhanced each other. She also thought the ecru Paul wanted to display was more in keeping with the store, but she wasn't about to muddle in that dispute.

"Where's Lance?" Paul marched toward the office.

"Seriously, Shirley," Vera said. "What do you think? Is the pink and black really too trite like he says? Should it be on a shelf, not in the spotlight?"

Shirley faced her and smiled. "Seriously? I'm the unsophisticated hick here, remember? If this were JC Penney, then my opinion counts."

Vera's face softened. "Don't do that—put yourself down. You've learned so fast. I'd like your input."

"Thank you. But this is between you and *Pauline*." She had far more important matters to worry about. The three miserable days since Stanley discovered the money theft left her barely able to eat or sleep.

Outside, a heavyset woman walked into view. She carried a leopard-print tote bag with a white tea cup puppy's head poking out from the front end. The woman opened the door.

"Vera," Shirley said. "We've got company."

Her head swiveled in that direction, then Vera's face became a polished visage as she smoothed her chignon.

Once again, Shirley directed her attention to the silk gowns.

"You know what we call her?" Lance whispered.

Startled, Shirley whipped around to see him standing close to her. She shook her head. "You scared me. I didn't hear you coming."

"Sorry." He leaned in. "Mrs. Frumproast."

"Who? That woman who just came in?"

Lance nodded. "She always smells like beef."

Shirley raised her eyebrows and waited.

"We don't know why. It's as though she stands in a kitchen all day while a roast is cooking. My Aunt Mazel smelled like that."

"Aunt Mazel? With an m?" Not caring, all Shirley wanted was to hang the nighties and try to figure out how she and Stanley would survive.

"But beyond that, the woman is forever hiring walkers, then trying to seduce them."

That stopped her. "I don't understand. What's a walker?"

"You're kidding me." Lance snickered. He took her by the hand, led her to the office, and closed the door.

Paul shifted his gaze from the spreadsheet on his monitor to them. "Something wrong? Did Vera switch that display yet?"

"She's with a customer." Shirley turned to Lance. "I have

work to do."

"Mrs. Frumproast is here. Shirley doesn't know what a walker is. I didn't want to explain it to her out there."

"You're going to tell her the Ernie story, aren't you." Paul rolled his eyes and went back to staring at numbers.

"As you know, there are a lot of staggeringly wealthy women of a certain age in the Sago Beach area. Especially on the island. Many are widows, more had their husbands dump them for young trophy wives, and all of them are desperate for male company." Lance sat on the sofa and swung his loafered foot on top of the opposite knee.

He'd bought the Italian leather shoes while on the shopping trip with Shirley. The pants he wore were fine linen and went quite well with the Egyptian cotton shirt. Now that she knew the kind of money Sago Beach people spent on clothing and shoes, it was hard to tamp down her growing resentment of them. Not Lance and Paul, of course. She'd always be grateful for their generosity, but she and Stanley could pay one month's bills with what they threw away on frivolous purchases.

"Shirley?" Lance said. "Where are you?"

She stirred and realized she'd drifted into a fog of thought. "Sorry."

"Have a seat." He patted the cushion next to him.

"No, thanks." She stifled a yawn. "It's no reflection on you. I haven't been sleeping. If I sit now, I'm afraid I won't get up."

"Get on with it, Lance," Paul said. "You're already boring her."

Lance made a face. "Walkers are older men that these women pay to escort them to charity balls and parties."

"I've overheard more than a few conversations about that," Shirley said. "I didn't know they had a name."

"It's an unwritten law, a code of conduct, that the walkers do not have sex with the women."

"Started by the men," Paul said.

Shirley turned to see the back of his head. Paul still stared at the screen. "That seems a bit odd," she said. "Don't men always want sex from women? What if a romance developed?"

Lance laughed. "Not likely. See, the walkers are gay. Not openly gay, but everyone knows it. They're not fooling anyone, but everybody goes along with the pretense they're straight."

"It's a formal custom. Just became a ritual, a canon," Paul said.

"Anyone who breeches that rule . . ." Lance waved a hand in the air. "Persona non grata."

"I take it Mrs. Frumproast committed such an error with this Ernie fellow?" Shirley chuckled at the nickname.

"Ernie's a dear friend of ours," Lance said. "He and his partner have been together for thirty years. He escorted the Frumproast to one of the balls last season, and afterward? She had him in for a nightcap. Most of these people know each other and consider them friends, so Ernie—being an amiable guy—said yes."

"She launched herself at Ernie," Paul said. "Tried to take off his clothes."

"When he refused her, she threw things at him, then tried to expose him. Began a whispering campaign against him," Lance said. "What she didn't realize was everybody likes Ernie more than they do her."

"Totally screwed up," Paul said. "Now she's a nonentity."

"Reduced to coming into our store and chatting us up."

"Which is why Lance is hiding in here at the moment," Paul said. "Be a dear, Shirley, would you go see if the coast is clear?"

She nodded, left the office, and from the end of the hall, scanned the sales floor. Mrs. Frumproast stood at the register counter petting and cooing to her puppy as Vera wrapped her purchases in tissue paper. The puppy licked Frumproast's hand.

She returned to the office. "Not yet. I'm sure the woman has no interest in talking to me, so I'm going back to work." She opened the door, then turned as a thought hit her. "Why don't these women just find a straight man?"

"At their age?" Lance sighed. "Sweetie, all the single straight men in the right age group and income level want younger women. The number of available older men is limited to begin with. Isn't it the same among your friends?"

"Well, yes," Shirley said. "But somehow I thought with wealthy people, it would be easier. They have so many advantages."

"No. Add in the factors. You being a notable and, I might add, lovely exception, most women over 60 are overweight and out of shape. The rich women are spoiled, too. They don't *want* Joe average, which shrinks their dating pool. They demand manners, polish, and a pedigree. Pool's shrunk again. They can't abide anyone who doesn't have money, because a less-well-off man might only want them for their wealth. No way to know, is there? God forbid they should date a man from a lesser station. They'd be dropped like thorny toads from the society register, and other people's opinions of them matter most, you know. Now they're fishing in an inflatable baby pool. They've boxed themselves into a nasty corner."

"And our friends, Lance," Paul said, "make good money from it, don't forget."

"Huh." Shirley closed the door behind her and headed for the sales floor. The conversation she'd heard months earlier between that Von Cletan woman and her friend echoed in her head. Von Cletan seemed desperate for sex, had paid a younger man, and felt humiliated. Her friend had given up the whole search. Shirley's friend Betty paid the lifeguard. Then there were the women she'd waited on at Pauline's. Lamenting the lack of sexual activity was a common, if veiled, topic among the older ladies.

Stupid rich women didn't know how lucky they were. She'd trade the sex for financial peace of mind. Or maybe not. Stanley hadn't meant for things to go so wrong. She had agreed to give the accountant the money to invest. For the thousandth time, she wished for a redo. To go back and not trust. To take the time and find out more about Alexander Weiss.

CHAPTER TWENTY-SEVEN

Fletcher drained the last of his Guinness, set the bottle on the coffee table, and sighed. He frowned at the dozen or so remaining boxes stacked against the wall. He'd finished unpacking and arranging the bedrooms, dining room, and kitchen. Books, CDs, and framed pictures were in the rest, and he dreaded trying to put them in order.

"This was way easier the last time." Then he remembered why. Janice had done most of the organizing when they bought their house four years earlier.

The doorbell chimed. The concierge hadn't called to announce a guest, so he wondered who was at the door.

The sight of the blonde from next door dressed in a white T-shirt and tight jeans surprised him. Adrenaline shot through his body. "Hi." He scrambled for her name—Mary? Molly?

"Hi. It's Maddy." Her eyes were light blue, and they sparkled.

"Right. Sorry. I'm Fletcher." He felt like an idiot.

"Yes. I remember." She waved several envelopes at him. "They put your mail in my box. Thought you might want them." She pointed to the one on top. "You shouldn't miss your opportunity to invest in Tennessee ranchland. You could split wood. Build your own cabin."

Laughing, he opened the door wider. "Yes. I've always pictured myself as the hardscrabble, live off the land type."

Doing an exaggerated up and down survey of him, she smirked. "Definitely my first impression of you."

"Would you like to come in?"

"I would." She stepped inside and placed the mail on the mahogany table against the wall.

He closed the door. "So? What do you think?"

She walked through the wide travertine foyer and into the living room.

Her perfect posture made her seem taller. His mother would approve—she bemoaned how young women *slumped around* these days. Maddy moved like a dancer. Fluid. She had poise. That was the word. Tanya's heavy, clunky stomp came to mind, and he shuddered.

"Nice." Maddy turned to him.

"You bought the end unit I wanted," he said, then realized that might sound wrong. "This is fine, though. You must have incredible views from every room."

A slight smile graced her face, and those blue eyes seemed to examine him. They were like a phrase from an Elton John song, *eyes like ice on fire.* An alarm went off in his head. This one's too young also, he screamed at himself. Don't even think about it. But his nerves were tingling, like he'd just injected caffeine. No worries, another part of his brain prompted—you were blinded by boobs before. Tanya and Janice were both stacked. This one wasn't.

"Would you like to come see for yourself?" she said.

"Sure." The word came out before he'd had time to think. Well, it wouldn't hurt to be neighborly.

"Great. Follow me." She sauntered out the front door.

He locked up and followed.

"This is my first place all by myself." She led the way into her foyer.

"Really. Guess that means you're divorced?" Despite

himself, Fletcher's heart did a twirl.

"No." She shook her head. "Almost got married. Thank God I came to my senses." She gestured toward the living room. "What do you think?"

He hadn't yet seen anything but her. Now he scanned the place. There was more square footage, he already knew that. The décor said *old sophisticated money.* The afternoon light illuminated the luster of the full-length silk draperies framing her Palladians. Extra moldings graced the doorways and ceilings. Matching sofas, covered in what looked like suede, faced each other perpendicular to a huge fireplace. On the marble coffee table sat a rare black swan Red Ware ceramic piece from Japan. "It's amazing. Comfortable, but at the same time elegant. I love the Japanese swan."

She gave him a peculiar look. "Are you gay?

"No." He laughed. "My ex-wife is an interior designer. I know way more than I should about many things. She's crazy for those Red Ware ceramic pieces."

Taking him by the hand, which sent erotic shivers cascading through his limbs, she brought him into the hall leading to the bedrooms. "Tell me, what do you think of this?" She pointed to the framed painting on the wall.

His eyes widened. "Sure looks like a Kandinsky. It's not real, is it?"

A smile lit up her face, and she nodded. "I just bought it."

"Who are you?" The girl had some money. "A Vanderbilt or a Rockefeller?"

That made her burst with laughter. "No. I wanted my first place to be something special, with everything I love."

"You must do okay for yourself." He was afraid to ask what she did to make that kind of money.

A grin slid across her lips. "I do."

***

A few hours later, Fletcher had Katie in the car with him. Lauren, Katie's mom, had asked if he'd watch her that Sunday night. It wasn't his scheduled visitation day, but since he had no plans other than hanging with his friend Vinny at Dave's Pool and Brew, he agreed.

Katie wanted to eat dinner at The Burger Flip. Despite knowing Lauren would not approve, Fletcher caved in.

At the moment, Katie's brown curls bobbed up and down, fingers tapping her thighs in time to whatever boy band's music poured from her iPod's ear buds. She stared out the window, lips moving during the parts she knew by heart.

Fletcher grinned. She seemed happy. He and Lauren were in a good place, finally—a friendship. It may have had a lot to do with Lauren's new boyfriend, Carl the cardiologist. Whatever it was, if Katie was thriving, then Fletcher was okay with it.

His thoughts drifted back to Maddy Forsyth. Her lithe body. Those amazing eyes. Her apartment blew him away. Classy, like her. But the mystery of how she managed to live the way she did intrigued him. His best guess was a wealthy boyfriend, despite what she said about saving her money. He hoped her effect on him would diminish as he became used to seeing her. Otherwise, living next door would be sheer torture.

"Daddy," Katie said. "You just passed it."

"Oops. Thank you." He pulled into the next left turn lane and executed a U-turn.

"Can we eat inside?"

"Why not." He turned into the lot and parked.

She scampered ahead and opened the heavy glass entrance door.

Fletcher hit the key fob lock, then followed her in.

Standing in line, staring at the orange menu board above the service counter, he saw what he wanted. A double Burger Flip with sharp cheddar, fried onions, bacon, and a secret sauce. He heard Janice's voice in his head nagging about his irresponsible food choices. Would he ever *not* have a woman's say-so ringing in his ears?

"Grandpa," Katie squealed. She darted out of line and over to the hallway leading to the restrooms.

He left the line and hurried in that direction, expecting to see either of Katie's grandfathers. They both loved fast food and often snuck away from their wives to indulge. It was an open secret. He hoped she hadn't trailed him into the men's room.

In the hall, Katie stood hugging Stanley, who bent to kiss her forehead. Something wasn't right about the image, though. It took a second for Fletcher to comprehend that his father wore an orange and red striped shirt, blue work pants, and an orange paper hat. A mop and bucket were in the corner.

"Dad?"

Stanley flushed red as he straightened to upright. "Hello, son."

"What are you doing?"

Spreading his arms in a *what-does-it-look-like* gesture, Stanley said, "Working."

"But . . . I thought you worked at Happy Mart."

"I quit. Now I work here." Stanley moved to reclaim the mop. "And I'd best get to it."

That didn't make sense. "I'm confused, Dad. You told me you and Mom were bored and that's why you got jobs. A soft job as a greeter, meeting people. That—I understand. You can't think this is enjoyable."

Stanley's face hardened.

"Can we get free food now?" Katie seemed excited about her grandpa working there.

"No." Fletcher grabbed her hand. "Come on, sweetie. Let's have our dinner. Dad, I'll call you later."

CHAPTER TWENTY-EIGHT

Nina's cell rang. "Crap." Keeping her eyes on the Cape Cod's lit front window, she stretched to the passenger seat and fumbled inside her purse for the phone. She assumed it was one of her children and answered on the fourth ring. "Hello."

"Nina? It's Fletcher."

She wouldn't have picked up if she'd seen the number. "Hi."

"I called the house first. Mary Ann said you were at a lecture? Why'd you answer? I was going to leave a voice mail."

Through the backlit sheers of the window, Nina saw the shapes of George and a woman embrace, then kiss. Damn it. The familiar blade of betrayal twisted in her gut.

"Nina?"

"Right. I'm here," she said, wincing from new stabs of pain. "I, uh, left the lecture early. I'm in the car."

"What's wrong? You sound strange."

"Nothing." She'd never told anyone in her family about her husband's affairs. She tried to calm her voice. "What's up?"

"I just got off the phone with Dad. He and Mom are losing it. Have you talked to them lately? He quit his job at Happy Mart, and now he's working at The Burger Flip. Katie and I saw him there tonight."

"So?" George and the woman disappeared from her view.

"So, the story about being bored is horse manure. They must need the money. I bought the weird argument that Dad liked the people-greeting job. Geezers like him do that all the time. But nobody works at The Burger Flip for fun."

George had promised he'd never stray again. He actually cried. She'd felt *sorry* for him. She focused her attention, tried to comprehend what Fletcher said while reeling from George's cruelty. "What do you want me to do?"

"Dad wouldn't come clean with me. Insisted he and Mom are working because they want to. I ran into a brick wall. Maybe you could find out more."

"I'll try. I'll call Mom tomorrow. You might be right about them being short on cash, but you could be wrong, too. I don't think it's that bizarre for them to be bored with retirement. I mean, wouldn't you go a little nuts if all you had to do every day was hang out with the likes of their friends? Well, not Dora. We love her. But the rest? I'd *pay* someone if it meant escaping Silver Sago Village."

Fletcher laughed. "Maybe. Maybe I'm worried for nothing. Okay, call me after you talk to Mom. 'Nite."

Nina threw the phone into her purse. A flickering dim light emanated from the house's upstairs window. Oh, that's ducky peachy, she thought. They're *doing it* by candlelight. She seethed. George told her he considered candles in the bedroom just plain hokey.

She glanced at George's car on the other side of the street. He'd parked three houses down, then walked back. Knowing her burgundy minivan would give her away, she'd borrowed her best friend Evelyn Asbury's Camry—a car so ubiquitous, no one would ever think they were followed in one. She'd found a spot in the deeper darkness under an enormous sycamore tree and watched him walk into the Cape Cod's side door by the garage. He didn't even knock first.

She reclined the seat and wondered what to do. Part of her

wanted to sneak through the shadows and let the air out of his tires. Another part wanted to douse the porch with gas and throw a match into it. If she got away with it, there'd be his insurance money. Why hadn't she left him after the last affair? It was before the recession. They had lots of money in investments then. His commercial real estate business was now down by half, and she'd lost her consulting job. To leave him today would be a financial disaster for them both. Timing was everything.

Her reasonable mind won. She'd go home. It looked like one of those nights where George would be out late, then give her another plausible bullshit story about entertaining clients.

She started the Camry, eased from her spot, and braked for a pair of yellow eyes in the middle of the street. The cat scampered away. Getting a flash of inspiration, she pulled over in front of his car, put the Camry into Park, and fished her key ring from her purse.

With the key to his BMW in hand, she glanced in both directions and unlocked it. She lowered the back passenger side window, then popped the trunk. Inside, she found his emergency food supply. George had a phobia, one she once found endearing, that no matter what happened, he'd be able to eat. He also kept a supply box in the basement and one in the attic. Having bought and packed the items for him, she knew there'd be a can of tuna.

She found it and pulled up the metal tab and lid. Its fishy stink hit her nose. She didn't like tuna. Pinching a chunk from the can, she placed it in the grass near the sidewalk. Then she set another on the asphalt by the passenger door. The last piece went under the floor mat. She closed the trunk, locked the car, and hustled back to the Camry. A mile later, she tossed the tuna can into some tall weeds.

On her way home, to take her mind off George, she considered what Fletcher said. Could their parents have money problems? Of course they could, she reasoned. Everybody was hurting. Shirley and Stanley were notorious for not sharing any detail of their finances. They never had. If they did, in fact, need a little more income, then God bless them and their independence for going out and getting it, instead of whining to their kids. Evelyn's parents did that—piled the guilt onto Evelyn and her husband about the high cost of living. She and John contributed every month so her parents could maintain their lifestyle. John joked about it being better than the alternative—having his in-laws move in.

Nina shuddered at that idea. Evelyn's house was dark when she parked in the driveway. She locked up and put the key under the flowerpot on the kitchen porch, as arranged. Then she walked to the next block and reclaimed her minivan. John was out of town, but Nina didn't want Evelyn's kids asking questions about the car switch. Their children knew each other, and word would get back to George.

She made the turn onto her street. What to do about George? Even if they could afford to split, would she be able to leave? The man had a strong hold on her. Whenever she confronted him in the past, he sweet-talked her into forgiving him. He was charming, still handsome as hell, and knew she'd melt. Every time. She craved him in bed. He made her tremble from anticipation, and weak from exhaustion when they finished. He gazed into her eyes and swore she was the only woman he'd ever truly loved. She believed him—or wanted to believe him so much that his argument worked. The other women were mere curiosities. It was just sex. It didn't mean a thing to him. He didn't intend to hurt her.

"Bull Twinkies." She had plenty of backbone and willpower to stand up to his garbage—as long as he wasn't anywhere near her. She sighed, pulled into the garage, climbed out of her van, and headed into the house.

***

Nina sipped her coffee and checked for email on her laptop at the kitchen table. Mary Ann nibbled her bagel, and Charles slurped as he shoveled cereal and milk into his mouth.

"Mom," Mary Ann said, "make him stop. That's so gross."

"Charles, stop." Nina glanced at Mary Ann's plate. "You might want to wrap that to eat on the bus. It's getting late."

George came down the stairs with his briefcase and paused in the doorway. He wore a charcoal suit and a red and navy striped tie. He'd come home around two. Nina pretended to be asleep, but detected the distinct odor of animal urine when he entered. He went straight to the shower.

She stifled a laugh. "Good morning."

"Morning." He went for the coffee.

His stainless travel mug, as always, waited for him next to the pot.

Nina turned to the computer, knowing her face would give her away. "How'd your meeting go last night?"

"Fine." George placed the lid on the mug. "The client wants to meet with us again tonight. They're thinking of buying that old strip mall, where the pancake house was, on the highway. Want to put a jazz club in, so they need to see what the scene is like after midnight."

"I imagine that would be important." *Lying son of a bitch.* She checked the time. "Bus in five minutes, kids. Get a move on."

Mary Ann pushed back from the table. Charles groaned, took his bowl to the sink, then raced upstairs.

"I'm bringing in my car for a detailing today," George said.

"Oh? Didn't you have that done a few weeks ago?"

"Um, yeah. Something got in there, though."

"Something? Like what?"

"Cat. Raccoon. Squirrels. Who knows? Whatever it was, it peed on my seats."

"Ewww. How disgusting, Dad. Now I have a choice between a dorky van or a pee-mobile. Thanks." Mary Ann left the room.

"How in the world did it get in?" Nina asked.

"I left the window open," he mumbled.

"In that neighborhood?" Nina glanced at him, feigning shock. "You're lucky you still *have* a car."

"What?" George's face paled for a moment.

He'd obviously forgotten where he *said* he'd be. "By the tracks and the old depot? I'm surprised you didn't find a wino sleeping it off inside. Or the shell of your car sitting on blocks."

"I must have hit the button with my elbow and didn't realize it." He shook his head. "You'd think I'd have noticed."

"You had more pressing matters on your mind, I'm sure." Nina composed a sweet and supportive expression.

George flashed his million-watt smile. "Yes. It *was* a crucial meeting. Very satisfying. Got quite a lot accomplished." He bent to kiss her forehead.

The smile froze on her face. She watched him go out the door to the garage. Watched it close behind him. Watched his car back onto the road and drive up the street.

"I'll have to kill him," she muttered.

CHAPTER TWENTY-NINE

Shirley recognized one of the two women entering Paulina's as the Von Cletan woman's friend she saw during lunch at Alfred's in the summer. Vera made her way to them.

What was her name? Shirley tried to recall as she lifted the empty box from a shipment of cashmere scarves and carried it to the storage room.

"It's a total waste of money." Paul's voice drifted from the office. "Tell him no."

"He says he'll only sign the lease if we paint and install new carpet," Lance said. "Otherwise, no deal."

"Then no deal. The rent's lower than anything else on the street."

She heard muffled whispering. After placing the empty in the pile to be crushed, she took a deep breath and reminded herself to take one step at a time. All morning, she couldn't get her mind off her money troubles. She'd finish the day and let the panic overpower her later. At bedtime, which was commonplace now.

"Fine." Paul's voice sounded strained. "It stays empty."

Her employers were no doubt speaking of a tiny store they owned in the less desirable section of town. She scoffed and let out a low groan. Less desirable in Sago Beach merely meant further away from trendy Pearl Avenue, not a blighted area. There wasn't any such thing as blight on Sago Beach Island. She'd heard them argue over how much to put into their investment properties.

Intense frustration made her hands shake. She battled back tears. How unfair it was. She really liked Lance and Paul and could never repay their kindness, but hearing the financial talk aggravated her. It was a constant reminder that so many people had no clue how fortunate they were. Including those two charming young men. She'd give anything to have such problems instead of her own.

A huge yawn overtook her. She felt disorientated and a little dizzy. She gripped the edge of a shelf to steady herself.

"Shirley? You okay?" Lance appeared in the doorway.

She nodded. "Just tired. I haven't been sleeping well."

"Things seem to be on the slow side today." In his eyes was real concern. "Do you want to leave early?"

I'd love to, she thought, but I need the money. She put on a big smile. "No, thanks. I've got a feeling it'll get busy in the afternoon. It usually does on Fridays. That'll perk me up."

"Well, take some extra time at lunch, then." He went back into the office.

She found the next box needing unpacking and moved it to the sales floor. Vera was with Roberta. That was her name—the Von Cletan woman's friend from Alfred's. Roberta. How the heck had her brain conjured that in the midst of a near breakdown?

Vera held a demure pink silk robe, and Roberta looked like she loved it. The woman with Roberta made a dismissive face.

Shirley set the carton on the floor near the register. She found the cutter for the packing tape and sliced it open. Layers of bubble wrap, then pink tissue paper, guarded the contents. The waste of perfectly good packing materials irritated her. Inside were silk panties in several shades of lavender. Taking one from the top, she held the frilly underwear up and referenced its tag to a list on the counter. Each pair would sell for eighty-five dollars. She tsked.

"Those are quite lovely."

Startled, Shirley turned to see Roberta's companion beside her eyeing the panties.

"Yes," Shirley said. "Aren't they? Can I find you a size?"

The woman's face blanched. "No." She smiled, then smirked. "I have no reason to buy or wear such things, as much as I'd like to pretend I did." She did a subtle head tilt in Roberta's direction. "Like some people."

Shirley didn't know how to react, but before she'd figured it out, the woman let her off the hook.

"I'm a widow. Twelve years now."

"I'm sorry." Shirley guessed her age as early seventies.

"Me, too. I miss the company. Among other things, if you know what I mean."

"I can imagine." The woman's inference wasn't unusual. Turned out, rich women complained constantly about no sex. Shirley heard frequent little *wink-wink* asides, which backed up what Lance and Paul had told her. She figured the ladies felt safe confiding in her because her age was close to theirs. A sisterhood of sorts. She doubted thirty-something Vera ever got an earful of such commentary.

The box of panties wasn't unpacking itself. She needed to get back to work if this lady wasn't buying anything. "Can I help you find something?"

The woman snickered. "You don't have what I want in this store. What I wouldn't give for a good roll in the hay. A little bumpa dumpa."

Shirley chuckled along with her, pretending to share her view. In fact, Shirley could have a *roll in the hay* any time she wanted. But what *she* wanted was a roll in the dough. A sudden idea buzzed into her mind.

"Excuse me. Did I hear you right?" Shirley asked. "I mean, are you serious?"

The woman's eyebrows rose. "About?"

"You'd pay money," Shirley whispered. "For that, um, roll in the hay?"

Glancing toward Vera and Roberta first, a conspiratorial grin bloomed on the woman's face. "Actually, I have in the past. It's a mite uncomfortable, though. The men tend to be younger. My friend over there has no idea."

"Really."

She nodded. "Really."

"What if I told you I know of a gentleman? A very discreet gentleman who's around our age."

The woman shot her a deadpan look. "I already know every walker in the area. They're all gay, no matter what you've heard."

Shirley shook her head. "This one isn't a walker. He doesn't escort anyone to any functions. He only does one thing."

The lady's eyebrows shot up.

"But he's expensive."

"What's expensive?"

A jumble of figures raced through Shirley's mind. How much was it worth? "Four-hundred dollars."

"That's not too bad. Do you have his number?"

Panic hit. She scrambled for a response. "No. He calls you. Give me your number, and I'll pass it along." She took a pen from the counter and offered her the back of a Paulina's business card.

"I'd like to find out a little bit more about him," the woman said.

So would I, Shirley thought. "I'll call you when I'm not at work. We can talk about it then."

She wrote her name and number on the card, then handed it to Shirley. "Have you had occasion to take advantage of this man's favors?"

Blood rushed to Shirley's face. She hoped the woman didn't notice. "Indeed. I have."

CHAPTER THIRTY

"Excuse me, please," Shirley said to the woman. Feeling faint, she hurried to the store's bathroom, locked the door, and sat in the upholstered chair by the full-length gilded mirror. Perspiration beaded on her forehead, and she lowered her head between her knees.

What had she just done? An insane flash of an idea, and she blurted it out? The lack of sleep and her financial stress had deactivated her normal decorum filter. She took a deep breath and opened her eyes. An ant ambled across the marble tile. A stray scrap of tissue lay beside the braided bamboo wastebasket.

Advice that Paul often recited echoed in her head. *Find out what people want, what they're willing to pay for it, and provide it. That's how to make money.* She'd spent the sleepless nights racking her brain for a product or service to offer that could save her and Stanley, and it was right there the whole time. The valuable commodity was Stanley himself.

Shirley straightened. That woman in the store thought four-hundred dollars was a fair price. How long would such an encounter take? Twenty minutes? Thirty? An hour?

"Oh, but what am I thinking?" She stood and stared in the mirror. Prostitution? Asking her husband to sleep with other women?

"Shirley?" Lance called from the other side of the door. "You all right, honey?"

Shirley sighed. "Yes. I'll be out in a moment."

"O-kayee."

Shaking her head, she went to the sink, spritzed some water on her face, and dabbed it dry with a paper towel. Her make-up looked not-great, but passable. She opened the door to see a concerned Lance in the hall.

He approached her and put his hand on her shoulder. "Paul and I agree. You're a wreck today. Go home and get some sleep, for heaven's sake."

"But I—"

"Don't worry about the money. We'll pay you for the rest of the day. We insist."

She nodded. "Thank you."

"Do you need me to call a cab?"

"No. I dropped Stanley off this morning for his early shift. I have the car." She moved toward the break room to retrieve her purse.

"You drive slow and carefully, now." He handed her a shiny pink Paulina's paper bag. "Here. I put some relaxing teas together. I use them all the time. Some earplugs, too. I buy them by the gross." He lowered his voice. "Paul snores like a son-of-a-gun."

"I heard that," Paul called from inside the office.

***

Shirley pushed her racing thoughts aside and concentrated on driving home. She unlocked the door, set her purse and the pink bag on the counter, took off her shoes, and flopped into Stanley's recliner. Expecting the crazed frenzy of conflicting thoughts to invade again, it surprised her when a wave of exhaustion took over instead. She glanced at her watch. Twelve-ten. Stanley's shift ended at three. She closed her eyes.

***

The phone's ring jarred Shirley awake. She felt for, then grabbed the handset on the end table.

"Hmmm?" she said, eyes still closed.

"It's me," Stanley said. "I called Paulina's, and they said they sent you home. What's the matter? Are you sick?"

She became more alert. "No. Tired." Maybe sick and tired?

"I'm glad you're not ill. The bus will be here in a few minutes. I'll see you soon."

"Now that I'm home, I can come get you."

"No. Just rest. I'll be there in about a half hour."

Shirley set the phone in its cradle, stretched, then went into the kitchen. It was three-fifteen. She'd slept for three hours and felt much better.

Her idea came knocking again, beckoning for her attention. Four-hundred dollars. For an hour at the most? That was more than Stanley brought home in a week. If he had a few customers a week, that was twelve-hundred. What if he did one a day?

She dug for the calculator in her purse and saw the card with the woman's name from the store. Could she handle Stanley having sex with that woman? With lots of other women? She had to admit, the thought upset her. But was it because, every time she'd considered the idea of Stanley being with another woman before this, the imagined scenario involved lust and desire? An affair of the heart? Stanley's being in love or even lust with someone else would kill her.

Stanley loved her. She loved Stanley. These were indisputable facts. He'd never strayed. They had a good sex life. Or they did until this financial mess made both of them too stressed out. They were a rock-solid couple. If Stanley had sex with women he didn't care about, only performed a *service*, did that make the idea more palatable to her? Yes, she decided. It did. It made a world of difference.

Taking a sheet of paper and the calculator, she wrote the pros and cons of the plan. On the pro side, she listed the money he might make and how fast they might be able to recover. On the con side, there was the problem of it being against the law. And the not-so-slight problem of convincing her Dudley Do-Right husband to do something very wrong.

Ten minutes later, she was in their bedroom changing when she heard the front door jalousies rattle.

"Shirley?" Stanley's voice carried up the stairs.

"I'll be down in a second." She took a last glance at her list, then folded the paper and tucked it into her pocket. She went downstairs.

Stanley smiled at her when she appeared. "You do look a little better."

"Than what?"

"Um. Than you did this morning?" His eyes widened.

She laughed. "Relax. I know the fatigue is wearing on me." It was important to get him in an easygoing state of mind.

The expression on his face changed from apprehension to relief.

He grinned and walked to her. Hugging her tight, he whispered, "I love you."

"I know." She kissed him. "I love you. More than ever." She gave him a gentle push. "What can I get for you? How about a beer?"

"Sure, thanks."

"Go sit in your recliner. Get comfortable. Being on your feet for eight hours is tough." She smiled.

"Wow. You should take naps more often." He went into the living room.

Letting the comment pass, she opened the fridge and found the *special* bottle of imported ale that Fletcher had left when he moved into his own place. She didn't understand what made it so special, even after Fletcher explained the process. It looked like any other beer to her. She removed a glass mug, now frosted, from the freezer and poured the ale into it.

She brought the mug and bottle to him and placed them on a napkin on the table to his right.

His face lit up. "Fancy schmancy. Thanks." He took a big sip. "Boy, that hits the spot."

She sat near him on the sofa. "Tell me how your day went."

While he told her about the deep fryer on the fritz, the customer who berated a cashier, and a lady who insisted her teensy dog was a service animal—although it was obvious it wasn't—she gathered her nerve.

"Seems the customers at The Burger Flip are as nutty as the ones at Happy Mart," she said.

"'Fraid so." He finished the beer. "Guess that's unavoidable these days." His face took on a serious cast. "You know, we have to sell this place. Soon."

The word *sell* hit her like a stab in the heart.

"Like you've been saying," he said, "if only we could find something to market that would get us out of our money problems."

A perfect segue if she'd ever heard one, she thought that was her signal. "Funny you should mention it."

His eyebrows rose. "Selling?"

"No. I thought of something that has the potential to make us eight-thousand dollars a month, or more."

"Criminy. I didn't make that as an electrician. What is it?"

"It would only take five to ten hours a week, but if it works, we could expand that. We'd only be dealing with wealthy people, and you wouldn't be covered with frying grease." At least she hoped not.

"Eight grand a month for ten hours a week? Doesn't involve ski masks, guns, or bank tellers, does it?"

She faked a laugh. "No."

"You didn't answer an email from Nigeria? You can't take those seriously, honey. They're a scam." His face filled with alarm. "You didn't send them money, did you?"

She shot him a deadpan stare. "As if we had any to spare."

He blanched. "So, what did you think of?"

"The single, older women I wait on at Paulina's gave me the idea. There's a certain thing I found out is missing from many of these rich women's lives. They complain about it all the time. They're willing to pay well to get it. There isn't much of it available. That's where we, or you, enter the picture."

"You're talking in riddles."

"We could put at least six thousand dollars in the bank every month. That's seventy-two thousand a year, Stanley. In several years, we'd have more than we did before, and we could retire again."

"Stop dancing around it. Sounds like you want to do a Ponzi scheme of some kind."

"They almost always get caught." She sighed. "We wouldn't—because the women would never admit to paying us. That would ruin their status and reputations. It's a built-in safeguard."

"Pay us to do what?" Stanley's eyes narrowed.

"Have sex with you."

CHAPTER THIRTY-ONE

The bewildered expression on Stanley's face frightened Shirley. In almost fifty years of marriage, this was new.

"What did you say?" he said. "It's a trick, right?"

"I know it sounds ridiculous," Shirley said. "I know it doesn't make sense. On the surface. But when I started to punch some numbers, it could solve our problem."

"You *want* me to have sex with other women?" He pushed himself from the recliner. "You've lost your mind." He walked toward the stairs.

"Not young pretty ones. Women our age who don't have anybody."

"Oh. Well, *that* sounds enticing."

"What does that mean? You'd agree to it if they were more attractive?" Shirley felt a flutter of uncertainty.

"No. Of course not." Pivoting, he paced into the living room, then stared at her. "Are you trying to trap me somehow? Is this a test from one of those women's magazines? 'Cause if it is, then—no. I don't want anyone else. I'm very happy with you. I love you."

Forcing control of her rising frustration, Shirley took a deep breath and re-thought.

Stanley kept looking at her with concern. "Are we done

now? Or do I have to make an appointment with a psychiatrist for you? Stress-related trauma causes brain cells to go haywire. And honey, you are stressed."

"I'm no more stressed than you." She stood. "I don't *want* you to be with other women, but it's a way to make a lot of money quickly. I know you love me. The only reason I can handle the mere suggestion of your being with others is because it wouldn't be something you desired. One appointment that took maybe an hour of your time would give us more money than you make at The Burger Flip in a week."

His face softened, and she hoped maybe that meant he'd consider it.

"If we could build your cliental to one visit a day," she said, "five days a week, at four-hundred each, that's two-thousand dollars. In a week." She threw her arms wide. "We could not only save our home, but put money aside. We could recover from this."

"Have you forgotten a little detail like it's illegal? I could go to jail."

"Have *you* forgotten what I told you earlier? These are society women. They'd rather die than admit to the police they hired someone. It would ruin their status."

Wiping his brow with the back of his hand, he grimaced. "If this is such a good idea, why don't you do it?"

Shirley pointed to the window. "Have you seriously never noticed what's out there? Eight gazillion old women and six old men. The women are like lionesses, waiting to pounce on the first available male. It's the same in the world of those wealthy women, but worse. Any single men their age go after the younger, hotter women because their money allows them that option." She gestured down the length of her body. "I do not have what the older rich men want. I do not have what the older women want. Wrong equipment. I am not a commodity. You are. And you won't consider using it to save us? Besides, I thought it was a well-known but never mentioned secret that all men loved the idea of getting a taste of something different."

"You're serious? You want me to be a male prostitute? What would that make you? My pimp?"

A shuffling on concrete sound at the front door made them glance in that direction. They exchanged worried looks.

"Yoo-hoo?" Dora called.

Through the jalousies Shirley saw her and the wavy outline of another person approaching.

"Hello," a male voice said.

"Hello," Dora answered with a flirtatious flair.

"I forgot," Stanley said, lowering his voice. "I asked Tim to come over to watch the ball game. I'll tell him it's not a good time."

"No, then Dora will know something's wrong. I hope she didn't hear us."

Stanley opened the door.

Shirley composed herself and managed a benign smile. "Hi. Come on in. We were just, uh, talking about a television show."

"Yeah? Which one?" Dora sauntered in, using her *sexy* walk.

Tim followed, his eyes on Dora.

"Um . . ." Shirley hesitated, trying to conjure a show name, then dropped the effort as she observed Dora's sudden flirtation toward Tim. Case in point—the lioness. Shirley glanced at Stanley. He didn't seem to get it.

"Tim," Stanley said, "this is my wife, Shirley."

Shirley nodded. "Pleasure to finally meet you. Stanley told me you made his time at Happy Mart tolerable."

"And this," Stanley turned to Dora, "is our dear friend, Dora Flynn."

Dora's face blossomed with a huge smile. Her eyes glittered. How did she do that? Shirley wondered.

"You work at Happy Mart?" Dora gushed. "No wonder you look so familiar. I'm sure I've seen you there."

"I would have remembered you," Tim said, smiling.

"Have a seat, you two," Shirley said. "Stanley, come help me get drinks and snacks in the kitchen." She grabbed his hand and led him there.

"Thank God Dora stopped by," she whispered. "No more Morty. He's toast."

"What?"

"She likes Tim. I can tell. She'll break up with Morty the minute she gets home, I guarantee it."

"How can you switch gears so fast?" Stanley opened the fridge. "I'm still reeling from our conversation about your nut-ball idea."

"It's not a nut-ball idea, and I'm a woman." Shirley took a box of crackers from the cabinet. "Hand me that cheddar cheese on the shelf under the milk, would you? We women try to compartmentalize. How else could I have managed my mother's horrible bout with cancer, Fletcher's broken leg, and be happy at Nina's college graduation, all at the same time? Sometimes it works, sometimes it doesn't."

Passing her the cheese, he then placed two cans of beer on the counter. He reached for the chardonnay. "I assume Dora will want this?"

"Pour her a big glass. She'll flirt more."

"You really don't like Morty, do you?"

CHAPTER THIRTY-TWO

Shirley had never witnessed instant attraction before. As she, Stanley, Dora, and Tim sat exchanging pleasantries in the living room, she found herself fascinated by the chemistry between Dora and Tim.

Tim was an average-looking man of around seventy, with perhaps an extra twenty pounds on him. Although bald, deep smile lines and kind eyes made up for his lack of hair. Shirley liked him, and Dora seemed transfixed. The electricity felt palpable to Shirley.

"What did you do pre-retirement?" Dora asked Tim. "In your *real* life, as we call it around here."

"Plate spinner in a carnival." Tim grinned.

"Huh?" Stanley's brows rose.

Dora exploded with laughter. "Oh, he's kidding, Stanley." Then she appeared unsure. "You *were* joking, weren't you?"

"Sort of," Tim said. "It was a hobby. My actual business was rather mundane. My wife and I started a cleaning company when we first married, then it grew. We did okay." His eyes closed for a moment.

"You miss her," Shirley said, touched by his sentiment.

"Yes." He looked up. "Been three years since she passed."

There was *the* moment of silence—the understood ritual of

respect at the mention of deceased loved ones. It seemed universal in the retirement world. Having waited the correct amount of time, Shirley reached for a cheese-topped cracker and broke the pause. "Tell us about the plate spinning. I've never met anyone who could do that."

Tim chuckled. "I taught myself when I was a teenager. Managed to get on Ted Mack's Amateur Hour."

"I used to watch that show," Dora said.

"Sunday nights. Everybody watched it," Stanley said. "We probably saw you on it, Tim."

"If you ever catch old footage of the show, and there's a gangly sixteen-year-old kid spinning plates, it was most likely me. I didn't have a suit of my own, so my mother made me wear my older brother's. Way too big. With a bow tie, no less. I had a great DA going on, too." He touched the back of his neck. "She was embarrassed by my hair style and told the barber to give me a flat top instead. Instead of cool, I looked like a fool."

"Why, you're practically a star." Dora batted her eyelashes.

Cutting his glance to Shirley, Stanley rolled his eyes.

Another knock rattled the jalousies. Shirley turned to see two obscured people beyond the pebbled glass slats. "We're popular today." On her way to the entry, the dreaded thoughts of impending financial disaster ruptured from her squared-away imaginary box. A split second of panic threw her, then she shoved those worries away to be dealt with later. She opened the door.

Agnes and her aged man-toy Jerry smiled at Shirley. He greeted Shirley with a kiss on the cheek. Agnes' targeted assault must have worked. He looked happier than she'd seen him in years.

Wearing her signature cut-off jeans and black high-top sneakers, Agnes held a tiny black dog in her arms. The straps of a blue diaper bag hung on Jerry's shoulder.

"Meet my new puppy," Agnes said, walking in. "He's three months old."

Gathering around Agnes and the squirming bundle in her arms, Shirley joined Dora in issuing oohs and ahs. Agnes lifted him.

"Are you sure it's not a rat?" Stanley asked. "What's that thing weigh?"

"A pound and a half," Agnes said. "When he's full grown, he'll be around four pounds."

"It's called a tea cup dog," Dora said. "Very trendy. The celebrities carry them around in their purses."

"Does he have a name?" Tim asked.

Setting the diaper bag on the sofa, Jerry frowned. "I want to call him Buttons, but Agnes doesn't like it."

"Buttons is cute," Dora said, taking the puppy from Agnes and cuddling it to her chest. "He is precious. I may have to get one of these."

Agnes scowled. "Buttons is the name of a washed-up clown fired from Ringling Brothers who's now doing summer schtick for octogenarians in the Catskills."

Tim and Stanley laughed.

"Sorry, Jerry," Stanley said. "But that was funny."

"Wasn't meant to be." Agnes plopped onto the sofa. "I dated the son of a bitch until he ran off with one of my painting models."

That made everyone laugh.

"Wait a minute," Dora said, stroking the puppy under its chin. "I thought you told us that when you do paint people, you only do men."

Agnes smiled. "Then I guess—*that* would be the funny part."

Though going along with them, Shirley's effort to quash the frightening reality of her life took more energy than she anticipated. Paying attention to the conversation suddenly felt exhausting. She looked at Stanley. Their eyes met. His expression went to serious, then he seemed to dismiss her and turned toward Tim.

"I haven't properly introduced my friend Tim here," Stanley said. He went on to do the requisite intros.

Shirley walked into the kitchen, feeling drained. With both hands, she leaned on the counter and took deep breaths.

"How long have you kids been an item?" Shirley heard Agnes from the other room. She could imagine both Dora's and Tim's faces reddening.

During the pause that followed, Shirley rejoined them, a forced smile on her face.

"We actually just met," Tim said, indicating Dora. "Not a half an hour ago."

Eyebrows raised, Agnes nodded. "Wow. I'm picking up quite a vibe here. Guess Morty's going to be available." She glanced at Shirley. "You should let Edna know. She's always had a thing for Morty."

Dora's face showed surprise and maybe a bit of shock.

"Oh, for Krypton's sake," Agnes said. "Tell Edna, Shirley. Her attention will cushion the blow when Dora dumps him. And maybe the rest of us will get a break from Edna's incessant gossiping, if she's got a life of her own going on."

Looking bewildered, Tim said, "Who's Morty?"

"Nobody," Dora said.

"Dora's boyfriend," Stanley said.

Right was right was right. Shirley could hear the thoughts in Stanley's mind. He didn't like Morty much either, but her husband's inner Dudley Do-Right probably felt a proper statement of fact was in order. Her hopes for convincing him to go along with her scheme sank further. Yes, it scared her. Yes, she hated the idea of him with other women. But why couldn't he see that, handled well, it could save them?

Smiling, Dora shook her head. "Morty's hardly a boyfriend. We've gone to dinner, a few movies. That's all."

The puppy whined, and Agnes took him from Dora.

"I think he needs to wee," Agnes said. "I'll take him outside." She fetched a plastic bag from the diaper bag and moved toward the door. "Shirley, why don't you come with me? Make sure I don't upset any of your neighbors by letting him go in the wrong place."

"Hah," Tim said. "The local squirrels probably make bigger messes."

Agnes turned to him. "I'm sure you're right, but there are a couple of busybodies around here. Seems all they do is stare out the window and pray for something to report to the homeowner's association."

Dora snickered. "Very true."

Shirley and Agnes walked past the parking lot to a grassy area that led downhill to a pond. Agnes set the puppy down, and he sniffed, then stepped with great care around the stiff St. Augustine grass blades.

"Goodness, he's so—"

"What the hell's up with you and Stanley?" Agnes said.

Though caught unaware, Shirley wasn't surprised Agnes observed the tension between her and Stanley. "Boy, you don't miss a thing, do you?"

"Life-long keen study of people," Agnes said. "Keeps me sharp."

The puppy found a place he liked and squatted.

Knowing Agnes would see through any quickie excuse she made up, Shirley decided the thinnest top layer of the truth would do. "As you know, we're both working now. It's not because we *want* to, as we told everyone. It's because our investments haven't rebounded from the big drop as well as we'd hoped."

"Duh. News flash. You didn't fool anybody." Agnes bent to scoop the tablespoon-sized poop into the bag. "Good boy." She held the bag up high and waved it at a third story window in the building across the parking lot.

Following her gaze, Shirley saw a curtain closing in the window. "Mrs. Tolaski."

Agnes petted the dog, who ventured another few feet

toward the pond. Two Muscovy ducks in the water squawked and took flight. The puppy scooted back to shelter against Agnes' ankle.

"I thought people might guess the real reason," Shirley said. "It was a face-saver to say that. Mostly for Stanley's sake. He's feeling like a huge failure."

"Men." Agnes chortled. "Such egos. As if he'd any control over what those maniacal idiots in the New York banks did to tank the economy. You're not the only ones, you know."

"I know." However, she and Stanley might be the only ones they knew who'd wiped out what was left by trusting a crooked accountant.

"Well then, for Stanley's sake, we'll keep on pretending he loves flipping burgers."

"Thank you, Agnes." Shirley blinked back tears and wished she could tell her the whole truth.

"Talk about timing." Agnes nodded her head toward the parking lot. "It's like she's got extra-sensory perception."

Edna was speed walking her way to them. Shirley chuckled. "If only she would use it for good and not evil."

CHAPTER THIRTY-THREE

Fletcher waved goodbye to Tyler and Alice as he backed down the driveway. They stood in the open front doorway waving back. Alice blew kisses. Janice, with a definite frown, scooted them into the house and shut the door. It was Sunday afternoon, and he'd had the kids since Friday.

Janice had signed the divorce papers. They were done. In order to avoid court, he gave her the house and a very generous alimony—which Florida usually denied to spouses of less than twenty years. Despite that, the frost in her eyes and brimstone in her voice hadn't let up one iota.

He and Agnes had met for coffee several times since she insinuated herself into his business at his parents' townhouse. She'd explained about characteristics in others that infuriated people. Most times, she said, it was because the person getting pissed off actually possessed that characteristic themselves, but chose not to see it, much less acknowledge the possibility of its presence. The more he examined the theory, the more it made sense. Janice's fury at his cheating on her, no matter that he'd also cheated *with* her, seemed to be worse now. Somehow, Janice recused herself from the same scrutiny, perfecting the role of the wronged victim to all who would listen. Fletcher received more than a few hate-spewed calls from Janice's sisters and friends.

He drove home thinking about how he missed the clues when he and Janice first embarked on their affair. Her inner resentments and simmering temper. Maybe he'd chosen not to see them, blinded as he was by her amazing body and her willingness to please him. In a way, he owed Tanya a bit of gratitude for luring him away. Janice, in retrospect, really wasn't the sweet girl she'd pretended to be. She could be mean and vindictive.

Pulling into his parking spot, he promised himself he would only date women closer to his own age. "No one under thirty-five," he shouted, hitting the dashboard with his fist. He blanched. Although still in the car, he glanced around to see if anyone could have heard him. The garage seemed empty. He went to the elevators.

Upstairs, as he unlocked his door, the soft *ting* of the elevator sounded. He turned to see Maddy and a fortyish man exit and head his way. Maddy wore a low-cut flowered sundress and four-inch espadrilles that made her legs look like they soared to her waist. Combating his devilish instinct to conjure an image of her naked, he made himself stop. *No one under thirty-five*, he lectured to his overactive imagination.

"Hello, neighbor," Maddy said.

Her melodic voice caused an eruption of those disabling quivers again. He could be sixteen all over again.

"Did you have a nice weekend with your children?"

Fletcher had not seen her in the week since they exchanged apartment tours. "How did you know I had my kids?"

Maddy and the man laughed.

"We heard childish squealing and shrieking, and you told me you had little ones, so I put two and two together. I'm clever that way." She said it with a touch of sarcasm.

"It was either that, or you had one kinky party," the man said.

Fletcher stared at him, realizing the guy had to be older than him and might be in his fifties. He'd obviously spent the night with her. He took an instant dislike to him. A stab of wild jealousy hit him, too. "Are you Maddy's father?"

Her eyes widening, Maddy blushed. "I'm sorry. Fletcher, this is Bill Previste. He's not my father."

Bill smiled. "Jeez, I hope not. We'd have an Oedipus-type crisis on our hands." He laughed. "Nice to meet you." He extended his hand.

Shaking the man's hand, Fletcher forced a smile. "Well." He turned his doorknob and opened the door. "You both have a good day." He walked into his place, closed the door, then with arms outstretched, shook his entire body to rid himself of the unnerving sensations coursing through him.

Throwing his wallet and keys on the entry table, Fletcher went into the bedroom, threw off his shirt, and put on a pair of gym shorts. Ignoring the mess made by Alice and Tyler, he grabbed a beer from the fridge and plopped onto the sofa. He'd relax for a bit, then muster the energy to clean up the child debris.

Bill Previste was a jerk. Fletcher saw right through him. He hardly knew Maddy, but the thought of her having sex with Bill upset him. Why? Perhaps it was nothing more than his competitive spirit kicking in. If she'd go for an old guy like Bill, then why not him? "Argghhh." Fletcher slapped his head. "No one under thirty-five." He repeated it a few times.

Bill could be the answer to the questions he'd been asking himself about Maddy's upper-crust taste and lifestyle. Maybe Bill was her sugar daddy. Whatever she did for a living probably didn't cover her housing, much less her expensive art and furnishings.

He closed his eyes for a few minutes. The doorbell chimed. He stretched, ambled to the entry, and checked the peephole.

Maddy stood there, arms crossed, facing the elevators.

"Just a second." His pulse racing, he ran to the bedroom, found a T-shirt, and wrestled it on while hustling back to the door. He let her in. She'd changed into jeans and a loose button-down shirt that hung to her hips. She was barefoot, and her painted toenails were a soft pink. Even her feet were pretty.

"Had to hide the evidence first?" She smiled.

"Evidence? Of what?"

"Whatever it is you didn't want me to see. It was just a joke. I read too many mysteries."

"Worried about guests tripping over toys is all. Come in." He started toward the living room, scooped up a stuffed turtle and a Tonka truck on his way, then placed them at the beginning of the bedroom hallway. "I was having a beer. Can I get you anything?"

"A beer would be wonderful, thanks." She moved a doll from a club chair and sat.

Fletcher hurried to get another bottle, popped the cap with an opener, and returned to see her leaning in and assembling Legos on the coffee table. Her shining blonde hair brushed the table top, and he caught a glimpse of a pink lace bra under the shirt, which puffed out as she bent to place a block.

She looked up. "I used to love these things."

He handed her the beer, then sat on the sofa. "Me, too. To what do I owe the honor of your visit?"

Shrugging, she took a sip. "I thought I should get to know my neighbor better. If that's okay with you."

"I think it's a great idea. Where's your boyfriend?" It was a struggle not to stare at her.

"You didn't like Bill, did you?"

"You always this direct?"

"Pretty much. It drives my mother crazy."

"I don't know Bill, therefore I can't say." Had he let his disapproval show when he met the man? He decided to be direct right back at her. "You have a thing for old guys, huh?"

She laughed. "I have a *thing* for men who interest me. Age has little to do with it." She took another drink from her beer. "Bill has accomplished fantastic things in his life. He's a fascinating man."

"But?"

A slow grin crept onto her face. She seemed to be deliberating whether to tell him something. "He's got an, um, issue. Or two. Ones I can't overlook."

"Why don't you break up with him?"

Her eyebrows rose. "Break up with him? We're not a couple." She blushed again. "This was the first time I let him stay the night. There won't be a second time."

"Poor sucker. He's on his way home thinking he's the luckiest SOB around, and you're going to dump his ass, aren't you?"

She nodded and a naughty cast came over her. "You and I are going to get along. You're not afraid to be honest, are you?"

"I wouldn't go that far. I'm not an idiot. It's a rare woman who wants to hear what a man's really thinking."

"I do." She squinched her face into a thoughtful expression. "I'd love to have at least one man's honest opinion. How refreshing that would be."

"Here, here." Fletcher lifted his bottle in a toast. "A friend to be honest with." Not a chance he'd be completely honest, he thought, but he'd give it a good shot.

Raising her beer to meet his, they clinked bottles and drank.

"You know . . ." She set her beer down, straightening in the chair. "In high society, you don't *ever* do that. Strictly a no-no."

"Do what? Tell the truth?"

A chortle of laughter escaped her, and she threw her head back. As she moved her head down again, she brushed her hair away from her eyes with a huge smile. "Yes. That, too. In fact, truth telling may be the biggest no-no. But I was referring to the toast by touching bottles. Or touching glasses." She made a face resembling a rich and snotty cartoon character, disapproval emanating from the pinched expression. "It's *pedestrian.*"

Fletcher smiled. "I'll keep that in mind for my next invite to Buckingham Palace. Thanks. You know a lot about that world, do you?"

She flinched, seeming flustered for an instant. "I have friends who travel in those circles."

"Lucky them. My friends tend to gather at the pool hall."

"I've never been to a pool hall." She drained her beer, licked her lips, and stood.

Lost in the beginning of a fantasy after watching her pink tongue do the quick circuit on her mouth, Fletcher snapped out of it in time to not make a fool of himself. "You're not missing much. You belong in far classier places."

"Thank you." She stepped around the coffee table and covered a yawn. "Sorry. Very little sleep last night, and beer makes me drowsy. If you'll excuse me, I need a nap. I have a dinner tonight."

He stood, disappointed. "Of course." He followed her to the door, then opened it for her. "I'm glad you came by."

She smirked, then gave him a little kiss on the cheek. "Me, too. Bye."

His heart went into jackhammer mode. He admired the view as she walked toward her apartment and shut the door. She left because I bored her, he thought. He thudded his head against the door. "And I'm in the effing *friend zone.*"

Resuming his previous prone position on the sofa, he slapped himself again. That was good. She was too young. She obviously considered him a non-contender, for whatever reason. Maybe because she had no interest in a man with small children. Maybe he wasn't worldly enough. He'd never had to think about that before. Women always threw themselves at him before they knew much about him. He was good-looking for his age, he'd been told that enough. Coupled with his making a six-figure salary, albeit a low six-figure—okay, it barely crossed that threshold—he was hard to resist. For most women. Maddy was no average woman.

This is good, he told himself again. The friend zone. Perfect. It would keep him out of trouble. Yet, the image of her clear eyes with their intriguing shades of light blue, and those moist lips, and those long, long, legs, and the shiny so-soft-looking hair beckoned him. He yanked the pillow from beneath his head and slammed it over his face. "No one under thirty-five," he screamed. "No one under thirty-five!"

Disgusted, he jumped from the sofa and stormed into the bathroom for a cold shower.

CHAPTER THIRTY-FOUR

Stanley sat with the other employees listening to Jason, the red-pimpled assistant manager of The Burger Flip, explain the new hairnet policy. Stanley stifled a yawn. It was another early Saturday morning. He glanced at his Timex. The fancy watch Fletcher gave him for his birthday wasn't the kind of thing to wear when expecting a day full of greasy fumes. He'd worn it once and now wondered if he should sell the damn thing. He didn't know how he'd ever explain its absence to Fletcher without hurting his feelings or revealing the severe money shortage. There might be no way to hide it much longer anyway. He flushed with shame at the utter humiliation headed his way.

Standing in front of the register counter, Jason opened the cleaning manual and demonstrated with a paper towel the proper motions for removing the water spots from the milkshake machine after cleaning. It was important for it to shine. He stroked each cylinder gently with the towel. Several of the teen employees tittered in the back of the restaurant, making Stanley stifle a chuckle. Jason did seem to be enjoying it a tad much.

Finishing the dregs of his free coffee—the perk that was supposed to compensate for a six AM meeting—Stanley wished he were home in bed. Then he remembered the jumbo fight he and Shirley had and knew he was better off at work. Two days before, he'd invited a real estate agent—described to him as a real go-getter shark—to the townhouse. Shirley refused to let the man in, and for the first time Stanley could recall, she was rude. Slammed the jalousies in the guy's face. Then she laid into Stanley about her cockamamie male prostitution idea. He shook his head.

"Stanley?" Jason's irritating whiny voice broke into Stanley's thoughts. "You disagree with that?"

"No. Sorry," Stanley said, waving a dismissive hand. "Thinking about something else."

When Jason finally wrapped it up, Stanley felt relieved to get to work. He stocked the condiment mini-packs, wiped thc tables and counters, and checked the restrooms. The Saturday crowds began at seven for breakfast. The entire crew whirled through the continuing rush for lunch.

It didn't let up until after two-thirty. Stanley sighed at the aftermath trash on the floor and went for the broom.

"Mr. Nowack?" a young female voice asked.

He turned to see his co-worker, Jessica, standing behind him. She was a high school junior, smart and attractive in an athletic way. He'd had a few conversations with her. She seemed to be a great kid with a bright future and reminded him of his granddaughter, Mary Ann.

"I was wondering if you could take my closing shift on Friday night," Jessica said. "I'm taking the SAT Saturday, and it's really important that I get a decent night's sleep."

"Sure, Jessica." Stanley smiled. "You want to get into Harvard, you need good test scores."

"Actually, my first choice school is Stanford. Then Brown." She smiled back at him. "Thank you *so* much. I did ask Jason for the night off, but he screwed up my schedule. You're really saving me. Thanks." She turned and joined a group of two other girls and three boys seated at a booth close to the doors.

Stanley gathered cleaning supplies and went into the men's room. After any weekend lunch rush the bathrooms needed cleaning before the dinner onslaught, but this was a mess of new proportions. He grabbed a garbage bag and put on a pair of latex gloves. Swirls of paper towels littered the floor like enormous snowflakes. Food wrappers, drink containers, lids, and straws added to the disorder. "What in the name of Jehosephat?" he said.

A sweat and mud stained muscle T-shirt lay near the sink. He used two fingers to lift it, finding a set of ear buds underneath. Technically, his job required him to sort through and place left-behind items in the lost-and-found. He wasn't in the mood for it and used his free hand to push the counter debris into the bag, then dowsed the surface with disinfectant spray. He let it set there to do its lemon-scented deodorizing and opened the first stall door. Besides the expected paper shreds on the floor, there was a used condom on the edge of the toilet.

"For crying out loud," he muttered. "It's a zoo." With the broom bristles, he knocked the offensive item into the bowl, then flushed the toilet with a shiver of disgust.

When the bathrooms were clean, Stanley took his broom into the dining area. Jessica and her friends were munching French fries in the front booth. Two other lunch stragglers occupied tables by the window, one reading a book, the other texting on his phone.

Stanley started sweeping at the back of the dining room, working his way toward the front door and registers. A few minutes later, the *ting* of the entry signal prompted him to glance at the door.

Walt Jenkins, the owner, smiled as he walked in. He wore white sneakers, khakis, and a lime green Polo shirt.

A chorus of "Hi, Mr. Jenkins," came from the teenagers behind the counter.

"Good afternoon, everyone." Walt surveyed the area, nodded, then locked eyes with Stanley and strolled to him.

Stanley stilled his broom and held it in his left hand while he shook hands with Walt. "This is a nice surprise. I thought somebody said you were out of town this week." He was relieved he'd done the restrooms first.

"The trip was cancelled." Walt gestured around him. "Heck of a clean up, isn't it?"

"Takes me by surprise every weekend."

Walt grinned. "I can't tell you how many times I cleaned this floor. Over and over. The customers' ability to make a mess always amazed me. I was over the moon when Margie and I decided we could afford to pay someone else to do it. Tell me, how's it going?"

Stanley spread his arms wide, the broom in his hand. "What's not to like?"

Laughing, Walt said, "Good. Keep it up and learn the business. I could use a mature, wiser head around here. I'll be expanding next year, adding two more locations. Going into management sound agreeable to you?"

"It sounds fantastic." An image of himself in a respected position and the far bigger paycheck gave him new hope for the future. "Thanks."

"Last time I we met, you said you play golf?" Walt asked.

"Yup. Can't say I'm as good as I used to be, though."

Jason emerged from behind the fryer and scurried toward them.

"We've had a foursome for a few years," Walt said. "But the wife of one of the guys is very ill, and he cancelled on us. You interested in being the fourth?"

"Sure, Walt," Stanley said as Jason joined them. "It does depend on whether I'm scheduled to work that day."

"I'm sure Jason will accommodate us on that," Walt said.

The anxious expression on Jason's face looked like a squirrel twitching for an acorn.

"Yes, Mr. Jenkins," Jason said. "So glad you stopped in, sir. If you'll step into the office, I have the current sales figures. We had a spectacular week. I think that milkshake promotion really made a difference."

"Wonderful," Walt said. "Now, if you'll—"

"Freeze," a male voice yelled at the same time the entry *ting* sounded.

"Nobody move," a second man said.

Audible gasps came from both customers and employees.

Stanley's gaze flicked to the door. Two men dressed in black T-shirts and jeans with black ski masks and holding handguns ventured toward the registers. The taller of the two went to his right, sweeping his gun back and forth, threatening the seven customers in the dining room and Stanley, Walt, and Jason. The shorter man held a duffle bag and kept his gun aimed at the three employees behind the counter.

"Shit," Jason said.

"Shut up." The tall one pointed his gun at Jason. "You, in the middle with the broom, drop it. You three put your hands up."

Stanley let go of the handle, and it clattered onto the tile. He, Walt, and Jason raised their arms. He looked at the booth of teenagers and saw with relief that at least Jessica wasn't there. Maybe she'd left while he spoke with Walt. He willed the remaining kids and other customers not to do anything stupid.

"Empty the registers," the shorter robber said. "You." He pointed the gun at Emily, a sixteen-year-old. "You do it. Put it in here." He threw the black duffle onto the counter. "The rest of you behind there move back and lay on the floor."

They were teenagers, also—a boy named Alonzo and a girl named Valerie. They did as they were told.

"Now you kids in the booth," the taller one said. "One at a time, get out and lay on the floor where I can see you." The boy closest to the end slid off the seat, crawled a few feet to the center of the dining room, then lay down on his stomach. The second teen followed.

"You two at the tables over there," the man said. "Do the same thing. Down. Now."

Stanley heard chairs scraping the floor behind him.

"Hurry up," the shorter man said to Emily.

Emily began to cry, and her hands shook as she took the cash from the first register drawer. A bill fell on the floor, and she stooped to retrieve it.

"No. Leave it. Stand up."

Sobbing, Emily nodded and moved to the second register.

Hang in there, Emily, Stanley thought. He snuck a glance at Walt, whose face remained composed, but his eyes darted to the hallway that led to the restrooms and grew wide.

Stanley looked in that direction. Jessica stood in the hall, head down, texting on her phone. She'd apparently been in the bathroom.

Jessica looked up, took a few steps toward the dining room, then froze. Her mouth dropped open. She screamed.

"No, Jessica," Jason yelled.

She screamed louder.

"Get down," Walt snapped.

The taller robber pivoted in her direction and fired.

Jason moved in front of Stanley and Walt and pointed at Jessica. "No!"

The robber swiveled back and fired at Jason.

The crack of the second report hit Stanley at the same instant blood flew into his face. Knocked to the floor, his head slammed against the Mexican tile. Walt landed on him.

A few seconds of silence passed, then more screaming started. He saw the robbers run out the door. He tried to move Walt, but couldn't. His head hurt. He stopped straining and rested his cheek against the tile.

CHAPTER THIRTY-FIVE

Stanley had a headache that hurt like a jackhammer had drilled into his skull. There was a pillow under his head, and the surface he lay on wasn't hard tile anymore. He opened his eyes. Hospital-blue curtains formed a private space for him. Through a gap, he saw and heard Shirley having a quiet conversation with a nurse.

"Hello?" His voice came out more like a squawk. Speaking made the ache worse.

Shirley turned and looked at him. She flew to his side, her face inches away from his. "Thank God you're all right." A tear escaped from one eye as she grasped his hand with both of hers. "I've been so worried."

The nurse approached him from the other side. "How are you feeling, Mr. Nowack?"

Her cheerful, but booming, voice made him wince. "Please don't talk so loud. My head is killing me."

She frowned and held up a penlight. She shined the light into each eye. "Good."

Stanley winced. "Don't do that again. It hurt."

Nodding, she wrapped a blood pressure cuff around his arm and pumped it up. When she finished, she stuck a thermometer attached to a curly wire into his mouth and grabbed his wrist while looking at her watch.

"How long have I been out?"

"Shhh."

Clamping his lips shut, he waited.

She removed the thermometer. "Tell me your name."

"Abraham Lincoln."

The nurse's eyebrows rose. "Very funny."

"My name is Stanley Nowack."

She went on to ask him the day of the week, the year, and the current president's name.

Fletcher came into the curtained cubicle with two take-out foam cups. He smiled wide. "Dad? You're awake. That's great." He handed one cup to Shirley, then walked to Stanley's other side beside the nurse.

"Everything seems fine," the nurse said. "The results of your CT scan were okay as well. The doctor doesn't think you have a serious injury, and there are no signs of bleeding. He wants you to stay for twenty-four hours observation, just to be sure. I'll see if your room is ready, then we can get you moved upstairs."

"Thank you," Shirley said.

"My pleasure," the nurse said with a small chuckle. "It's not every day I have the great Abraham Lincoln under my care." She hurried away.

"What time is it?" Stanley asked. "And how are the others?"

Shirley's eyes cut to Fletcher, and Stanley turned to look at him.

Grimacing, Fletcher took an audible breath, and blew it out. "It's after ten. You've been unconscious for about seven hours. The good news is everything looks fine."

"And the bad news?" Stanley sensed it was awful.

"Walt Jenkins, the owner, died. I spoke to the police. They said the bullet went through the manager kid's arm, then hit Walt in the chest, and that's why he fell on you."

Grief struck Stanley, and he closed his eyes. "He was such a good man. Gave me a chance. We were headed toward being friends—asked me to play golf with him. Crap." A replay of their last conversation reminded him also that Walt mentioned the possibility of Stanley managing his new restaurant. His only hope for climbing out of the financial abyss vaporized into the ether.

Then he remembered seeing the gunman swing toward Jessica and fire. "Jessica?"

Fletcher shut his eyes and shook his head. "She's dead, too."

"God damn it," Stanley said. "Son of a bitch." That beautiful young girl with so much promise. He couldn't imagine the anguish her parents felt. "Did they catch the scum who did this?"

"No. Not yet." Shirley touched his cheek.

"Would you mind if I spoke to your mother alone for a moment?"

"Sure, Dad. I'll take a walk around the halls." Fletcher lifted his foam cup from the floor where he'd placed it and stood. "I'll call Nina while I do. She'll want to know you're awake."

Watching his son amble away, Stanley reflected on the fragility of life. "You know, we're so lucky we have both our children. Six grandchildren. Every one of them in good health. We're in good health."

"Yes," Shirley said. "You're right."

"It's all so tenuous, isn't it?"

She nodded, smiling.

"Whatever problems we have seem inconsequential compared to losing a child." He wiped a tear from his eye. "Or each other."

"I couldn't agree more." Shirley's wonderful face had an angelic cast.

"Funny, isn't it? Funny strange, I mean. Not funny—haha. You don't really appreciate what's most important until you lose it, or think you'll lose it."

"Absolutely." She took his hand and squeezed it.

"Our money troubles are small issues compared to people who've lost their loved ones."

"Right." She kissed his hand.

"Whatever I have to do to get us back on track, I'll do."

"Does that mean you'll continue working at The Burger Flip?"

He thought for a moment. "My guess is that place will be in limbo for a while. Walt's wife or kids would have to run things. I've never seen his family visit. Makes me doubt there's any interest on their part. If my job there is gone, I'll hit the employment trail again. As soon as my head doesn't feel like someone's in there with a hammer and chisel."

"Thank you, dear. It means so much to me to know you realize what's really important."

Gazing into her eyes, he felt a wave of overwhelming love and tenderness. "I would do anything for you. For us."

She grinned. "Good. I think you just agreed to give my money-making idea a try."

"Cri-min-ent-ly."

CHAPTER THIRTY-SIX

Catherine Von Cletan and Pookie Minton exchanged air kisses in front of The Breakers hotel in Palm Beach. Catherine watched Pookie's husband accompany her to their Bentley where their chauffer waited by the open door.

"Shall we?" Count Alfonse de Albreccio gestured to Catherine's S600 Mercedes where Hector stood exchanging pleasantries with the head valet.

She smiled at him. "Yes." Her left foot twisted a little as she stepped forward, and she wobbled. "Gracious me."

The count grabbed her by the arm and steadied her.

Perhaps she'd had one glass of wine too many at dinner, but it had been such a lovely evening. She walked with the count and allowed him to help her into the back seat.

He got in on the other side, and Hector steered the car toward Sago Beach.

Taking her right hand in his, the count brought it to his lips. "Thank you for your enchanting company tonight. Rarely have I enjoyed such engaging conversation."

Feeling the blood rush to her face, she studied him. For a man in his early seventies, he was in good shape. Tall and thin, he had what her mother would have called an elegant stature. In spite of his rather large hooked nose, she decided his was a face full of character.

Leaning closer, he whispered, "I find you quite alluring."

"Thank you." The blush seemed to spread throughout her body. Then a stab of disbelief hit her. She'd done her homework and knew the truth about his family's estate being greatly diminished, but the de Albreccio name still carried great prestige. Did he like her or the idea of her money best? Did her extra pounds bother him? "Although, I'm sure you're accustomed to more *delicate* women."

He laughed. "Aren't you the fisherwoman." His eyes narrowed. "More *delicate* women, my lady, aren't nearly as much fun to play with." He winked. "If you'll please forgive my bluntness."

Fun? He had to mean in the bedroom. She couldn't stop the wide-eyed look she gave him.

Placing his lips on her ear, he flicked his tongue on the bottom of her ear lobe.

She shivered from the sensation.

"I know this is only our second date," he whispered, "but I am getting the feeling that you and I are very much of the same mold. You *are* a sexual creature, aren't you?"

"Oh," she squealed. The excitement building inside her made her dizzy. "I am certainly not going to answer that, dear sir." She batted her eyelashes. "I suppose some things you simply have to find out for yourself."

"Grrrrrr." The low, deep growling sound emanated from him as he kissed her neck. "I *love* strong women."

"Stop now," she whispered as she remembered Hector in the front seat. She gave him a gentle push away. "Wait until we're inside."

The rest of the way home, the count teased her by walking his fingertips up and down the length of her thigh, venturing toward her restricted zone several times. He chuckled when she gasped.

She felt giddy with the excitement coursing through her as

they exited the car and made their way to her private study. Catherine sat on the loveseat.

The count closed the door behind them, then leaned against it, staring at her with a lascivious leer. "Come here."

"Just a moment." She walked to her desk and pressed a button on the wall-mounted intercom. "Michael?" While she waited, she whispered, "My new majordomo."

A few seconds later, static buzzed, and a man answered. "Yes, Mrs. Von Cletan?"

"Give the staff and yourself the rest of the night off."

"Thank you, ma'am."

"We'll need to give them a little time to disperse," she said. "I do like my privacy. How about a night cap?" Though she already felt ready for action—in fact, she was incredibly turned on—she wanted another drink for courage, and intensifying the booze goggles on the count might help him overlook her weight. She moved to the bar and opened the cabinet doors.

"Allow me," he said, coming close and brushing the back of his hand across her breast. "The way you take charge, it's drawing me like a moth to flame." He gestured to the array of bottles. "What is your pleasure?"

"Macallan. Two fingers, then ice." She took two Waterford club glasses from the shelf and placed them in front of him.

"Excellent taste in scotch I see." He poured the same for both of them, plunked a few ice cubes in, then handed her one. "To us." He raised his glass and drank.

She took a long sip and savored the burn in her mouth.

He set his on the granite bar and touched her shoulders, slowly stroking up and down. "Anticipation. I love it." His hands moved to her breasts, circling and circling on the black silk of her dress, until . . .

Even through her bra, the sensation of her hardening nipples under his fingers thrilled her. "Alfonse." She sucked in a breath and moved away. "Let me . . ." Her voice came out shaky. She cleared her throat. "Let me check the hall."

"Whatever you say." He grinned. "You're in charge tonight."

Still holding her glass, she opened the door and stepped out. All seemed quiet. "Would you like to finish your drink upstairs in my suite? There's a spectacular view of the ocean from my balcony."

Picking up his drink, the count nodded. He stopped at the doorway to retrieve a leather briefcase he'd left there earlier before going to dinner.

"That's perfectly safe there," she said. "No one is here to touch it." He'd explained earlier that there were contracts he'd needed to review on his way to her home.

"I need to have it with me," he said. "You'll see." He winked again.

She ignored his odd response, assuming he was as swayed by lust as she and not thinking clearly about anything else. Taking another hefty sip of the scotch first, she took off her shoes and led the way to the grand staircase.

"I'm right behind you," he said in a low voice as they mounted the stairs. "And the view is fantastic."

"Dear heavens," she said, stopping and turning to see his face, then having to grab for the banister railing again as she felt the stairs tip to the left. "Truly?" She straightened and realized she was drunk. Well, good.

"Keep going. It's everything I can do to contain myself."

She had finally found the man who appreciated her. All of her.

Sensing his intense stare on her backside, she swayed a little more as she reached the second floor and really flaunted it on the way to her suite. The heavy paneled double doors stood open, revealing a sitting room with French doors leading to a spacious balcony, and beyond it, more French doors leading to her bed. She switched on a lamp.

"Fit for a queen," the count said. "How perfect." He set his drink on a side table beside a chair in the sitting area and placed the briefcase on the thick carpet.

Gesturing toward the balcony, Catherine waited for him to look at her. He seemed to be more interested in gulping the remnants of his scotch. "Alfonse." She put her hands on her hips.

Staring at her from under bushy brows, his lids narrowed to slits. "Yes?"

"I was trying to show you the view."

"I see all the view I want to from right here."

"Oh." That flummoxed her.

He took a step closer. "What do you want, my dear queen? I am your servant." He bowed.

"I, um, I don't . . ."

"Come now," he said, his voice sounding husky. "You didn't lure me up here to show me an oceanscape. Command me."

"I don't know how." She worried the spell was breaking. "I'm not sure what it is you're implying."

"Yes, you do." He moved forward, caressed her hips, then he pulled her tight against him. "See? Nothing yet. You command me, and I'll obey."

She didn't understand why, with all his aggressive fawning over her, his ardor hadn't reached the most important area yet. "I'm not sure I—"

"I know you do." He broke from her, retrieved the briefcase, and took it into her bedroom, plopping it onto the bed's silk coverlet.

Maybe he was one of those older men who needed a pill. She entered the bedroom. "Can I get you a glass of water?"

He gave her a curious look. "No. Come here and kiss me."

That was more like it. Her pent-up lust took over, and she nearly knocked him backward onto the bed. She kissed him.

"Harder," he said. "Kiss me harder, like you mean it."

A peculiar feeling rushed through her that mixed with the lust, and she forced her tongue into his mouth.

He whimpered and unzipped his pants, letting them fall. Taking her hands in his while she continued her assault, he placed them lower.

It felt like he wore a type of loin covering. She glanced down. In the dim light, it looked like a black leather sheath, and beneath it, his interest grew. She stopped kissing him.

"See?" he said. "It's working, it's working. Don't stop now. Caress me. Kiss me." He opened the briefcase and removed a leather whip.

"What is that for?" She took a step back.

"Like you don't know." He held it out, then placed in her hand. "I've been horribly bad. Wicked, even."

Alcohol glazing her mind, it took a moment to register. "You want me to hit you with this?"

He growled again. "A strong woman like you. Feel it. It's softer than you think and won't hurt me. Yes, hit me. Wait until you see what happens when you do." He chuckled. "I'm rather large. A beast. You won't be disappointed."

"Ewww." She dropped it, grabbed the bedpost, and steadied herself. "No. Absolutely not." She walked backward toward the sitting room. "You're a pervert."

He laughed. "For God's sake, woman, wake up. This is how grown-ups play. You want some action? This is how it works." He lay on the bed, aroused now. "Go ahead and get mad."

His erection was huge, but disgust filled her. "You despicable man. Get out of my bedroom. Get out of my house."

"That's it. Get mad. Get furious. You want me. You know you do. Look at you, ordering me around like I'm a servant. Big, fat women like you love to be in charge. Admit it."

"I will not." She shivered. "You have me all wrong."

"Do I?" He rose and stepped toward her. "We're perfect for each other. You are big and bossy. I happen to love dominating women like you. You turn me on."

She backed away further into the hall, then headed for the stairs. "Get out of my house right now, or I'm calling the police."

Laughing, he disappeared back into her bedroom. "All right, my dear, porcine darling. You win this time, but I'll wager you'll rethink this and realize I'm right. You're going to beg me to come back."

CHAPTER THIRTY-SEVEN

Shirley guessed she was, for the most part, invisible to the women she waited on at Pauline's. A forgettable clerk—a pleasant member of the servant class. Still, for the task of approaching *clients* for Stanley, she wanted little chance of recognition—zero, if possible.

"How about this one?" The middle-aged sales woman gestured to another wig on the shelf behind the counter. It had short, strawberry-blonde curls and sat atop a black velvet head and shoulders stand. "It's been very popular with our mature customers."

"I've never thought of myself as a blonde." Shirley scanned the rows of wigs, all on the same head forms. She'd tried on four. "Don't you have one that looks like it *belongs* on someone my age?"

The woman screwed up one side of her mouth. "Nobody *ever* comes in here and wants to look her age." She shrugged. "They think they're fooling people if they've got young hair."

"The only ones they're fooling are themselves." Shirley pointed to the light brown one she'd tried on first. "Is there any way to have some authentic-looking gray streaks put in? That cut and length seemed good, but I'd feel like a nitwit in it."

"We do have a colorist." The woman pulled a white binder

from under the counter. "Let me make a call and see."

Wandering toward the store's mall entry while the sales lady used the phone, Shirley checked her watch. She had ten minutes before she was to meet Dora at the food court for lunch. Dora had driven because Stanley, the stubborn ox, insisted on taking the car to go job searching. Why couldn't he see that even if he found something, which seemed more unlikely every day, it would pay at a piddling pace—nowhere near the amount needed to rescue them in time. "I can't lose my house," she muttered as she tamped down yet another wave of sheer terror.

"Good news," the saleslady called.

Shirley turned and approached her.

"The colorist said she could have it done in a few days." The woman held up the wig. "Want to try it on again to be sure it's the one?"

"Probably a good idea." Shirley set her purse down and allowed the woman to position it on her head. Backing away from the counter, she studied her reflection in a full-length mirror on the opposite wall. The wig looked believable. She imagined heavier, different make-up and nodded.

"Shirley? Is that you?" Agnes' voice came from the doorway.

Suppressing the shocked *eek* sound she felt coming, Shirley swallowed and faced Agnes, who wore a knee-length, embroidered denim skirt with her black high-tops. *So much for my disguise.* "Why, hello." She whipped the wig off her head and yelped when a few of her own hairs snagged.

"You've got to be more careful. You haven't bought it yet." Frowning, the saleswoman took the wig from Shirley and smoothed its locks on her way to the register. "I told you. Gently on and gently off, and it'll last a lot longer."

"I'm sorry. I'll have to think about buying it and get back to you." Shirley faked a smile, then walked toward the doorway, leading Agnes into the mall. "Agnes, what are you doing way up here in Palm Beach Gardens?"

"You're hair's all messed up in the rear," Agnes said. "Looks like a bird nested there." She took off her backpack, sat on the marble slab edge of a burbling fountain, and patted the space next to her. "Sit. You know, when you turned tail and left that store, that lady looked like she was about to jump over the counter and tackle you."

Shirley stroked her hair into place, then sat. "I was trying to avoid embarrassment—didn't want anyone to see me. Then you came in, and I panicked. How did you recognize me?"

Agnes shrugged. "You're wearing a Shirley outfit. Then I checked the body build and your profile."

"I have a *Shirley* outfit?"

"When you go out during the day, you always wear either starched white or khaki pants, white sneakers, and your nubby-knit beige sweater over a T-shirt. It's your uniform."

"I hadn't realized I was so predictable."

"Eh, don't give it a wrinkle in time. If you're comfortable, then who cares?"

Shirley glanced at her watch. "I have to meet Dora in a few minutes."

"She know you're sick?"

"What?"

"Don't worry, I won't tell anyone." Agnes bent and rummaged through a side pocket of her backpack. "Ah. Here." On her open palm, she presented a polished piece of lapis lazuli about the size of a quarter. "Helps the immune system and purifies the mind, body, and spirit."

"Thank you, but I'm not sick."

Closing her fingers over the rock, Agnes gave Shirley a sideways glare.

The silence between them made Shirley twitch as her mind scurried for a viable explanation.

Agnes' eyes widened. "Then why the wig? Costume party?"

"Yes." That was a great excuse. Shirley wished she'd thought of it.

"Yeah? Who's having the party? It's not at the clubhouse."

"No. I, uh . . ." Shirley felt the blood rush into her cheeks.

"It's not a party is it?" Agnes' left eyebrow rose. "Oh." She snickered. "No wonder you're turning six shades of purple." She slapped her knee. "Didn't think you and Stanley had it in you."

"Had what in us?" Shirley stared at her.

"Role-playing bedroom games keep a relationship fresh. Good for you." Agnes lifted her backpack and stood. "Don't worry, you know me. I'm no gossip. Your secret's safe. Everyone will go on believing you two are the original missionaries. And I'm very relieved you don't have the big C." She winked at Shirley, then lowered her voice to a whisper. "That wig will work. Try being the dangerous female spy from the French Resistance. Jerome loves to play that one. See you back at the ranch, adventure-girl."

Open-mouthed, Shirley watched Agnes saunter away, then realized she was late to meet Dora. As she hustled toward the food court, she shivered when unwanted pictures of Agnes and Jerome in various costumes invaded her head.

Dora waved to her from a table in the center when Shirley rounded the corner.

"I'm so sorry I'm late," Shirley said.

"Only five minutes." Dora gestured to the Italian food stand. "I'm in the mood for a chicken parm sandwich. What about you?"

"I'll need a moment to decide."

"Good. You can watch my stuff while I'm gone." Dora pointed to a huge white paper shopping bag on the floor beside her seat. "Wait 'till you see what I got." She went to get in line.

Shirley sat, then leaned to peek into Dora's bag. There were smaller bags from Saks, Nordstrom's, Crate & Barrel, and a few other unidentified ones. She straightened and took a deep breath. Dora had always been able to afford more than Shirley, but fate's clobbering took its toll, and now it irked the tar out of her. Each tank of gas for the car made Shirley cringe. The electric bill sent chills through her. The wig she'd picked out equaled a month's grocery money, but not getting caught was the most important thing. If only Stanley would agree to it, she was sure they could bring money in fast.

CHAPTER THIRTY-EIGHT

In the two weeks since he and Maddy spent that Sunday afternoon hour getting to know each other a bit, Fletcher found multiple excuses to call her. He needed a woman's opinion of paint color. What did she think of the draperies for his little ones' room? How did one pick the best produce? And the corker that brought his ruse to an end—*come over here and taste this*—when he'd only heated jarred spaghetti sauce.

He couldn't help himself, and he didn't want to. Maddy was mature, sophisticated, drop-dead gorgeous, and she thought he was fun to hang out with. Not exactly the adulation Tanya had poured on him, but Tanya turned out to be a phony. The difficult part of being anywhere near Maddy was trying to hide his rapid pulse and elevated adrenaline rush.

Then something great happened. Maddy asked *him* out. On a date. She said she'd drive, and where they were going was a surprise.

Now, as he pushed shirts on their hangers back and forth on the rack in his closet, he felt a slight twinge of guilt. He'd told his father he'd never date anyone under thirty-five again. He'd told himself the same a thousand times since meeting Maddy.

"Too bad," he shouted at the mirror in the closet. "I'm not Superman. *No one* could say no to this girl." He lowered his voice and shook his head. "Least of all, me." Imagining his parents' reaction, he decided there was no way he'd tell them about Maddy, much less introduce them. He took a blue, short-sleeve button-down off its hanger and put it on. His cell rang, and he ran to the kitchen where he'd left it on the counter.

"You ready?" It was Maddy.

"Yes, ma'am. You going to pick me up at the door, nice and proper?"

She chuckled. "I'll be in the hall in five minutes. Be there or be square."

Grinning, he walked to the bedroom. He took two condoms from his nightstand drawer and put them in his wallet. He didn't expect anything, but he could hope. The tossed blankets caught his attention, and he made up the bed—in case luck and life showed mercy toward him at his place instead of hers.

When he emerged from his front door, she stood with one hand on a hip, tapping her foot. She looked beautiful, as always, wearing tight jeans, strappy high-heeled sandals, and a stretchy fabric sleeveless top that made her smallish breasts seem bigger.

"What, no flowers for me?" He frowned. "I'm an old-fashioned kind of guy."

That earned him an eye-roll.

"Come on," she said, gesturing toward the elevators. "Your chariot awaits." She plucked a yellow rose from a table arrangement on their way down the hall. "Here you go. Happy now, princess?"

Fletcher accepted the flower and adopted his best effeminate sway. "I could get used to this."

She laughed. "You do that a mite too convincingly." She pressed the elevator button.

There was about a minute of silence as they waited, and Fletcher's brain scrambled for a safe topic of conversation. He didn't want to seem nosy or too anxious. Normally, he had no problem conjuring witty repartee, but his mind seemed to have just short-circuited. The elevator dinged. The doors opened, and they stepped inside, joining an elderly couple in formal dress.

Maddy smiled at them. "Student competition night at the opera?"

The woman nodded. "Yes. How did you know?"

"Darling," the man said, "where else would we be headed in this attire? It's not Season." He smiled at Maddy. "No offense, Miss." He cut his eyes toward Fletcher. "And yourselves? Where are you taking your beautiful daughter this evening?"

Maddy's eyes widened, and Fletcher nearly choked. Did he appear old enough to be her father? He was eighteen years her senior, so technically, he *could* be her father, but—ouch. He didn't think he looked the part at all.

"He's my date," Maddy said. "But we get that a lot." She leaned toward the couple and spoke in a conspiratorial whisper that Fletcher had no problem hearing. "He looks really old for his age, and I look really young for mine. He's only five years beyond me. He tends to get a little sensitive about it."

The woman gasped and put a hand over her mouth. "Really?"

The man didn't seem to buy it and stared harder at Fletcher.

Another ding, the doors opened to the lobby, and the man hustled his wife away.

Ushering Maddy from the elevator, Fletcher shook his head. "You—are a devil."

She laughed. "You aren't the first to tell me. My mother could make your ears bleed and your eyes glaze over with stories of how I exasperate her."

They started toward the garage decks.

"Speaking of your mother, you mentioned she lives in South Florida?"

"Did I?"

"I think so. Whereabouts?"

"Doesn't matter." She waved a hand. "Every retirement mecca looks like the next one down here."

"That's true."

They stopped in front of the exit to the garage, Fletcher opened it for her, then followed her out.

"I don't want to talk about my mother." Maddy led the way to her parking space.

He lagged behind to admire the way her long legs connected to her swaying taut butt, imagining each hand cupped onto a firm, but soft, cheek, then slowly inching inward—

She glanced back. "You're staring at my ass?"

"Not my fault. It's magnificent."

Stopping short, she waited for him to catch up, then held his arm as they walked together.

"Tell me about your parents," she said. "You told me they moved from New Jersey."

"Nothing much to say about them." It took effort to refocus. "They're as ordinary as white bread and vanilla ice cream. They're nice, retired, senior citizens. Dad plays golf. Mom plays mah-jongg. They're not rich, but comfortable enough, although you'd never know it. They've always been frugal. And now that they're getting older? It's become even more pronounced and annoying. I've heard some old people do that. Whatever habits they had intensify as they age."

A visible shiver shook Maddy. She stopped and rubbed her arms. "God, I hope that's not true. Can't imagine what I'm in for if it is."

"My parents won't go to a movie unless it's at their clubhouse for fifty cents."

"They sound sweet. You shouldn't mock ordinary. There were years I'd have given anything for a few crumbs of white-bread-and-vanilla ordinary."

"It's weird. A few months ago, they decided to find jobs. Said they were bored."

"Maybe they were. It's always good to climb out of a comfortable rut and do new things, meet new people. Maybe there's more to them than you think."

He snorted. "Yeah . . . no."

Maddy pointed to a white Mercedes SL550. "Here we are."

"Well, it's no pumpkin carriage, but it'll have to do." He opened the driver's side door for her.

She exuded grace as she slipped into the seat.

He got in the passenger side. "After seeing your apartment, this comes as no surprise." He gave her a stern look. "What, exactly, is it you do at that marketing firm? You don't own it, do you?"

While starting the car, then selecting some jazz, she wore a bemused grin. "No, I don't."

***

Nina scraped the last of the cake batter into the second eight-inch pan, then ran a finger along the edge of the bowl to get what the spatula didn't. She licked the finger. The extra rum she'd put in packed a punch. She put the bowl in the sink, then washed her hands. Her cell rang as she finished drying off.

"Hey there, sexy." It was George.

"Are you drunk?"

"What? No." He laughed. "Can't a man call his wife sexy without alcohol being involved?"

She chose not to make the easy wisecrack about his lack of calling her anything in the recent past, drunk or sober. "Don't tell me. You have another *meeting* tonight."

"Wrong." He sounded giddy. "I closed a big contract today. You know that empty warehouse next to the fire station? Yours truly found a five-year tenant. I'll tell you all about it at dinner tonight. Whatcha making?"

"Well, honestly, it's plain old burgers. I've kind of gotten used to you, uh, working late, and Charles is eating at a friend's for dinner, so it was only Mary Ann and I."

"Put one on for me. I'll be home by six. And honey? I plan to do some celebrating with you. Be ready."

Honey? She closed the phone and tucked it into her back pocket. Either the mistress finally had enough of him or she went out of town. She hoped it was the former. The situation had become almost unbearable for Nina—knowing where he went and what he did. She did not want to confront him and enter another huge conflict stage like the last time. She just wanted the affair to end and for their lives to go back to a semblance of normal. As much as she knew she should have faced him and kicked him out, her heart wouldn't let her. It infuriated her, but she loved the man and didn't have the inner strength to live without him. He still made her melt inside.

Be ready. She knew what that meant. He said it when he wanted sex. After a business victory, he always wanted sex. How many victories had there been lately? Only the bimbo cheating with him would know. She glanced at her watch—four o'clock. Noticing the cake pans, she placed them in the waiting wall oven, set the timer, and headed upstairs to shave her legs and attend to more personal grooming. As mad as she'd been at George since discovering the latest affair, there was no way she'd throw away the chance of an epic night of sex. Celebration nights in the past sometimes brought encore performances.

Loud, raunchy-sounding music rattled Mary Ann's bedroom door. Nina banged on it. "Turn it down." There was no turn-down and no answer. She banged again and shouted this time. "Turn the music down."

Seconds later, the sound lowered, then the door opened. Mary Ann, headphones around her neck, stood there reading a text on her cell. She looked up. "What?"

Nina mentally counted, but didn't make it past three.

"What, Mom? I'm busy."

"Listening to it that loud will ruin your hearing. And why are you wearing headphones, but not using them?" She scanned the room behind her daughter and saw no textbooks out. Mary Ann's zipped-up backpack leaned against the dresser. "Is your homework done?"

"I don't have any." Mary Ann's cell made a silly *boing-boing* noise, and she conducted a furious assault on the miniscule keys.

"That seems hard to believe, but all right. Keep the music down, even with the headphones on. I mean it."

"Okay." Mary Ann diverted her attention from her social life long enough to grab the door with one hand and began to shut it.

Nina placed a palm on it, stopping the motion.

Mary Ann glanced up with questioning eyes.

"Come downstairs for dinner at six-thirty. Your father says he'll be here."

The sixteen-year-old gave her mother a scathing, sarcastic look. "Right. Holding my breath for that one." She closed the door.

"Me, too," Nina muttered as she went into her bathroom. She locked the door and shed her jeans, hanging them on a wall hook. Lifting her T-shirt, she checked herself out in the mirror. The comfortable white cotton panties would be changed to something lacy later, when she took a quick shower after dinner and dishes. Her body looked pretty good for a forty-eight-year old woman. Tiny bits of cellulite showed on her thighs, but who didn't have that? She held the T-shirt higher and studied her breasts. Even with the padded bra, they didn't amount to much. Her conversation with Fletcher's idiot ex-girlfriend, Tanya, came to mind. She'd said men became stupid around her monstrous-sized boobs. Nina wondered if the little gold digger was right—maybe she *should* have her breasts enhanced. Was that all George really needed from her? Was he afraid to hurt her feelings by asking her to have it done? The women she'd seen—well, spied on—that he fooled around with all had bigger chests than hers.

Nina nearly slapped herself. Why hadn't she realized it before? He was a big boobs man, and she was a small boobs woman. It made sense. On occasion, he said he loved her and looked like he meant it. Giving him the gift of the woman he loved with the added bonus of his favorite female attribute was a no-brainer.

Lowering the T-shirt, she resolved to broach the subject. Casual—like she'd been mulling it over for some time. She couldn't wait to see his face when she asked for his opinion.

She hummed while gathering the shaving cream, razor, and a washcloth. "I'm taking my husband back," she sang, trying to make her improvised lyrics fit into the tune from *My Boyfriend's Back*. "And I'm having sex tonight. Hey la, hey la, I'm taking my husband back." She smiled at herself in the mirror.

Lifting her right leg over the counter and placing her foot into the white porcelain sink, she turned on the water and adjusted the temperature to warm. She preferred to shave her legs this way, taking her time and being able to see anything she'd missed, making sure they were silky smooth. Midway through shaving, Nina's phone rang. The cell was in her jeans. Thinking it might be George, she swung her leg to the floor—a little too fast—and lost her balance. She scrambled to grab the counter as she fell, but puddles of soapy water made it slippery, and her tailbone hit the tile.

"Ow!" Intense pain radiated from her back. She lay her head on the floor, took a deep breath, then tried to sit up. The pain kept her from making it halfway. The ringing cell stopped.

Pushing with her hands this time for another attempt, it still hurt far too much, and she lay back down.

"Mary Ann," she yelled. "Mary Ann, come help me."

A bleep noise from her cell indicated a voice message. She remembered she locked the bathroom door. And there was a cake about to burn in the oven.

"Mary Ann!"

CHAPTER THIRTY-NINE

The jalousies rattled in their frame as the front door slammed. Shirley raced to the landing and called down the stairs. "Stanley? Are you all right?"

A garbled reply included several choice curse words.

"I'll be right down." In the midst of changing, she flung her work suit onto the bed, then threw on a T-shirt and shorts. When she rounded the bottom stair and headed to the kitchen, she stopped. Stanley sat at the dining table, staring ahead as if in a trance.

"Honey, are you okay?" She ventured closer.

He shook his head. "It's a horrible mess. All of it."

"What is?" What more could have happened?

"For the love of God, woman." He stood, shoved the chair backward so hard it hit the wall, and let out a heaving sigh.

She retreated a few more feet away from him and waited.

When he looked at her, there were tears in his eyes. "I . . . I don't know what to do."

Keeping her composure, she sat at the table and concentrated on staying calm. "Because of our situation? What's different about it today?"

"We're going to lose our house. We're going to live in a crapped-out apartment in the worst section of town. We'll probably get robbed and murdered in our sleep."

"What are you talking about?"

"I told you I went looking for a job." He turned and faced the door.

"Yes."

"I've done that several times now. There's no hope for me anywhere. So today, I went to see what was out there that we could afford after we sell this place. And it's all crap."

"I'm sure we could stay with Fletcher if we needed to." Shirley's first inclination was to argue there was no way she'd sign any paperwork for a sale, but it wasn't the right moment to flex her muscle on that one. She chose her words with care. "It wouldn't be ideal, but we wouldn't be around criminals." Having seen Fletcher's new apartment, she wanted to add a snide crack referring to the white-collar criminals who probably lived in that fancy building. Her resentment of people whom the bad economic times hadn't hurt grew every day. "Worst comes to worst, there's always moving back to New Jersey and in with Nina."

Stanley shook his head, and his breathing took on a raspy quality.

A long moment of silence passed. Still facing away from her, Stanley's arm lifted toward his face.

He was wiping away tears, she guessed.

"I failed you," he said, his voice faltering. "I failed us. I'm sorry, but I'd rather shoot myself than let my kids know how bad off we are. It's the way I feel. Sorry."

"I understand." She stood. "It's embarrassing, but it's not your fault alone, you know. I could have worked and contributed. The recession gets a big part of the blame, too. And a slime ball accountant."

He walked to the entry. With his back toward her, he placed his hands on either side of the front doorframe and leaned in, hanging his head. "Your idea. What exactly would I have to do?"

She wasn't sure she'd heard right. "You're going to do it?"

"Depends. Tell me *exactly* how you plan to arrange it so we don't get caught. And tell me how in God's name I'm supposed to act excited about women I'm not attracted to."

An instant of panic hit her. Maybe she'd pushed so hard for the idea because she thought, underneath it all, it would never happen. Now that providing sex seemed a real possibility, could she go through with it?

He turned around. "Well?"

"Um." She gestured toward the stairs. "I have a list I've been working on. A checklist of things we need to do and figure out."

Waving her onward, he moved to the table and sat. "Go on and get it then."

She hurried to the bedroom and slid the file folder from between the mattress and box spring. Hesitating at the doorway, she bit her lip, gathering her nerve. Could she know that Stanley, her Stanley, was having sex with other women and live with that?

"I'll get used to it," she muttered, then went downstairs.

***

"So I'm single and a handyman?" Stanley asked.

"In name only. We'll get those magnetic signs for the car, and you'll carry a tool box. When you drive up to the la-dee-da mansions over in Sago Beach, it'll be totally believable for our old car to be there. Their neighbors won't suspect a thing."

"What if someone we know sees me?"

"Who do we know in Sago Beach? Besides Lance and Paul, I mean, and you won't be going anywhere near Paulina's. You'll wait until you've crossed the Intracoastal, pull over somewhere inconspicuous to put the signs on, then take them off again before leaving the island. That way, our friends here won't know anything about it."

His lips tightened into a grimace. "How are you going to

find these *clients*? You can't tell women about this while you're at work, you know. And somehow, I don't think my standing on a street corner in Sago Beach doing my best to appear fetching and lonely is going to accomplish anything." He shoved backward in the chair, stood, then pulled one pant leg up while imitating a woman's *come hither* look. "Somebody would call the cops pronto. I'd be a cooked goose before I had a chance to shit in the yard."

Shirley laughed, and the awful tension in the air broke. He nodded, dropped the pant leg, and laughed with her.

"I have thought about that," she said.

He sat down again. "Do tell."

"I already have two potential clients. But they can't know it's me, Shirley from Paulina's. I'll be Mitzi, and I'll pretend Shirley passed along their numbers to me. I'm fairly certain they wouldn't recognize my voice. Those women don't pay any mind to a plain old saleswoman. I'm as forgettable as yesterday's cat litter to them."

"What if they don't want to hire me? I need more than two customers anyway, according to your figures here." He pointed to the open file folder with Shirley's notes. "How do you plan to get any more of them?"

"I'll wear a wig and dress in clothes I've never worn at Paulina's, then do what I've been doing. Eavesdropping. I'll go to the better restaurants, check out who is seated where, then ask for the table that's closest to a likely candidate. Believe me, the subject of male company comes up more often than how much they hate their maids. I don't think it'll be a challenge."

"They hate their maids? Why don't they hire ones they like?"

Shirley snorted. "New maids, old maids—doesn't matter. Some of these women are impossible. They don't approve of anybody who's not on their economic level. I don't think most of them even like each other. They take catty into the stratosphere."

Grunting, he leaned back in his chair. "The odds of them liking me don't sound very good. I'm definitely not in that league."

"You're providing a service, not escorting them to ritzy galas. As long as you . . ." The word wouldn't form on her lips. She cleared her throat. "As long as you *perform* that service, they don't have to like you. It's a good point, though. You'll have to tread carefully. Be very circumspect. Never reveal too much. Never assume you're anything more than, say, like their gardener or chauffeur."

"Cri-min-ent-ly, this is sounding better every minute," he said with heavy sarcasm in his voice. "Not what I expected. It sounds like work."

She nodded. "Think of yourself as a kind of actor. For the time you're there, you do have to work hard, acting as though being there with . . . whomever." She waved a hand. "Pretending there's no one else you'd rather be with. Then you collect the four-hundred dollars. Cash."

He whistled. "Thirty minutes?"

"I don't know. I'm guessing. How long do you think an encounter might take? I'm assuming it'll be different than when we do it."

"You can say that again." He rubbed his chin. "I need a beer." He rose and walked to the fridge. "Want one?"

"No. Alcohol makes me more depressed. I don't need any help in that department right now." Laying her forehead on the table, she sighed. A tinny plink indicated the bottle cap hitting the counter.

He returned. "This has to be the strangest conversation we've ever had. *I've* ever had." He took a big gulp.

She lifted her head. "But you do see how fast this could lift us out of our mess?"

"Unfortunately. How soon would we start?"

"The way we're charging things on cards, tomorrow would be great. I need to order the signs, though. That'll only take a few days. If I can, how about scheduling the first one on Monday? The widowed Mrs. Daniel Manning seemed anxious. I'll call her first."

"All right." Picking at the edges of the beer label, he exhaled. "We haven't talked about the naked elephant in the room." He took another long sip, then set the bottle down. "How do I make something happen . . ." He gestured to his lap. "Down there? If I'm not interested?"

Sighing again, Shirley stared at him. "I appreciate your saying that on my behalf, I really do. We both know, with stimulation, a man's body reacts automatically. You don't have to pretend for my sake. You love me and would never cheat on me. I know it like I know my own face. You're the heart of my heart. My everything. Knowing that is the only reason I can consider this crazy plan. Let's not bring it up again, okay?"

He leaned in, cupped her chin in his hand, and landed a soft kiss on her lips. "You are the most amazing woman. I am so lucky I have you."

"Thank you."

Standing, he picked up the beer, took a drink, and began pacing to the living room and back. "What about the calling part? There's caller ID, and if they don't have that, our home number listing will be easy for anyone to find."

"Fletcher gave me that cell phone with the big numbers on it last Christmas, remember? He's been paying the monthly fee, in hopes I'll take it out of my dresser drawer and actually use it. We'll use that and keep the number for our new business only."

"Okay." He placed the bottle on the table. "Mitzi, huh?"

"I love Mitzi Gaynor, you know that. I thought it would be a fun name. You have to think of a name, too. You can't go by *Stanley.*"

"Like what?"

"It has to be something common, but very masculine."

"Tony." He made a *voila* hand gesture. "Vito."

Shirley shook her head. "Sounds like you're from a mob

movie."

"What's wrong with a tough-guy name?"

"I was thinking maybe Ed or Jim."

"Nah. Too milk-toasty." He went back to pacing. "What about Sam? Johnny? No. Wait." He smiled. "Mack. That's it. A man's man name. Mack, like the truck."

Or The Knife, Shirley thought. Still a mob name. Men.

CHAPTER FORTY

Catherine sat at her desk, combing the lists of potential VIP donors for the upcoming My Brother's Keeper charity ball. Few of the people listed were what she'd call VIP's. But it was better than the previous year. Slowly, the recession's impact on the luxury lifestyle was receding. She and Pookie had joked—in private—at the last committee meeting. The old-guard money people, such as they, regained everything and much more. The nouveaux rich, who'd been so desperate to prove they belonged, got taken to the proverbial cleaners by charlatans and the stock market.

"Fourteen percent guaranteed, my hiney," she said. "What fool would believe such rubbish?"

Her cell rang with the music to a French lullaby. She smiled as she answered. "Muffin. How are you, darling?"

"I'm fine, Mother. Calling to check in on you. Don't forget your doctor's appointment tomorrow. Have you been staying on the diet?"

Glancing at the opened box of Godiva chocolate truffles on the corner of her desk, she hesitated, then gulped vodka and cranberry juice from her cut-crystal glass.

"Mother?"

"Yes, yes. Sorry, had a dry throat. Needed a sip. Of course

I'm going tomorrow. You'd be very proud of me. I'll bet I've lost five pounds."

"Really." Maddy didn't sound like she believed it.

"You'll see." Catherine promised herself she wouldn't eat another bite until after the appointment. Maybe by some miracle, she would have lost a few pounds. "Ooh, I have some news for you. Pookie's nephew, Clarence—you remember him, don't you? He and *his* fiancée ended their engagement, too. He heard about your break-up, and—he's interested. Isn't that wonderful?"

"I'm seeing someone." Maddy's voice was flat.

"Well, I wish you had told me." Catherine eyed a dark chocolate truffle drizzled with raspberry icing. "Who is he? Tell me *all* about him."

"Uh-uh. Unless and until there's a reason for you to know more, you're not going to."

A knock sounded on the door of Catherine's study.

"*Un moment*, darling," she said to Maddy, then lowered the phone. "*Entrez*."

The door opened, and Lucinda came forward, placed a pile of mail on her desk, then backed out of the room, closing the door after her.

"It was just the mail," she said, thumbing through the envelopes. "You were saying?"

"Nothing of importance."

A linen-weave ecru envelope addressed in flowery handwriting caught Catherine's attention. "If you're not wanting to talk about this man, then how special could he be? Why don't you at least agree to have drinks with Clarence? There's no harm in that." There was no return address, only initials she couldn't quite make out. She opened it and pulled out the note.

"I remember Clarence. He was a jerk. Rude, cocky, and only talked about how great he was. No, thank you."

Catherine skimmed over the writing on the note, then yelped and dropped it.

"Mother?"

She composed herself. "I'm so sorry. It's . . . there's a note from a man I rejected recently, is all. He didn't take it very well."

"You *rejected* someone? Who? Since when are you dating?"

"You're not the only one being pursued. I'll have you know I'm a hot ticket." Catherine didn't understand why that particular lie escaped her lips. It had to be the vodka talking.

"Oh—kay. I meant no insult. You surprised me. You've never mentioned dating anyone. I thought you'd moved past that phase of your life."

"You're never too old for love."

"Good to know. I've got another call coming in. I'll phone tomorrow to see how the doctor's visit went."

They ended the call, and Catherine picked up the note. It was from Count de Albreccio.

Dearest Catherine,

I hope this finds you well. I wanted to tell you in person, but felt, since I hadn't heard from you, that you haven't forgiven and wouldn't have seen me. I know you most likely expected we would have another chance, but I met someone else while waiting for your call. I am moving back to Italy with my new love. Maria and I will be married there. I felt, since we shared such an intimate bond, that you would want to hear it from me and not from the Sago Beach gossips.

I wish you well. All my best,

Alfonse

Catherine finished off her drink. "Even that arrogant reprobate found love," she muttered, then grabbed the raspberry truffle and shoved it into her mouth.

***

Nina walked with care across the kitchen, wincing at the pain, and watched George's car back out of the driveway. Her expected epic sex the night before had turned into five hours at the emergency room. Luckily, she hadn't broken anything, though it felt like major bruising on everything below her waist.

Although George had taken her to the ER, he complained the entire time—when he wasn't outside the building making phone calls. When they got home, he acted like a petulant boy, locked himself into the bathroom, and proceeded to pleasure himself. Nina endured listening to his exaggerated moans—a peculiar custom of George's that started when they first married. She figured that was his way of protesting not having sex when he wanted. His attempt at letting her know what she was missing. From his attitude, it seemed somehow he blamed her for not being able to accommodate him, which she did not understand. She'd explained she was only trying to be her best for him, but he insinuated her fall was some sort of dodge.

***

"What do you think?" Shirley pointed to the magnetic signs on the dining room table. They were plain—white background, black letters, and a stock photo of tools in a tool belt. She thought they accomplished what was needed—a legitimate excuse to be in a swanky neighborhood, but nondescript enough to be instantly forgettable.

Stanley shrugged. "Mack the Handyman. Where did the picture of the tool belt come from? And . . . wait a minute. There's no phone number."

"The guy at the sign place found the photo. As for the phone number, we don't want anyone to see the sign and call you for the purpose of actually fixing anything, do we?"

"Ah." Stanley rubbed his chin. "There's an idea we hadn't thought of. I could be a handyman for real."

Taking a deep breath, Shirley waited for him to think that through. She cocked her head and placed her hands on her hips.

His eyes met hers, and he smiled. "Yeah, you're right. I'd get what? Thirty bucks an hour, and how long would it take until I built up enough business to work forty hours a week?"

She nodded. "If ever. They're getting about twenty an

hour. I grant you that's a lot more than you made at The Burger Flip—if you could get steady work out of it. I asked around the village. And, I check the paper every day. There are so many ads advertising handyman services. Seems anyone who used to be in construction is trying to freelance doing that. Which is good for us. It makes you and your sign blend right in. No one will pay any attention to you."

"Aw, shucks, thanks." He twisted his wedding ring. "It's going to feel mighty strange not wearing this."

"Don't get used to it."

Picking up one of the signs, he held it out in front of him. "I have to admit, I'm nervous about tomorrow."

"Don't worry. That's what we're doing now. We'll think of everything they could ask and practice your answers." She walked to the kitchen. "I definitely need wine first. You?"

Banging on the front door and the accompanying rattle of the jalousies startled her. She shot a glance at the door, which wasn't locked.

"Yoo-hoo?" Dora called. "It's me."

The handle began to turn. Dora and Shirley quite often let themselves into each other's homes.

Stanley looked frozen in place.

The handle finished its rotation, and the hinges squeaked as Dora opened the door.

"Quick," Shirley hissed. "Take the signs upstairs."

He whirled around, grabbed the other sign from the table, then ran.

Dora entered and looked astonished at Stanley disappearing up the stairs. "What was that all about?"

Composing a calm front, Shirley ignored the thumping in her chest and gestured to where Stanley had been. "Bad tacos. For lunch." She tsked. "I warned him." Turning back to the kitchen, she motioned for Dora to follow her. "Wine? I was about to pour a glass."

"Sure, doll." Dora dragged a chair out from the dinette and

sat. "I can't stay long, though. Tim's taking me out to dinner, then dancing." She smiled.

Shirley took the chardonnay from the refrigerator, poured two glasses, then handed one to Dora.

Dora held the glass aloft. "To love."

Gently clinking her glass to Dora's, Shirley stared at her. "Love? Really? Already?"

After sipping the wine, Dora set it on the table with a goofy grin. "I think so. Can you believe it? I haven't felt like this since I met Lester all those years ago."

"Congratulations. Does Tim feel the same?"

"Seems to. Maybe that's what tonight is about. I think he's going to tell me."

"I hope you're right." Shirley downed half her glass, then saw Dora's heavily-penciled eyebrows rise. "I'm thirsty."

"Can I borrow your gold necklace? The one with the green beads? It would look perfect with the new blouse I bought for tonight."

"Sure. Do you know where he's taking you?"

"La Maison de Fleur. Up in Palm Beach. On Worth Avenue, no less."

Shirley sat opposite her. "Even I've heard of that restaurant. It's very expensive. This must be serious."

Dora played with one of the silver bangles on her wrist. "I did try to suggest something less pricey. He wouldn't hear of it. I'm getting the impression that Tim is better off than he lets on."

Smiling at her, Shirley found herself at a loss for words as an unexpected stab of jealousy hit her. She wanted to be happy for Dora, but what she wanted more was to scream.

CHAPTER FORTY-ONE

Stanley steered the car into the wide brick-paver driveway and stopped in front of a set of imposing wrought iron gates with gold-tipped spikes at the top. There was a call box on his left, and he pressed the button.

"Yes?" a female voice said.

"Mrs. Manning? It's Mack—the uh . . . handyman."

"Oh."

The ensuing silence concerned Stanley. As he was about to press the button again, the gates began to open inward. He waited for a space wide enough to drive through, then proceeded toward the mansion.

His anxiety increased as he approached the enormous two-story stucco home. Rows of lush royal palms lined the driveway. Shirley told him not to park in the front of any house he visited, but to use the secondary areas. He was not a guest. He was a paid service provider, the same as the yard maintenance guys.

"Except I'm not trimming any bushes." He pulled into a lane alongside the four-bay garage and cut the engine. While grabbing his prop—a gray metal tool box—he noticed how quiet the house and grounds were. No other cars.

He marshaled his nerve, locked up, walked to the door closest to the garage, and rang the bell on an intercom box.

Again, it took too long for a response, and his unease grew. He knocked.

"I'm here. I'm here." The door opened. A short, plump woman in her late sixties wearing a dark curly wig stood there. "Hello. Please, come in." She moved aside to allow him access.

Stanley stepped inside, forced a smile, and offered his hand. "I'm Mack, Mrs. Manning. Very nice to meet you."

She placed her hand on his and gazed up at him. "You're tall." Her eyes widened and a crooked smile appeared. "Lordy." She closed the door.

The pronounced wrinkles on her face made the dark wig look ridiculous. Did she believe it looked natural?

"This way." She led him to a long hall off the kitchen. Three cats—one black, one ginger, and one gray—trailed her.

Stanley heard barking, and a shaggy gray and white dog raced to catch them. As he'd feared, he felt zero attraction to Mrs. Manning. He followed, studying her, trying to imagine what she'd been like as a younger woman, hoping that would help things along. Panic raised its unwelcome head instead.

She wore a pale-green patterned skirt, a green shirt, and a pair of sandals with little metal beads that jangled as she walked. Her hips were wide, wider than her bottom.

This is not going to work, he thought. What am I supposed to do?

"In here." Stopping in front of a door, she pushed it open, revealing what appeared to be a guest bedroom.

Stanley felt sweat bloom on his forehead. He entered, placed his tool box on the wood floor, then scanned the room. Done in Chinese-looking wallpaper, an Oriental rug covered most of the floor. A double bed with its spread and top sheet folded down awaited. The reaction from his gut was nausea.

The cats meandered in. The dog jumped onto the bed, still barking.

"You can call me Beverly." She walked to the window and closed the wood blinds.

"All right," Stanley said. "Beverly. That's a fine name." He went to the door and started to shut it.

"No." Beverly gestured for him to swing it open again. "My babies need to be able to see me at all times and come and go as they please. They get upset otherwise." She giggled. "I have to admit, I'm a bit nervous, too." She approached him and touched his chest. "Especially now, after seeing you. Goodness, you're quite the looker. And so . . . tall. That usually translates to other areas." She winked. "I can see why you'd be in demand."

His heart jammed up into his throat. The black cat rubbed against his shins.

"He likes you." She kicked off her sandals. "That's a good sign."

"Great. Well. I guess we'd better get a little more comfortable." He sat on an upholstered bench at the end of the bed and removed his shoes and socks.

The dog dropped to the floor and sniffed Stanley's feet.

Beverly pulled off her shirt, knocking her wig askew. She wore an enormous black lace bra to contain voluminous white boobs. Fat rolled from under the bra. Her stomach was as broad as her chest and sagged over the waistband of the skirt.

Trying hard not to let his revulsion show, Stanley forced another smile and fought the urge to straighten the wig for her. Was he supposed to think it was her real hair? Playing along was safer. He didn't want to take the chance of insulting her. Of course, if Stanley Junior didn't show up, that was a far more serious insult. He concentrated on conjuring the image of a Marilyn Monroe poster he'd worshipped while in the army. It served him well then.

Lowering her eyelids and fluttering her lashes, Beverly pointed to the zipper in the back of her skirt. "Would you be so kind, handsome sir?"

"Oh. Yeah. Sure."

She backed toward him, then thrust her butt out into his face and wiggled it.

Repulsed, he shrank further away. She seemed to be losing all inhibition and gaining energy by the second. At that point, he knew for certain. Absolutely nothing would happen. How in hell was he going to get out of it without embarrassing them both? "This is a very nice skirt." He unzipped it for her. "There you go."

"Give it a tug for me?" She wiggled again.

He pulled it down and gasped as a huge, deeply-dimpled ass wobbled in front of him.

"Surprised, huh?" She turned to face him. "Bet you didn't think I'd go commando." She made a naughty face. "I do it all the time. Makes me feel sexy, sexy, *sexy*. I walk around with no underwear on, and my staff hasn't a clue." She laughed. "Isn't that delicious?" Gesturing down her body with one hand, she posed with the other behind her head. "Look familiar to you? Botero is a dear friend. He used me as a model once. Now you. Clothes off."

Standing, he puzzled over the Botero comment—not recognizing the name—and grabbed his shirt ends and began to pull upward when he felt her hands caressing his upper thighs.

"Come out. Come out and play now," she said as her hands rose higher. "This is exciting. I never dreamed you'd be so handsome. And you're mine to do whatever I want with."

Throwing his shirt on the bench, he grabbed her hands. "All in good time. All in good time."

"You're so right. We're here to have fun. No sense in rushing." She pulled free, took several steps back, then charged him—knocking him off balance so he landed on his back on the bed.

The dog leapt onto the bench, and restarted his incessant barking.

A second later, Beverly was on top of him, her breasts bulging from the bra, threatening a prison break as she swept them back and forth across his face.

He felt buried in cold floppy flesh. A sandpapery tongue

flicked the toes of his right foot. “Ahh? What the—”

“Me, too,” Beverly cooed. “Me, too.” One boob burst from its confines, and she mashed it next to his mouth. It was bigger than his head. A cat meowed into his ear, and he felt soft fur against his neck.

“My husband used to love when I did this.” A shudder accompanied by a quiet moan escaped her. “Incredible. I’m getting so excited already. I may not even need the KY. Suck on my titty, Mack. Quick.”

The dog howled.

He ventured a tentative lick.

"Yes. More. You nasty boy. Stop teasing me."

Black, boiling clouds of doom engulfed him as he placed his mouth over her nipple. The most important participant of the party refused to cooperate. Maybe he could fake an injury. How was he going to explain any of it to Shirley? He felt like throwing up.

Suddenly, there was air and light again as she sat—straddling him—and gyrated. “Ooh, I can feel you.” She sounded giddy. “You won’t be able to hide much longer. I can’t wait to see what you’ve got for me.”

Oh, yes you can. He thought he should say something nice, then he’d conjure a back sprain. “You certainly have a lot of energy, Beverly.”

She leered at him and increased the motion. “You ain’t seen nothing, yet, tiger.” She growled.

In the distance, a door slammed.

“Surprise! Mom?” a male voice called. “Where are you? Mom? It’s me. Whose car is that?”

Alarm distorted her face, and she rolled away from Stanley. “Damn it. It’s my son.” She got off the bed and hurried to the bedroom door. The dog and the cats raced out to the hall.

Heart pounding and feeling like he’d been flattened by a steam roller, Stanley grabbed his shirt and gasped for air. "Thank you, God," he muttered.

Her voice took on a motherly tone when she called to her son. "Hi, darling. I'm . . . just . . . won't be a minute."

She shut and locked the door, then hissed at Stanley. "Get dressed. And for shit's sake, look like you're fixing something."

Listening to her curses while she struggled with her clothing, the expletives shocked him. He finished putting on his shoes, straightened his shirt, and opened his tool box.

Smoothing the bedspread, he checked for any other tell-tale evidence, then took a screwdriver over to the window valance and acted as though he'd been tightening the final screw.

"Okay," Beverly whispered. She pulled some folded bills from her pocket and tucked them into Stanley's. "That's good, what you're doing. You were fixing the blinds. Mountings came loose." She opened the door and left the room. "What a *wonderful* surprise, dear."

Her conversational-toned banter aimed at her son faded as she walked away.

Stanley counted to sixty, then went to the hall and called after her. "Mrs. Manning? I think we're all set here. Wanna come check it?"

"Certainly." Her voice came from a distant place and gradually became louder. "Let me see to this, sweetheart, then we'll visit." She entered the room and kept her voice loud. "Yes. That's perfect. Nice and tight now." Raising her eyebrows, she whispered. "It's too bad we were interrupted. You would have had something nice and tight, I promise you. I had a surgery."

He felt blood rush to his face. Reaching into his pocket, he took the bills and held them out to her. "You don't need to pay me," he whispered. "I didn't do what I was hired to do."

"You keep it," she said. "We'll make up for it next time."

Ain't going to be a next time, he thought.

CHAPTER FORTY-TWO

"Whoa." Shirley placed an iced tea in on the table in front of Stanley. He'd filled her in on the basics of his fiasco. "Talk slower. I couldn't understand the last sentence."

"It. Was. A. Freaking. Nightmare." He shuddered. "Did you hear *that*?"

She sat across from him. "No need to be hostile."

"If we go forward with this, you can't set me up with fat women. Stanley Junior not only didn't want to play, I think he retreated up inside of me. I'm afraid to look."

"Mrs. Manning *is* on the chubby side, but—"

"Where did you find that woman? She's certifiable. Then there were the cats, and her dog kept barking at me. It was insane. Like a bizarre episode of a reality show. If her son hadn't walked in, I don't know how I'd have gotten out of it. I might need therapy."

"She seemed perfectly lovely to me. There are men who love *ample* women, you know. But if you can't get over a few extra pounds? Shoot." What if their plan failed because of that fact? "You'll have to do something like picture a pretty girl in your mind."

"I'm telling you, it's not going to work. I can't fake it." He drank from his tea glass. "No way in hell."

"Calm yourself. Let me think." Part of her rejoiced that her husband experienced difficulty cheating on her, but the desperate-for-money other part felt panic coming on.

"She said she had surgery. It made her tight? What in blazes was she talking about?"

Shirley opened her mouth, then, drawing a blank, closed it. "I haven't got any idea. Maybe she had problems after childbirth or something."

"Arrgghh." He stood and rubbed his head. "I'm sorry. We have to sell the house."

"No." The solution came to her. "We'll go to a urologist and get you some of those erection malfunction pills."

"I do not have erectile dysfunction." Pacing toward the living room, he said, "And as soon as the horrifying image that's burned into my retinas goes away, I'll prove it to you."

"The pills will work. I know because Dora told me Morty had to take them, and when he did, even the slightest attention to his, uh, particular, made it stand up and count. Rather nicely, as a matter of fact."

"Shit. Too much information." He turned. "I can't look Morty in the face anymore."

"Big deal." Shirley laughed. "When's the last time you saw him anyway? Dora's dating Tim now."

"You women share a ridiculous amount of personal info."

"I've never shared information about *your* particular."

He gave her a doubtful look.

"On a stack of white Bibles." She raised her right hand. "Not a word. I don't want them knowing the intimate details of our marriage any more than you do."

Settling in his recliner, he lifted the remote, spurred the TV into action, flipped a few channels, and closed his eyes. "I'm traumatized. I need a nap."

"I'm going to find a urologist with an appointment time open for us in the morning."

"Us? I think I can manage on my own."

"I want to be there and hear everything the doctor says. You're not so great at relaying details. Remember when you had that wart removed and the doctor said—"

A loud snort-like snore stopped her.

***

The next morning at nine, Shirley and Stanley sat in the patient waiting room of Dr. Gloria Schwartz.

Stanley threw an ancient dog-eared issue of *Popular Mechanics* on the table in front of them, then picked up a fishing magazine from the pile. "Did you *have* to pick a woman doctor?" he said in a hushed tone. There was one other person there, a man across the room reading *The Wall Street Journal.* "This is difficult enough."

"I told you, I tried all of them. She was the only one who could take you so soon. Luckily, there was a cancellation. If you'd known in advance it was a female doctor, you might have backed out."

Slumping in the chair, he crossed his arms. "I'd rather sell the goddamn townhouse."

A few minutes later, a young and pretty nurse in an abstract-patterned uniform appeared in the doorway. "Mr. Nowack?"

Terrific, Stanley thought, announce my name. He glanced at the other man and saw him smirk. The obvious double-entendre had plagued him his whole life.

He and Shirley followed the nurse to a cubicle where she measured his height, weighed him, and checked his blood pressure and temperature. Then she took them to a private room.

She pulled some paper sheets from a drawer and laid them on the examination table.

"Get undressed, put these on, and the doctor will be in a couple of minutes," she said, then left. The door closed behind her.

"Can't we just order boner pills from Canada?" He cringed at the thought of the woman doctor touching him. What if she was attractive, and Stanley Junior *liked* her? "If she gives me an exam, I don't want you to watch. Promise?"

Shirley gave him a deadpan look. "That's childish. But, all right. I promise. You are turning redder than a stalk of rhubarb. Stop worrying. Let me do most the talking."

He stripped, put on the paper sheets, and sat on the exam table. Shirley kept reading an article in the magazine she'd brought from the waiting room.

Ten minutes passed while he counted the ceiling tiles, read the informational brochure about prostate symptoms, and studied a poster illustrating a cross-section of male genitalia until he heard a knock. The door opened.

"Mr. Nowack?" a male voice said.

Stanley glanced toward it. A man in his forties, wearing a white doctor's coat, stood there.

"Yes?" Stanley said.

"I'm Dr. Golden." He entered, closed the door, then offered his hand. "I hope you don't mind, but Dr. Schwartz had a family emergency. We often fill in for one another."

"Thank Christ," Stanley said, letting out an audible breath. They shook hands.

"He was nervous about seeing a woman doctor," Shirley said.

"You must be Mrs. Nowack? Hello." He sat on a green padded stool on casters, opened the manila chart in his hand, then flipped a page. "It says here this is an emergency? It was important you be seen this morning? What happened? Is there some sort of blockage? Are you experiencing pain?"

Caught without an answer, Stanley looked at Shirley.

She smiled at the doctor. "I'm afraid that's my fault. It sure felt like an emergency to me yesterday."

Dr. Golden stared at her.

"You see," she said, "Stanley and I have enjoyed a Monday

afternoon, um . . . *thing* for years. Since he retired nine years ago. A sort of let's-start-the-week-off-right thing. I can't tell you how much I look forward to it." Her face flushed. "Goodness, I can't believe I'm telling you this." She leaned toward him and patted his arm. "But you're a doctor. I'm sure you must understand. Anyway, imagine my alarm when my dear husband . . ." She gazed adoringly at Stanley. ". . . well, when nothing happened. There must be something horribly wrong. I hope you can help us."

Dr. Golden chuckled. "Mrs. Nowack, your husband is seventy-four. It's very common among older men. Quite honestly, I'm surprised this hasn't happened before now." He asked many questions about Stanley's medical history, then stood and placed the chart on the counter by the sink. "I'll examine you, Mr. Nowack, but your blood pressure is good, and you don't seem to have any other problems besides aging."

"Thanks, Doc," Stanley said.

The doctor donned gloves and began the exam. As agreed, Shirley kept her gaze on the magazine in her lap. Glad she must have thought his request was about modesty, Stanley wasn't about to tell her, *oh, never mind, you can look*. He'd have to explain his fear of having an erection caused by another female in front of her.

A few minutes later, Dr. Golden removed the gloves. "All set. I'm finished."

"I think he needs those pills." Shirley closed the magazine. "The ones that make something happen down there?"

"One occurrence isn't a cause for concern," Dr. Golden said. "We'll wait and see what happens in the next month or so. If it becomes a more frequent problem, then we'll revisit the pills option."

Letting out a loud gasp, Shirley covered her mouth with her hand. "A *month*? Oh, no, no. I can't wait a month. I don't want to wait a day."

The doctor's eyebrows shot to his hairline.

Stanley thought he'd better step in. "My wife is an unusual woman." He nodded toward her. "She's always had a healthy appetite, if you get my drift, and it's a very important part of our lives. It helps her fight her depression. It was an awful time. Wouldn't even bathe." He ignored her shocked reaction to his lie.

Dr. Golden nodded.

"You wouldn't believe the amount of air freshener the place needed. I would never forgive myself if she sank back into it."

"I thought you said it was only on Mondays," Dr. Golden said. "You manage to go six days without, then if you don't have relations on the seventh, you fall apart?"

"Heavens, no," Shirley said. "We do it every day. Mondays are simply special. We do, um, a little bit more for each other on Mondays. I don't even want to consider how I'll feel if we can't have sex for a month. Why, the very thought of it . . ." Her eyes welled with tears, and she pulled a tissue from her purse.

When the hell had she become such an accomplished liar? Stanley wondered.

"You two. Do it. *Every day*?" Dr. Golden looked shocked. "Congratulations. I know couples in their twenties who don't have that robust a sex life."

"It keeps us close," Shirley said, dabbing an eye. "Please tell me Stanley can have those magic pills. It means so much."

Consulting the chart again, Dr. Golden studied at his notes. "You have no heart problem history, no prostate enlargement. No diabetes. As long as you continue like this, well, I suppose I can grant your request."

Stanley cracked up inside because Shirley looked at Dr. Golden like he'd just saved her infant from the jaws of a beast.

"You are an angel," she said. "I have another question. I've heard about a surgery that makes a woman *tighter*. Can you tell me what that means?"

Dr. Golden gave her a puzzled stare. "My wife needs to meet you."

CHAPTER FORTY-THREE

Fletcher smiled when Maddy came in from his kitchen carrying a platter of cheese and crackers. They'd had the one date, during which he kept a respectful distance in all ways. Not only because he wanted to make the right impression, but also to hide his body's telltale signs—the sudden quiver, the hitching of his breath as he started to speak, the racing of his heart. His infatuation with her made him crazy. He knew he had no business going out with her. She was gorgeous, smart, well-to-do—out of his league—and too young for him. Even if things developed between them, his biggest fear was he'd fall in love, and she'd eventually become bored and move on, crushing him, like Tanya had.

Maddy had called earlier and asked if they could watch a movie together. He'd blurted out a *yes* before any conscious thought reached his brain. A half hour later, she'd arrived with a bag of snacks and a cold bottle of chardonnay, wearing a strapless white sundress.

She set the glass platter on the coffee table, then positioned herself on the sofa beside him, her right leg crossed toward him.

The hem of her dress slid higher on her leg, exposing lean, tan, and smooth-looking thighs. He wondered if he'd ever touch them.

"I found a new green market on Saturday," she said. "These artisanal cheeses are amazing. Wait until you taste them." Taking a slice of a white one, she placed it on a cracker and offered it to him. "See if you can identify it."

He accepted it and took a bite, forcing his gaze off her legs and onto her face. The taste of sharp cheddar and something else strong and familiar flooded his mouth as he chewed. "Was that beer in there?"

"Thought you might like that one." She laughed. "Yes. It's made with a stout, I believe. Pretty good, huh?"

Her silky hair shimmered despite the dimmed lighting, and her pretty pale-blue eyes sparkled with amusement. She wore a simple silver chain that directed Fletcher's attention to her breasts.

"Hey. Up here, mister." She laughed again.

He felt blood rushing to his face and lower, too. He laughed also, then realized his rapid shallow breathing betrayed him. "I'm sorry. Can't help myself. You're very beautiful."

"Thank you." She grabbed her wine, took a sip, then leaned in closer. "Honestly? You're a rather attractive specimen yourself." She stared at him.

Was that desire he saw in her eyes? Shit, he thought, I'm about to break my pledge. Could he? Should he? He was in deep, deep shit. He needed a moment to think and sank further into the back cushion, the better to hide his growing condition.

She looked away, cleared her throat, and reached for her wine again. "I suppose I should pop the movie into the player." Plucking the DVD from its case, she sauntered to the entertainment center and bent in front of the player. Her dress stopped just below her ass. "Which one opens it?"

The sight of the top of her bare legs at that angle made his breath hitch.

"Fletch?" She turned to him and grinned.

"Um." He swallowed. Something changed. Every atom of air in the room seemed tinged and crackled with electricity. All blood flow raged south. "I . . . um."

She straightened, left the DVD on a shelf, and took a couple steps closer to him, a dreamy cast in her eyes. "Anything the matter?"

"No." The word caught in his throat.

Approaching him, she leaned in. The silver necklace dangled near his mouth, framing a glimpse of the top of her breasts. She kissed the top of his forehead, then stood again.

"How about," she said, "instead of watching the movie, we dance. You like to dance?"

Consumed with the effort it took to not launch himself on her, he concentrated on keeping his hands planted on the sofa cushion. "I can't."

"You can't dance? That's silly. There's only us here. No one will see you."

He closed his eyes and said the words slowly. "No. I mean . . . I can't. Right now." He felt beads of sweat break out on his face.

Her eyes darted to his crotch. "Stand up." She held out her hand.

He couldn't hide it now, whether he sat or did as she asked. He put his hand in hers and stood. His monster erection pressing hard against his jeans felt like it needed its own zip code.

Her right hand brushed her cheek, then covered her mouth. "Ah-hah."

Casting his arms out to his sides, he tried for a nonchalant shrug.

"Guess that clears up whether or not you want me," she whispered. She seemed as affected by the static in the room as he was.

"I'm not supposed to. But, yes, I want you."

"Good." She took one step closer, bringing her body within inches of his.

His erection pulsated. "You're too young for me. We both know that."

"I don't care." With her right hand, she caressed her stomach, then moved up to her breasts.

"You'll tear my heart into pieces. I can't go through that pain again."

"No. I won't." She drilled into him with an intense stare. "I've wanted you since the moment I met you." Her hand touched his chest, then glided down, landing on his penis.

It throbbed under her touch. A small guttural sound escaped from her.

That was it. Making his own barely-contained grunts and gasps, he put one arm around her, pulling her close. With the other hand he touched her cheek where she had. Her lips were sweet, moist—perfect—and waiting for him. He kissed her, gentle at first, but the fire they shared took over. Tongues probed. She tasted like nothing he'd ever had before. Their breaths came in shallow bursts.

With one hand behind her head and continuing to kiss her hard, not letting her up for air, he slipped his other hand under her dress. Up those firm thighs that were as soft and downy as he'd imagined. He tugged down a silky pair of panties, then gently probed a finger inside her. She was smooth, soft, warm, and surged with a slippery wetness.

She whimpered, a sound so seductive and feminine, it nearly sent him into orgasm.

Fletcher lowered her onto the carpet, his heart hammering so hard he couldn't stop a desire-driven wail. The lust and the helplessness made him feel huge, made him feel strong, and at the same time, completely weak and defenseless against his intensity. He yanked his pants off.

She writhed beneath him, reaching for him. Her touch on the tender skin of his hyper-sensitive erection sent fireworks through him. She caressed, then clutched him, guiding him forward. Primal instinct crashed into reason and took over.

When he plunged into her, a hot and slick haven, it elicited another erotic whimper. He thrust, and she moaned. And he felt the foreign, bewildering, and amazing sensation that he'd found where he belonged.

CHAPTER FORTY-FOUR

Shirley stepped off the Greater Sago Beaches bus at the entrance to Silver Sago Village. Shuffling through the carryall bag containing her purse and her fancy work shoes, she found and used her pass card to open the pedestrian gate at the entrance, then waved at the uniformed woman on duty in the guardhouse.

She headed toward their section, about a ten-minute walk. It was four-thirty. Stanley was at his *appointment* with a Mrs. Stanhope—his first since their visit to the urologist. Had Stanley's little pill accomplished what it needed to? Wild emotional swings swept through her, knowing he went to have sex with another woman. She struggled to think of it as a service. He wouldn't be attracted to Stanhope. There was no way Shirley would *ever* let a good-looking woman have an appointment, but he didn't need to know that. No, he was stuck with the women who hadn't taken care of themselves. Which, as she pondered it further, worked to their advantage anyway. Perhaps the less attractive women would be more grateful and tip better. She winced at the twinge of guilt she felt for that thought. Before this ridiculous situation existed, she would have blasted anyone for expressing such a horrible notion.

Passing a gardenia bush in full bloom, she inhaled deeply. The flowers smelled like heaven. In the distance to her right, a group of women sat in lawn chairs by a man-made lake, talking and laughing. One of them waved and said something to her. Shirley squinted, then recognized Edna. She put her hand beside her ear, indicating she couldn't hear her and waved with a smile.

Edna rose from her chair and walked in Shirley's direction.

The sound of a car slowing made her look at the road. An orange Jeep pulled alongside.

"Want a ride?" Agnes' head appeared near the passenger window.

"Sure." Shirley shrugged in Edna's direction, then opened the door and climbed in. "Go. Quickly. I don't have the patience for Edna today."

Agnes put the Jeep into drive and snickered. "Happy to rescue you. The woman's a first class gossip for sure. Guess I'm quite the influence, huh?"

"What?"

She pointed to Shirley's feet. "Wearing sneakers with that beautiful suit? That's got me written all over it."

Shirley looked at Agnes' black high-tops and laughed. "Maybe so." She lifted the shoebox containing her low-heeled pumps part way from her carryall. "But these shoes are not made for the streets. They're too expensive to take a chance on being ruined by walking outdoors in them. I wouldn't dare."

Agnes made the turn into Shirley's neighborhood. "How come you're taking the bus to work? Car break down?"

"No. Stanley dropped me off this morning. He needed the car this afternoon. I've taken the bus before. Actually, it was pleasant. I had time to read my book."

"And how's that adorable gay couple you work for?"

"Not so adorable right now. They had a fight and made the rest of us miserable. I'm glad to be home. I did make a huge sale today. That was good."

Agnes nodded. "If the rich can't find it in their hearts to pay a tiny bit higher taxes, the very least they can do is go out and spend a whole lot more of that obscene pile of money they're sitting on. Helps the economy, you know."

"It's certainly helping mine."

They pulled into Shirley's carport.

"Want to come in?" Shirley asked as she exited the car. "I haven't seen you in a few weeks. We could catch up."

"Nah." Agnes eyed her. "I know when you're just being polite. You're tired. Get some rest."

"Goodness. How do you do that?" Shirley shut the passenger door. "Sometimes, it's like you can see right into my head."

Agnes gave her a Cheshire grin, then backed out and drove away.

After changing out of her suit, Shirley started dinner. Stanley's appointment was at four. She figured he'd be coming home soon. It surprised her to feel nervous to ask about the encounter. She sliced a green pepper and added it to the salad bowl.

At five-thirty, she went outside and looked up and down the street, thinking she'd see Stanley drive in at any moment. Ten minutes later, she went indoors and paced, unable to concentrate on anything else.

She was contemplating calling the police to see if there had been any accidents when she heard the car door shut.

Stanley came in soon after, one hand behind his back.

"Where have you been?" Her voice sounded shrill and demanding, even to her. She made an effort to calm herself.

He approached her, bringing the hidden hand and a bouquet of red roses forward. "For you. My wife. Whom I love."

All her anguish went *poof* and dissipated.

He handed her the flowers and kissed her on the cheek. "It took longer than you and I thought it would, but the lady was, uh, pleased. She gave me six-hundred."

"*Six-hundred?* You're kidding. What did you do to her? Wait." Shirley thrust out a palm. "Don't tell me."

"I don't really want to talk about it, either. I'm going to take a shower. Then can we eat? I'm starved."

***

They sat at the dining room table, eating in silence. Shirley tried to pretend it was a normal night. It was anything but. The sound of Stanley's silverware striking the plate seemed to echo off the walls.

Shirley put her fork down. "I can't stand this. I have to know what happened. How it went. Maybe if you don't go into details?"

"You said it yourself. I don't remember details. Remember?" He smiled at her. "I show up at her house. It's another huge honking mansion. Lots of expensive art and antique furniture. She's chubby and plain. Never mind, you already know what she looks like. We go into her bedroom, which you would have loved. I wish I could provide a place like that for you. You deserve it."

"Okay. I get it. Stop laying it on so thick."

"She tells me she needs some time to *get there.*" His face flushed. "Before she could uh, you know—"

"Yes."

"So for half an hour, she has me read to her from this book with sexy little stories in it. That did the trick for her, because she was ready when we . . . when I . . . well, you know."

"The pill worked."

He stared at his food. "Yes."

"Did it happen by itself, or did it take some handiwork?"

"Does it matter?"

She stared at him and grew wary. "By itself, then. You were attracted to her?"

"No." He blew out a loud breath. "Jeezus, Shirley. It was those stories. They were very suggestive and, well, sexy. Had an effect on me, too."

"I guess we're in business." Her stomach ached like she'd

been punched.

"It was weird. I felt like I was cheating on you."

"You *were* cheating on me."

"Only because you asked me to. Then I went and bought the roses, which took even longer."

She glanced at the flowers, now re-cut and arranged in her best crystal vase. "I can't recall the last time you bought me roses."

"They are pretty pricey. I figured since she'd paid me extra, you wouldn't mind that I spent the money on them."

"It was very thoughtful of you." She closed her eyes. "Gosh. The first woman paid you although nothing happened, and this one gives you two-hundred more than you asked for. Do you think they're all like that?"

"We should buy a copy of that book," Stanley said.

"Oh?" She opened her eyes.

"For us. It's something I'd like us to do together. With the woman I love."

CHAPTER FORTY-FIVE

"Fantabulous, Mack." Leticia Basslebrook flopped onto a pile of disarrayed pillows and giggled. "That was incredible. Absolutely wonderful. I haven't had an experience like that in years. Decades, maybe."

"I aim to please." Stanley rolled away from her to the edge of the king-size bed, then sat. He checked his watch on the nightstand. Three-thirty. He'd been at Leticia's for forty-five minutes.

"You know, the last time I tried this, it was a disaster."

"Tried this? Having sex?"

"No, no, silly. Paid *entertainment,* if you will. He was a young guy, too young. Maybe in his mid-thirties? I got his name from a good friend. Tony. He was a hunk. Gorgeous. At first I was so excited, but then I felt, I don't know, old?" She covered her eyes with her hands. "It was so embarrassing that I couldn't enjoy myself at all." She patted his back. "But you. I like that you're older. How old are you, by the way?"

"Old enough." He stood to avoid her hand on him.

"Can I make appointment with you for next Wednesday? Actually, can we make it a standing date? Every Wednesday? It's the day my staff has off. No one has to know that way. I won't have to make silly excuses to anyone."

"Gotta call Mitzi and ask her." Two weeks into the new venture, calling Shirley *Mitzi* continued to feel weird. Being in bed with other women was weird. His life had become weirder than he'd ever imagined it could. He walked to the nearby pink velvet chair to retrieve his pants. Now that the sex was over, he didn't want to turn and see her sprawling naked on the bed. Leticia appeared marginally attractive when she met him at the door. As he suspected, her tunic-type shirt hid a lot.

It was difficult to work up enthusiasm for his task. Nearly fifty years with Shirley's slim and trim body made it a challenge to deal with fat rolls and boobs bigger than his head. With Shirley, he loved to caress her smooth, still-taut skin. He knew where to put his hands. The extra pounds on these other women made him unsure of himself. How was he supposed to know where or how to touch them? He really didn't want to. To combat that, he'd found starting sexual encounters with the women while they were at least partially clothed made it easier for him to achieve an erection. Once things were under way though, it surprised him to find the sex was not objectionable. He chuckled to himself as he pulled on his work jeans, thinking the old adage was true. There was no such thing as bad sex. But there wasn't any way he'd ever let Shirley know that—he might learn to like this. A lot. "Mitzi's the boss." He'd switched from carrying a tool box to a tool belt. He fastened it and turned.

Leticia groaned. "All right. I'll clear it through your pimpette." She sat, then grabbed a white silk robe from a chair near her side of the bed and put it on. She brushed her dyed blonde bangs from her forehead and smiled. "Dear God, you're a handsome man. Did you know that?"

"So I've been told." Stanley smiled at her. "Thank you for the compliment."

"The same friend of mine told me Tony was gay and only keeping company with us women for the money. You're not pretending, are you? Masquerading like Tony?"

Stanley snorted a laugh. "No. Not a chance."

She shuffled to a large wood bureau decorated with gold fittings and opened the top drawer. When she faced him, she held a wad of cash. She peeled off four bills, gave him a devilish grin, then added one more.

"Here." She offered him the money. "I figure you deserve a little extra."

"Well, thank you." Stanley took the bills and pocketed them. "Guess I'd better go. You said your chef was returning at four, right?"

Her eyes darted to a clock on the nightstand, then widened. "Crap. And the maid, too. I sent her on errands. Yes, please hurry downstairs. Let yourself out through the kitchen door—same way you came in. If anybody asks, you were here about a leak in my bathroom faucet. Okay?"

"Faucet. Leak fixed. Got it." Stanley hustled from the bedroom.

"Don't worry about the security code, the driveway gate will open automatically for you on this side."

On the lookout for Leticia's staff, Stanley felt guilty sneaking out of the house—like he'd done something wrong. He'd had a few close escapes from some homes already, and each time he experienced a strange sensation of being dirty. Skulking around like a criminal. It was a new feeling, and he didn't like it. Then reality smacked him again. He *was* doing something immoral. He *was* doing something illegal. No matter how he and Shirley shaped the facts to appease their consciences, it was plain wrong.

In the car, he took a small bottle of antibacterial gel from under his seat and doused his hands with it. His version of a French whore's bath. He started the engine and drove out to Sago Beach Ocean Drive, heading to Paulina's to pick up Shirley. She was working until four and had timed his appointment that way.

He pulled into a spot behind the lingerie store, spread the hundreds on the passenger seat, and tapped his fingers along with *Take Five* on the radio, liking the coincidence. The shop's rear door opened, and Shirley came through the doorway, waving goodbye. She closed it and approached the car with a tired expression.

"Long day?" Stanley asked.

She began to sit, then jumped up, noticing the money. "Five hundred?"

Stanley shrugged. "I guess she was happy with the service. You were right about these women. They like to throw money around."

Gathering the bills, Shirley tucked them into her purse and sat. While Stanley drove out of the lot, she checked her cell phone.

"Huh. I have a voice mail," she said. "We should have started using this when Fletcher first gave it to us. Once you get used to how it works, it's not difficult. I had no idea how convenient it could be." After punching some buttons, she put it to her ear.

He stared ahead at the road. They were approaching the Intracoastal bridge. He felt a tap on the arm and glanced at Shirley.

"It's Leticia Basslebrook," she said, pointing to the phone with her free hand. "You just left there, didn't you?"

He nodded.

"Hope everything's okay. You didn't have a problem, did you?"

"No. I—"

"Shush. Her message is starting."

Half a minute later, Shirley set the phone down. "Goodness. She wants to have a standing appointment with you every Wednesday at two o'clock."

"She mentioned it when I left, and I told her to schedule through you, boss."

"She sounded very pleased. What did you do to her?"

Shirley's voice gained a suspicious edge on the last sentence.

"Nothing. It was like you said. She was happy I was around

her age, is all." He'd never tell Shirley the details. He was learning fast how to use his fingers to manipulate and stimulate. He'd needed to. It was taking too long for them to *get ready* otherwise. Shirley wouldn't want to know how easily he'd brought Leticia to an orgasm. And then another. And another. The woman knew how to relax and go with it, he'd give her that much.

"What do you think?" she asked. "Is an automatic appointment okay with you?"

"Sure. Lock her in. Guaranteed money is good, isn't it?"

"I think we should charge her extra. A premium for that. After all, it means we'd have to say no to anyone else who wanted a Wednesday afternoon."

He looked at her and grinned. "Wow. You are ruthless. I love it." He turned into Silver Sago Village, waved at the guard, then slowed for the first yellow-painted speed bump. To their right, a gaggle of women sat in lawn chairs by the lake edge. They recognized the car and waved. "Wave to your friends, honey."

Shirley lowered her window, flapped her hand in their direction, then shut it.

"You miss hanging out with them?"

"A little. Not as much as I thought I would. It does make me appreciate the time I do spend with them now."

"I notice Dora's spending a lot of time with Tim, so maybe it's a good thing you're working, huh?"

"Ugh." Shirley sighed. "Don't remind me. I'm happy for her, but Tim turning out to be as well-off financially as he is—well, it's hard not to feel some resentment."

The cloud of guilt and shame that plagued him since he'd discovered he'd screwed up their finances descended on him. "I'm sorry. That's my fault. I'm sorry I let you down."

She shook her head. "No. We're not dwelling on it. We're doing what we have to, and it's working. Three thousand dollars in the two weeks since you got your blue pills. If this keeps up, we'll have the credit cards paid off in four months. Then we can start saving again." She caressed his arm. "Got any energy left for me tonight?"

CHAPTER FORTY-SIX

Nina's tailbone didn't hurt anymore. It had taken a couple of weeks, but she finally felt normal again. Physically, at least. George was back on his *I need to work nearly every night* routine. Did that mean he'd found another girlfriend? She hadn't found the right moment to bring up the subject of getting a breast enhancement, but push was shoving things around in the most irritating way. It was time to launch her *I'm taking back my husband* campaign.

The doorbell rang. She closed her checkbook, placed it and the pile of bills she'd been paying into the kitchen desk drawer, and went to the door.

Evelyn Asbury stood there, dressed in tennis clothes. "I'm a little early, but we finished our match, and I thought maybe you and I could catch up. 'Been awhile, hasn't it?"

"Come on in." Nina led her back to the kitchen. "Want some coffee?"

"Wine would be better."

"At four in the afternoon? You're a bad influence. But, one glass only, okay? I'm driving your car tonight, remember?"

Evelyn glanced around, then lowered her voice. "Where are your kids?"

"One's at soccer, the other at a friend's. Why?"

Pulling a chair away from the table, Evelyn looked pensive. "Because I have to tell you something." She sat, placed her purse on the next chair, and stared at Nina.

"But you need a glass of wine first."

Nodding, Evelyn bit her lip.

While Nina retrieved the pinot grigio from the refrigerator and poured it into two glasses, her imagination went wild. What sort of news would make her friend so mysterious? Normally, Evelyn shared news without a fuss. Was it about one of Evelyn's children? Her daughter was a senior in high school and very pretty. Had the little flirt gotten herself pregnant? Nina placed the drink in front of Evelyn, then joined her at the table. She leveled her gaze at Evelyn.

"Don't worry," Nina said. "Whatever it is, you know I'll be here for you. Now tell me what's wrong."

Evelyn gulped about half the wine, then shuddered. She kept her eyes on the glass. "I've been going round and round in my head about how to tell you this." She burped. "Shit. I'm just going to say it. George is screwing around on you."

Nina couldn't stop the deer-in-headlights look she knew had taken over her face. How had Evelyn found out? Nina didn't even know if there was a new girlfriend, or if the old one was back in the picture.

"Now, before you tell me I'm crazy," Evelyn said, "hear me out."

Calming, Nina composed a poker face.

"Last night, I met an old college friend for drinks. She's in the area for a convention and staying near the beach. We met at the hotel bar about nine." Evelyn closed her eyes. "I saw George go into the elevator with a tall blonde wearing four-inch stilettos, and they were all over each other. She's looks half our age." She exhaled. "Now you can start your denials."

Rattled, Nina digested the information. George had come home for dinner the night before, but said he had a meeting afterward to show a property to a lawyer for a New York City restaurant group. He hadn't said whether the lawyer was a man or woman.

"Nina? Did you hear what I told you?" Evelyn waved her hand in front of Nina's face.

"I heard you." She knew all too well it was possible, but the only way she could hold her head up among her friends was if she pretended George's betrayals didn't exist. If Evelyn knew, how long would it be until others knew, too? Nina felt blood rush to her face.

"Honey, it's not your fault. You still look amazing. You've been married for twenty-plus years. Men get weird in middle age. They do stupid things."

"Have you told anyone else?" Nina said.

"Me? Of course not. I wouldn't. And my friend doesn't know either of you, so I didn't explain it to her."

"Explain it to her?"

"She asked me what I was staring at in the lobby."

"Exactly what do you mean when you say they were all over each other? Is there a chance you misinterpreted what you saw?"

Evelyn made a face. "No."

"Because maybe they were headed to a second-floor meeting room. Hotels have those, you know. And if he accidentally brushed against her in a crowded elevator—"

Grabbing her drink, Evelyn emptied the glass, then set it down. "Wasn't crowded. Only two in there. His hand went up her dress. They were swapping spit as the doors closed. Happy?" She plunked her head onto the table.

His latest had been a brunette. During her spying, Nina had caught glimpses of her. So this was a new one?

"Did she have big boobs?" Nina asked.

"What?" Evelyn raised her head.

"You heard me. Tell me."

"There was a whole lot of cleavage showing from her skimpy little dress. Whether that was padding or real, who knows? Why do you care? Don't torture yourself."

"We need more wine." Nina rose and went to the fridge.

"What about the driving?"

"I won't go out tonight."

"Why do you borrow my car anyway? Mine's not so much better than yours. People at these lectures you're attending aren't going to care if you drive a minivan."

Making up her mind, Nina poured more for both of them. "I don't go to lectures. I spy on George."

"You knew?"

"I need someone to talk to about this. You're my best friend. Promise you won't tell even your husband what I'm going to tell you."

Two refills of wine later, Nina finished her synopsis of George's infidelities.

Evelyn, gape-mouthed, stared at her. "The bastard. Why haven't you kicked his sorry ass out? Don't you have any pride?" She blanched. "I'm sorry. I didn't mean that. Must be the wine talking."

"Apparently, I *don't* have any." Elbow on the table, Nina cradled her chin in her hand. "The issue is—I'm in love with him. After all these years, he stares at me a certain way, and I practically orgasm on the spot. I don't know if I could ever find that with anyone else. It's so rare. *You've* admitted that you and Dan hardly ever do it anymore, and when you do, it's routine and boring. I can't count the times you've said it."

"That's life. Sex gets boring with the same person after several decades. You deal with it."

"Sex is infrequent for George and me, too," Nina said, "but at least when we do it, it's fantastic."

"I'm kind of foggy here. It sounds like you don't mind that he's cheating?"

"I mind. It's killing me. But I want him back. I'm going to win him back. I finally figured out why he strays. It's the boobs."

Evelyn cocked her head. "Say again?"

"George loves big breasts. He can't bring himself to tell me and hurt my feelings. I never knew—it just dawned on me recently. I have tiny ones. I'm going to get big ones. Problem solved."

"Um . . ." Draining the last of her wine, Evelyn shook her head. "What if that's not it? If it doesn't stop him?"

"It'll work. I'm sure of it."

"No offense, but I think you're in denial. As much as you believe the opposite, there are some things you can't control."

"No. This is the answer. It's been the problem all along. I can feel it. And I don't want to control him."

Evelyn rolled her eyes. "Yes, you do. You try to control everything. It's what you do. You arrange things, organize events, tell us all who's to bring what, at what time, and in what order. I'm saying this as gently as I can—maybe he fools around because he likes the freedom of it?"

A flash of anger hit Nina, and she stood. "I keep this family in order. I work so hard to help them make the right choices. And I can't imagine how half our gatherings would have turned out if *someone* hadn't taken charge of things. No one else wants to, so it always falls on me."

"I've said too much." Evelyn rose and put her hand on Nina's shoulder. "I didn't mean to upset you further. I'm your friend. Let me know what I can do to help."

Twisting away from her, Nina cringed when her eyes filled with tears. "You should leave now."

Nodding, Evelyn headed for the door. "I'll let myself out. Call me tomorrow, okay?"

"Just go."

CHAPTER FORTY-SEVEN

Catherine's phone rang. She fished into her purse with one hand. The other held a champagne flute. "Hello?"

"Darling, it's Leticia. Do you have a moment?"

"Barely." Catherine glanced around Roberta's living room. The ladies seemed engaged enough in their conversations that she could duck out for a minute. "I'm at my book discussion group. We're just wrapping up."

"Good. Guess what I found."

"A new spa?" She left the room and went into the hall.

"Better. A man."

Allowing disinterest to creep into her voice, Catherine said, "How wonderful for you."

"And for you."

"I fail to see why it affects me. Although I'm pleased for you, of course." She checked her watch. "I'll call back later, and you can tell me all about him." Much later, maybe *never*.

"He's for hire. He's perfect. You're going to love him."

"Really, dear, I thought I made it crystal clear how I feel about the subject."

"This one's different. He's older. Got to be in his late sixties at least. And he has serious *talent*." She giggled. "Rock-solid talent, if you know what I mean."

Catherine checked behind her, then walked further down the hall. "You're shameless. Go on."

"I'm only sharing him with my closest friends."

***

Stanley had gone to shower. Shirley sat at the dinette table and dialed Leticia's number.

Leticia picked up on the first ring. "Mitzi, I'm reserving Mack's services every Wednesday at two."

The abrupt phone manners most of the women used while speaking to *Mitzi* threw her off a little, but she figured she'd have to accommodate them. She and *Mack* were no different than any other servants to them. "I'll have to check with him, and—"

"He already agreed."

"Did he? Well, that's why he needs me. You see, he has an appointment next Wednesday," she lied, "and I don't know—"

"Tell the other person she needs to reschedule. I'm willing to commit to a regular time. It's guaranteed income."

"I can try, but I can't promise anything. Mack's clients are all very important to us."

"I'll pay double. Even on the days when a holiday falls on a Wednesday, or if one of us is ill, I won't expect him to be here, and I'll still pay him for the time. How's that sound?"

"That's a generous offer. Let me discuss it with Mack, and I'll let you know."

"I can get him a lot of referral business. In fact, I've recommended him to a friend. But I won't continue to do so unless I get my guaranteed time."

The phone went dead. Shirley stared at the cell. "How about that?"

"How about what?" Stanley walked into the kitchen, wearing clean clothes and smelling like soap.

"Leticia will pay you double for an every Wednesday appointment."

His eyebrows rose. "Go figure."

"What in God's creation did you do with her?" Shirley looked at him with skepticism. "Level with me."

"I swear. Nothing unusual. I think it really is what you said. She likes that I'm older. She told me something along those lines. You nailed it, sweetheart. You were right." He went to the fridge and took out a bottle of beer.

"What, exactly, did she say?"

He gave her a funny face. "I don't recall. Wasn't important. 'Cept I know she liked the fact I'm old. Please tell me you're not expecting me to remember everything they say." He opened the beer, took a swallow, then smiled at her. "Unbelievable. Eight-hundred bucks for one hour a week?"

Shaking her head, Shirley stared at him. "I always knew there were rich people. But I never, in a lifetime of Sundays, would have guessed how many there were, and how much they'd splurge on frivolous things. In the middle of a recession, no less. Can you imagine what they spend in good economic years? It boggles the mind."

Stanley adopted a feminine model pose. "I—*am not*—a frivolous thing."

Laughing, Shirley's worries fell away. "I love you."

"I love you, too." He set his beer on the counter and opened his arms. "You are so beautiful. I realize that now even more."

Feeling the electric charge of desire between them, she shoved her chair back and went to him. He folded his arms around her and kissed her neck. She shivered with the erotic tension surging through her, loving the thrill of it.

His breathing quickened. "You're all I want."

They hurried upstairs to their bed.

***

"I can't believe this." Shirley sat up. "For *her*, apparently, things worked just dandy."

"I had to take a pill or nothing would have happened with her. I never needed help with you. Maybe it's my age. I don't remember the last time I tried to do it twice in one day."

"Take another pill."

"I can't. You know the doctor said no more than twenty-four hours apart. I'll make it up to you, I promise. I don't have any appointments tomorrow, do I? It'll be our special day."

Shirley got her robe from the hook on the bathroom door and put it on. "I may as well go make us some dinner."

"Don't be mad, please?" he called after her.

Pounding the steps as she descended, she didn't know why she was so angry. She felt hurt, insulted, undesirable, and at the same time—guilty and infuriated with herself. He was right. At seventy-four, once a day was probably all he could muster, even with the pills.

She took the leftover chicken casserole from the refrigerator and slammed the door shut. She grabbed two plates from the cabinet and let them clatter onto the counter. Yanking open the utensils drawer, she found a spatula, began to portion out the chicken, then stopped. With a scream of frustration, she threw the spatula across the room where it smacked into the hanging calendar, splattering chicken bits all over the smiling faces of her grandchildren and everywhere else.

"Shirley?"

She turned.

"I'm really sorry." Stanley peeked from around the kitchen wall. "Forgive me?"

Taking a deep breath, then blowing it out, she grimaced. "There's nothing to forgive. It's not your fault. We're going to have to understand what our new *normal* is." She forced a smile. "We'll do what you said. Have one day in the plan that's for us."

"Or two." He grinned. "I don't plan on working weekends, remember?"

Her anger subsided. She chuckled. "Never thought we'd be

one of those couples who had to schedule in a sex life."

"Is it safe to hug you?" He approached her.

As he held her close again, her cell rang. "I'd better see who it is." She broke away and plucked the phone from the table. "It says *Private Number*." She hit the button to answer. "Mack the Handyman. Mitzi speaking."

"Yes. I'm interested in your *handyman* service."

The voice was deep and raspy and sounded somehow familiar to Shirley. "I see. May I ask how you were referred to Mack?"

"A friend."

"Wonderful. But as you might expect, in our particular line of work, it's important that we are very careful. I'll need the friend's name, please."

A tiny grunt sound followed. "Basslebrook."

"Thank you. What is your name?"

"Catherine."

The voice and the name clicked. Dora would flip out if she knew. "I'll need a last name and an address, please." To Stanley, she mouthed, *you're not going to believe this.*

"I'd rather not. Have him meet me in the Sago Palms Hotel lobby tomorrow at six. I'll be wearing a lavender suit and matching hat."

"We don't do that."

"Excuse me?" Catherine sounded impatient. "That isn't my understanding. He *is* for hire, is he not? And what is the *we*? I don't want *you*."

I don't want you, either. "No hotels. No motels. Mack the Handyman only works in private homes. It's his specialty. And we require appointments in advance."

"That's what I'm trying to do." The—*you simpleton*—end of her sentence was implied. Arrogance dripped from the phone. "Set up an appointment. Tomorrow. At six. I don't think I could make it any clearer."

Catherine's attitude annoyed Shirley. "Mack is already

engaged tomorrow. Just a moment while I look at his schedule." She hummed a bit while she pretended. "He has next Tuesday afternoon or next Friday morning."

Stanley raised his arms in a *what are you talking about* gesture.

She waved him away.

"Well. I'll have to rethink this whole thing."

The phone went dead. Shirley stared at it. "She hung up on me. I suppose I'd better get used to that. They seem to do it a lot."

"I could go tomorrow," Stanley said. "Why'd you act like I was busy?"

"A—you, not two minutes ago, promised me that I could have you all to myself tomorrow. B—that was Catherine Von Cletan. Dora and I saw her in action once, on a trip to Sago Beach. She's haughty and rude. Thinks she owns people. If she's going to be one of your customers, you'd better start from the get-go not letting her run the show."

"What if she never calls back?"

"I have the feeling she will." The conversation Shirley overheard at Alfred's restaurant came rushing into her head. Catherine Von Cletan was desperate. "If not, as we're finding out, there's lots of other women and not so many men like you."

"Jeezus. I'm glad you're doing the phone calls. I'd have said okay and met her."

She held his hands in hers. "Promise me. Don't break the rules we set up. No exceptions. We do *not* want to get caught. And these women will talk to each other. If you make an exception for one, they'll all expect it."

CHAPTER FORTY-EIGHT

Fletcher paid for two insulated paper cups of coffee, grabbed them, and headed for the back of the crowded KrakaJava shop where Maddy waited. On his way, while negotiating a path through a lengthy line of waiting customers, he felt a tap on the arm. He stopped and turned to his right. Agnes, her shock of curly white hair sticking out from a Dolphins visor, and an old man sat in a booth with newspapers spread on the table.

Agnes smiled. "Fletcher. Good to see you."

"Hi. Thanks. Same here." He glanced toward Maddy. She looked like pure sunshine in a blue and white print dress that emphasized her slender waist. She was making her way to him. He motioned with one of the coffee cups. "I need to get over there."

"Got a morning date, do you? What's it—a meet and greet? Did she match her picture?"

"No. I mean, it's not a get-to-know-you meeting." Another quick check, and Maddy was almost to them. "Nice to see you."

"Tell me first, how do you like your new place? Your mother said it's a very fancy building. I know someone who bought there, too."

"Can I fill you in another time? Right now, I have to—"

"You have to what?" Maddy came to stand beside him.

Too late. "Give you your coffee, of course." He handed the cup in his left hand to her.

Agnes whistled a long, low tone, which made the man look up from an article in the Miami Herald. His eyes widened when he saw Maddy.

Maddy laughed. "You should introduce us, Fletch."

He sighed. "Maddy Forsyth, this is Agnes Graber and . . ."

"This handsome gentleman is Jerome Simms," Agnes said with a huge smile. She touched Jerome's hand and winked. "He's mine, Missy, don't even think about it."

Jerome rolled his eyes. "Sweet Jesus, Agnes. I barely have enough energy to keep up with you."

"Why don't you join us?" Agnes scooted to the end of the bench seat to make room.

"We can't. I—"

"I'd love to." Maddy cut across Fletcher, set her cup down, and sat next to Agnes.

Fletcher looked to Jerome for help, but the older man shrugged, then shook his head. Resigned, Fletcher took a seat beside Jerome and silently prayed Agnes wouldn't say anything about his Tanya disaster.

"You're not *the* Agnes Graber. The artist?" Maddy said.

Agnes grinned. "I am an artist. You've seen my work?"

"Yes." Maddy's face lit up. "A friend of mine had one of your paintings in his flat. In London. It was wonderful."

Fletcher couldn't quite figure out why Maddy was so animated about Agnes, but any subject other than his past was fine with him.

"After that, the next time I was in Sedona, I made it a point to search out your paintings."

"I'm flattered," Agnes said.

"Fletch, do you know who this is?" Maddy said.

"Um. A good friend of my mother's?" Fletcher and Agnes had discussed her art briefly, but he'd assumed she was just an old woman who sold a couple of paintings here and there as a hobby.

"No. This woman is an artistic genius."

"Oh, please." Agnes waved her hand in dismissal.

"Wait a minute," Fletcher said. "Whose flat?"

"Doesn't matter," Maddy said. "Ancient history. Anyway, I nearly bought one of yours, but my ex-fiancé talked me out of it. He didn't like the sharp contrast in the piece. He wanted something that wouldn't *fight* the neutral tones in the room. Everything about that man was bland and ordinary. I can't imagine what I saw in him or why I listened to him, and I've regretted it ever since."

"Thank you," Agnes said. "Would you like to come by the studio? I work out of my townhouse at Silver Sago Village."

Crap, Fletcher thought. Don't mention my parents living there, too. He willed Agnes to understand. Please, for the love of God . . .

"You feeling okay?" Jerome said to him, nudging him on the arm. "You're turning kind of pale."

"I'm fine," Fletcher said.

"I'd love to," Maddy said. "Wouldn't that be great, Fletch?"

"Sure." Fletcher checked his watch. "We really need to go." He shuffled out of the booth.

Agnes handed Maddy a business card. "Call me, and we'll set up a time."

Beaming, Maddy took the card and placed it in a side pocket of her purse. "Thanks. I'm so excited. Can't wait. So nice to meet you both." She slid along the bench and exited the booth.

As Maddy made her way toward the door, Fletcher trailed her, then backtracked. He leaned in toward Agnes.

Agnes had a quizzical expression.

"She doesn't know where my parents live, and they don't know anything about her, including the fact I'm dating her. I'd love to keep it that way. At least for now."

With a smile, Agnes nodded. "I deduced that from the panic on your face. Give me a little more credit, will you?" She gestured toward Maddy. "She seems like a gem. How long you two been an item?"

"Three weeks. I know she's young. But in some ways, I swear, she's older than me. I'm in heaven."

"Hope it lasts." Agnes cocked her head toward the door. "She's waiting."

He hustled to Maddy. "Agnes is a piece of work, isn't she?" He opened the door, then followed her out.

They walked to his car.

"You don't have a clue who Agnes is, do you?" Maddy asked.

"I thought I did. She's a hippie-dippy cosmic kind of person who paints. And I guess, judging from your reaction in there, she's pretty well-known as an artist."

"The powers-that-be running Art Basel in Miami every year would give their first-borns to have her participate. She lives an hour away, and they've never been able to talk her into it."

"Who or what is an Art Basel?"

"Never mind. I don't feel like explaining the art world to you." She crossed her arms and waited by the passenger door.

He hit the key fob, unlocking the car, then opened the door for her. "You seem irritated. Not everyone knows or cares about the art world. I know enough basics. Hey, I *did* recognize that Kandinsky in your apartment, didn't I? I'm simply not as into it as you."

Sliding into the seat, she made a gruff sound. "I'm aware of that."

Fletcher got in and decided to stay quiet. Not knowing her well enough yet to understand what had ticked her off, he figured it was safer to let her break the strange dynamic that had changed their mojo.

He made his way out of the parking lot, taking surreptitious peeks at her. A few minutes into the drive, she uncrossed her arms, shook them, and stretched.

"I'm sorry," she said. "Sometimes I forget."

"Forget?"

"Yes. You're right. Lots of people don't follow contemporary art."

That wasn't what bothered her. He could tell. He didn't know how, but he knew it was something else. "Thank you. Can I ask you something?"

She stared at him. "Ask away."

"It's obvious you grew up in pretty privileged circumstances. We've been dodging around the subject since we met, and I'm wondering why. You never mention any family—said you didn't want to talk about your mother. You don't have to tell me details, but—did something unpleasant happen? Something that upsets you to think about?"

For a moment, she appeared to be considering the question. She pursed her lips and closed her eyes. When she opened them, she shifted her torso toward him. "Nothing awful happened to me. My upbringing *was* among the wealthier class. But I began to despise it. It's a shallow world that celebrates whoever has more. A competition for who can spend the most. Four-thousand dollars for a custom shower curtain? Two million dollars on a wedding? It's stupid-crazy. Some—no—most of the people in my mother's world inherited what they have and have no idea how hard life can be for others. The lower classes, even the middle class, are regarded as weak and defective in some way, because they aren't resourceful enough to become rich. I choose not to live in that world anymore."

"You're not going to relinquish what you've got, don a toga, and climb up some remote mountain to meditate, are you?" He grinned. "Although, I'll bet you'd look damned fine in a toga."

Chuckling, she shook her head. "No. Don't misunderstand. I like having money. I love the things I'm able to do with it."

"That's a relief."

"Now let's forget about it, okay?"

"Deal."

CHAPTER FORTY-NINE

Stanley zipped his jeans, then pivoted to face the woman in the dim bedroom. A distant window in her bathroom provided just enough light to see.

With a plump finger, Lily Wentworth stroked the ivory silk bed sheet now gathered and covering her body. The toes of one foot swished against the underside of the sheet. She smiled a small, timid smile. "I'm so sorry about the screaming. I've never done that before. I truly don't know what got into me."

He cringed at the reminder. She'd scared the crap out of him. "I'm happy I didn't hurt you somehow. That's what I thought happened."

"No. It wasn't pain. It was . . ." Using one arm, she pushed into a sitting position while still clutching the sheets around her. Her blonded short hair, styled in orderly curls when he arrived, now resembled a palm tree suffering from frizzle-top. "It was enlightening." Staring toward the black-out shade over the window, she shivered. "I was married for thirty years."

He nodded and reached for his tool belt. "You were young then, when your husband passed."

"Passed?" She sighed. "He's very much alive. On his fourth wife now. She's younger than our daughter. They're having a *baby*. Can you believe it? The man is seventy-one."

Buckling the belt around his hips, he checked that his tools were secured and walked to her side of the bed. "I'm sorry. That's got to sting."

"Not anymore." She pointed behind him. "Will you hand me my purse? It's on the dresser there."

"Sure." He lifted the beige leather bag, surprised at its heft, then set it beside her.

She fished around inside the purse, finding an envelope. "My husband, Gavin, was my only lover until he abandoned me. Although, calling him a lover at all is ridiculous. Sex always felt like a chore, but I did it because I was supposed to. I was a virgin when we married. What did I know? It was in, out, in, and done. Over. I had no idea women were capable of *enjoying* it." From the envelope, she took four hundreds, counted them twice, then handed them to Stanley with a sheepish look.

"Thank you." He pocketed the cash.

"Gavin seemed to like it, but I didn't understand what all the fuss was about."

"I think that would be a reasonable reaction." He moved toward the door.

"Then I had a succession of boyfriends, and I learned how bad a hand I'd been dealt with Gavin. I felt so cheated."

Stanley had the feeling she needed to talk, but no desire to be the therapist. She hadn't wanted him to see her naked until the lights were off and the shades down. Her strange combination of shyness and wildness in bed struck him as a bit unstable. "Understandable. Well, guess I'd better be on my way."

"Can you wait down in the kitchen for a moment? Give me time to throw my clothes on? There's something I'd like to show you."

"All right." He left the bedroom, took the same back staircase he'd followed her up earlier. The kitchen was typical for the enormous house. He'd seen his share of them already. Huge rooms—some as big as his own entire downstairs. Cabinets with exotic wood doors, shiny stainless extra-huge refrigerators, multiple ovens, eight-burner gas stoves. Gleaming granite countertops so long they resembled air strips. Shirley told him none of these women ever cooked, they had chefs, and used caterers for parties. The place smelled antiseptic clean, and the lack of homey clutter gave it a clinical aura.

"Thank you for waiting." Lily entered the room in a cloud of musky perfume. She wore a low-cut clingy top that exposed a whole lot of her breasts. The same breasts she'd tried to hide under the sheet at first.

"Over here." She smiled and gestured to him. "In the laundry room."

Opening the door and turning on the light, she led the way into another large room. This one had rows of stark white cabinets along two walls, two sets of washers and dryers, and a four-foot by ten-foot worktable in the center.

"You must have a lot of laundry," he said.

"See that?" She pointed to the air conditioning vent in the ceiling. "It's hanging out on that one side. I had my gardener look at it, but he said it can't be fixed. It's driving me crazy. Any chance you'd know how to fix it for me?"

"Do you have the screw?" Stanley asked, thinking it wouldn't take him but a second.

"I saved it." Lily pulled open a drawer, shuffled inside, then found it.

"What about a step-ladder?"

"In that closet to your left." She clapped her hands. "Thank you so much. I was afraid the thing would fall out and hurt one of my maids."

"You wouldn't want that." He liked that she was concerned about her staff.

"No kidding. You know how fast they'd turn around and try to sue me? Everybody's out to take money where they can now. Not like the old days. My mother's servants were beyond faithful to her."

So much for the admiration he almost felt. He set the stepladder in place and climbed to reach the vent. The screw slipped in too easily, then fell out. "The hole for the screw is stripped. I need something to place behind the ceiling drywall to make a new screw hole."

She stared at him with a blank expression.

"Maybe you've got something I can use in the garage." He scanned the room and spotted another door on the opposite side. "That lead to it?"

"Yes. There's a workbench of some kind on the far side, I think. My mechanic uses it when he comes to work on the cars."

Stanley entered the garage. He felt for a light switch, found one, and flipped it. He glanced at his watch. Four-fifteen. His appointment with Lily began at three. Shirley would be expecting him home soon. Then he looked up. And across. It was an extra-deep three-door garage. Each bay had room for two cars. He whistled in amazement as he took in the sight. Lily Wentworth had an antique Mercedes coupe, a black SL65, a white Audi A8, a silver Bentley Flying Spur, and a pale-bluish Rolls Royce Phantom parked inside. Shaking his head, he walked past the cars, being careful to not brush against any of them. He wondered if this was typical of the women. Did they all have treasure troves of luxury cars?

The workbench top had nothing on it. Tools hung on pegboard hooks above. There were drawers underneath, and he began a search through them. He found a three-inch long piece of a one-by-four, grabbed it, and went back inside.

The laundry room was empty. He walked into the kitchen. Lily stood at the counter pouring vodka into a tall glass filled with ice and lemon slices.

She turned. "All fixed?"

"Not yet." He held out the piece of wood. "Okay if I use this?"

"I don't know what that is, but if it'll do what you need it to, then use it." She placed the cap on the vodka bottle, then lifted the glass. "To Mack. My new *handy* man."

He gave her an unenthusiastic smile and retreated to the laundry room. A clock on the wall ticked to four-thirty. Placing the wood on the work table, he took his Phillips head screwdriver from his tool belt and, using the screw, tried to pre-drill a hole for it.

Lily came in, placing her drink on the other end of the table.

"You wouldn't own a drill, would you?" he asked.

"I can't imagine why." She lifted the glass and downed about half of it.

Regretting that he'd been sucked into helping her, he climbed the step ladder, removed the remaining screw, and took the vent down. He put the wood piece in place, reinserted the vent, attached the good side screw, then slowly made the second screw bite into the wood. He heard a crack, and the screw fell out.

"Crum crud," he said, thinking far worse expletives. "The wood split. Guess I'd better go hunting in the garage once more."

***

Shirley looked at the clock again. Ten after five. Stanley should have returned by four-thirty. Even if he'd left the Wentworth place a few minutes after four, he would have stopped to call her on the way home. It had happened once. He'd used a pay phone at a gas station on Sago Beach Island. Before they started their enterprise, Stanley being occasionally later than expected bothered her, but waiting to use their only car was a simple inconvenience then. Now, his being late scared her. What if he'd gotten caught? Like the time Mrs. Manning's son surprised his mom with a visit at precisely the worst time, the uncertainties of the things they couldn't control drove Shirley's imagination wild.

The wall-mounted kitchen phone rang. Shirley ran to it. "Stanley?"

"No, Mom. It's me. Nina. You sound upset. Where's Dad?"

"He went out running errands for me." Shirley composed herself. "Everything's fine. How are you?"

"I wanted you to know I'll be having outpatient surgery tomorrow. Nothing major. Something cosmetic."

"Surgery? What on earth for?"

"It's a little procedure, is all. Nothing to be concerned about. I thought you should know in the off, very very off, chance that something goes wrong. The doctor has done this thousands of times."

"Getting your ears pierced is a little procedure. Not surgery. What are you having done?"

"I'd rather not say."

My Lord, Shirley thought, she's doing the vagina-tightening thing that Stanley's urologist described. She steeled herself. "Darling, I know that after three children things down below probably aren't like they used to be, but—"

"What?"

"It's been fourteen years. Surely George is accustomed to, um, well, you know—a more uh, looser . . . Wait. A more *relaxed* area."

"Good God. Are you talking about a vaginoplasty? How do you even know it exists?"

Feeling her face flush, Shirley kind of wished Nina hadn't let her know. "I'm old, not dead. I've heard talk about such things. Anyway, is it really worth the risk to have surgery? Aren't you scared? What if something *does* go kaflooey?"

"For crying out loud, I'm having my boobs done."

"That isn't much better. What for? You have lovely breasts."

"You haven't seen my chest since I was fourteen. They are small and droopy. I hate them."

Shirley took a deep breath. "I'm a bit confused. Weren't you the one who made fun of Fletcher's girlfriend Tanya because of her boob job? I thought you had no patience with women like her. Now you want to become one?"

"Tanya *was* a big boob. I'm not going to make mine ginormous. Give me some credit."

"What does George think?"

"That's the best part. He doesn't know. He left for a real estate conference in Las Vegas. I told you Mary Ann got her license last week, right? She'll drive me home when it's over. I'm going to surprise George."

CHAPTER FIFTY

Stanley checked his watch again. Five-fifty. Shirley would be mad as hell. He wanted to call her, but couldn't from Lily's house. How would he explain it?

Lily sat at the work table, draining the last of her second drink. She clunked the glass onto the granite. "It's wonderful you can actually fix things, you know that?"

She sounded toasted. With his left hand reaching over the vent, he steadied the wood scrap in place as his right hand held the screwdriver and tightened the aggravating thing into place. It held. He let out a huge sigh of relief.

"I was beautiful." She leaned on an elbow. "When I got married. I was thin, and sexy, and cute as all get out."

With no safe way to respond to her, he grunted an agreement. "Almost done here."

"So unfair." She tilted the glass to her mouth, and the ice cube remnants raced downward, clinking against her teeth. After sucking on the ice, then spitting it back into the glass, she lowered it to the counter again. "I wasted thirty years of my *fabulousness* with Gavin, the one-minute wonder. Can you believe it? I'll bet he hasn't gotten any better, either. This new young wife of his? Just a matter of time 'till she cheats on him. Probably already did. I bet that baby isn't even his."

Stanley finished with the second screw, stepped to the floor, and sighed. "Wow." He made a show of checking his watch. "It's late. I've got to go. You're all set here."

"Trust me. She ain't getting no satisfaction." She snorted out a guffaw. "Get it?"

He faked a laugh. "Yes. Very clever of you. Well. You have a good night. I'm going to let myself out. Okay?"

She waved him away, looking like she was about to cry.

Once past the kitchen and out the servants' entrance, he ran to the car.

***

Shirley jumped when the cell phone rang. She dashed to the dining room table where she'd left it. "Mack the handyman. This is Mitzi."

"Hello."

It was the husky voice of Catherine Von Cletan. Shirley's wish that it was Stanley fizzled.

"I would like to make an appointment with Mack."

"Of course." Shirley grabbed her clipboard and a pen. "He has Friday at two open this week." If he's not already in jail, she thought.

"Really."

The woman sounded ready to hang up, just like the last time she'd called. "I'm afraid so," Shirley said.

"I'd have to shift a few things. I'd prefer Thursday."

Shirley stared at Stanley's weekly appointment chart. He had nothing on Thursday, but she'd be damned if she'd cater to Von Cletan. She'd only seen her once, but something about her made Shirley want to piss her off. "Sorry," Shirley said. "It's Friday. Unless you'd like to wait until next week."

"No." A few seconds of silence ticked by. "I'll make the needed arrangements."

"All right. What is your address?"

"2000 South Sago Boulevard."

That address resonated in Shirley's head. Why?

"Did you hear me?" Catherine said.

"Yes. Just a moment." It sounded so familiar. A second later it came to her. The sneaky witch was trying to trick her. "That's the Sago Palms Hotel. I looked it up after you called the last time. I'm sorry. It's either at your home or not at all."

A loud harrumph filled Shirley's ear. She stayed silent, waiting.

"Very well." Catherine sounded exasperated. "19244 Bougainvillea Lane. I'll expect him at two."

"His fee is five-hundred dollars an hour. Cash only."

"I was told four-hundred."

"And he was told by several clients that he was not charging enough. From what we understand, he could easily get more."

"Fine. Goodbye."

"Wait, you haven't given me your name," Shirley said to the sound of the call disconnecting. She looked at the cell. "Well I *know* your damn name. You just don't know that I know. Hah." The dislike she held for Catherine Von Cletan quadrupled.

She shook off the negative feelings, hating what she and Stanley had to resort to. Smile and bear it, she thought. At least it was working. Part of her wished she'd been wrong. Sharing her husband with other women required a huge effort on her part every day. One day at a time. That was the way to stomach it. He loved her and no one else. And one day in the future, their debts would be paid, and their retirement would be secure again. Mack would hang up his tool belt for good.

The jalousies rattled as the door opened, and Shirley whipped around to see Stanley coming in. She raced to him.

"Hi, honey," he said. "Sorry I'm so late." He hugged her.

"What happened? You didn't call. I thought maybe you'd had trouble—gotten arrested."

"Arrested? No. Kind of held hostage, though. It was weird. She asked me to fix something."

"What?" Shirley pushed away from him. "Why?"

"I don't know. It was only a stripped screw from an air conditioning vent. It should have been simple. I thought it would take a minute at the most. Turned out to be a royal pain." He removed the tool belt and set it on the tile. "I think she's cheap. She counted the money twice before she'd hand it to me." Fishing in his pocket, he produced the four hundreds. "Here. No tip. Not even for fixing the AC vent. She must be one of those people who want to see what they can get for free."

"Like Morty." Irritated, Shirley went into the kitchen. With a quick snap of her wrist, she turned off the oven. "Dinner's going to be dried out."

"Also like Morty." Stanley chuckled.

She glared at him.

"You're not laughing," he said.

"It's not funny. You had me worried to death. Why didn't you call?"

"How could I? Ask to use her phone, then say, 'Honey, I'll be late for dinner?' I'm supposed to be single, remember?"

"You should have stopped at that gas station on the way home to call, like you did the last time."

"By then it was so late, I figured you'd pepper me with questions, like you are now, and I'd rather answer them here than standing at a pay phone. I'm heading to the shower." He walked up the stairs.

"I'm not the one who messed up here," she called after him. "You're not supposed to be an actual handyman, you know."

"Maybe we need to get *me* a cell phone," Stanley shouted.

Shirley stared at the empty landing above her in disbelief. He'd rejected Fletcher's offers to get him a phone and pay for the service plan more than a few times. She only agreed to Fletcher providing hers to make him stop bugging her. Then she'd let it sit in a drawer for a year before finding a use for it. She shuddered, wondering if Fletcher could somehow find out what she was using it for.

CHAPTER FIFTY-ONE

Stanley craned his neck to the left, searching for Von Cletan's driveway. Supposedly, it was hidden until the last second. An ear-blasting horn sounded, and a brilliant-yellow Lamborghini zoomed around him, throwing dust and leaves into the air. The man in the passenger seat flipped Stanley the finger as they passed.

"Christ. Like my nerves weren't already shot." Scanning the road ahead, he saw the side of a wall that could be it. A ten-foot-high fieldstone privacy wall. He slowed and put his turn signal on.

According to Shirley, he needed to be more careful with this client than all the others. Von Cletan was the richest woman in the town of Sago Beach, which was the richest in the state. Or at least that's what Dora told Shirley. She didn't know if there was a way to verify it. He'd made the argument—did it matter? What did he care? As long as she paid for the service.

Turning into the drive, he checked the number. It was the right house. A heavy, ornate iron gate awaited him about twenty feet further. The three-story stucco mansion was easily another hundred yards beyond that. Stanley whistled to himself as he took in the immensity of the estate. It dwarfed all its neighbors.

When he braked to stop at the call box, the gate began to open inward. He drove past the circular turnoff to the front portico, and continued past the main house to the garage. Although *garage* hardly described it. A huge building in its own right, it had five separate bays. From its size, he imagined Von Cletan might have the capacity to store her cars three deep inside. Above it, the second floor windows had curtains and flowers in the planter boxes. Apartments for her live-in staff, he assumed. He'd learned so much about the super-wealthy class, their privileges no longer shocked him.

The grounds seemed deserted. His recent education taught him that as well. Rich women gave their staff time off when they wanted the utmost privacy. And even those who lived on the grounds had better find something better to do, somewhere else to be.

He parked in front of one of the bays, took his tool belt from the passenger seat, and got out of the car. Putting it on, he glanced at the servants' entrance door—a face appeared, obscured by the pebbled glass, then went away. He walked to the door and rang the bell, remembering how Shirley warned him that Von Cletan hadn't left her last name. He was to play along until she introduced herself.

It opened within seconds. A gruff voice said, "Come in. Quickly."

He did and stood in a darkened anteroom. Adjusting from the glaring sunlight outdoors to the dimness inside, it took a moment before he could see her. She was about five-four, very rotund in the middle, with better than the usual fake-blonde hair, a stern expression of disdain, and blue eyes so focused he felt she could laser him in half at will. She wore a lavender suit with a round diamond brooch attached to the jacket. Her heavy perfume smelled familiar, but he never remembered the names of those things. She reminded him of his frumpy fifth-grade teacher, and he wondered whether the blue pill he'd taken would be enough to enable him to have sex with her.

"Ma'am?" he said. "I'm Mack. Very pleased to meet you." He did a subtle nod of the head.

"You're on time. I like that."

The raspy, low tone of her voice made her sound angry.

She left the anteroom and walked toward a winding staircase at the end of a hall, her low heels making a soft clacking sound on the beige marble floor. Stopping to turn and stare, she motioned to him. "Follow me."

He checked out the rooms on either side of the hall on his way. One had a stainless counter, another lots of glass-fronted cabinets stacked with dishes, and another filled with silver serving pieces, like the ones Shirley used at Thanksgiving. The house smelled like roses.

"This is the back staircase." She stopped at the first step. "From now on when you arrive, you'll let yourself in this way and report directly to my suite—where I'm taking you now. When you leave, you'll exit immediately the same way you came in. I have security cameras covering every area."

Duly noted, *your highness*, he thought, feeling insulted. He trailed behind her to the second floor, where she made a right turn into a huge room with furniture groupings and an enormous television mounted on the wall.

"Your living room's upstairs?" He regretted blurting it out the moment it escaped him.

"This section of the house is for my personal use only. I entertain guests in the public rooms downstairs."

They passed a few more closed doors, then she made another right into a smaller area with comfy-looking chairs, a desk, and a balcony with French doors. Past the balcony, Stanley saw the pale-aqua blue ocean and people playing on the beach.

She opened a pair of solid double doors on the opposite wall revealing her bedroom.

Cri-min-ent-ly, he thought, by the time you hiked all that way from the kitchen to your room, you'd be exhausted. "You must sleep well."

Giving him a strange look, she gestured to the chairs in the entry area. "Have a seat."

The fabric looked expensive. He removed his tool belt, placed it with care on the carpet, then sat.

"I think you should understand what I expect," she said.

"All right."

She sat opposite him, the suit skirt staying just below her knees, legs together, but not crossed. She had thick ankles.

"I'm glad you're an attractive man," she said. "It will make this easier for me."

"Thank—"

"Up until now, it hasn't been easy." She closed her eyes and put up a palm to hold him off. "I am quite a sensuous woman. My husband died some years back. I have certain needs. Seeing to those needs has been difficult. One gets weary of *going it alone* shall we say? Are you with me so far?"

"I believe so."

"Because of my position in society, discretion is not only required, but crucial. And although I certainly wouldn't do anything publicly, if you reveal anything about our encounters, even the fact you've met me, I do know the right people to make your life a living hell, and they wouldn't ask for a reason."

That was enough. Stanley stood and reached for his tool belt. "I'm sorry, ma'am, but this won't work. I don't like the implications you're making. You're acting as if I'm some scumbag low life. Money or no money, you can kiss my ass." Shirley was going to kill him, but too bad. "I'll let myself out. You watch me on your cameras to make sure I don't swipe your damned silver on the way." He stepped out to the main area.

"Wait."

He stopped, then turned.

Her face softened a bit. "Forgive me. I've been so battered all my life by those who want to take advantage of me, sometimes I forget there are decent people."

If she wanted sympathy from him, she wasn't going to get it. "Just the same, I don't like being treated like that. I still think we should forget the whole thing. Don't worry. I'll never tell a soul I was here."

"Please, don't go." She stood, then approached him. "I'd like to find out more about you. I'll pay you a thousand dollars if you'll simply sit once more."

A thousand dollars to sit? "Okay." As he sat, he wondered if she also threw money from the car windows for the fun of watching poor people fight for it.

"What's your last name?"

"I can't tell you that."

"And why not?"

"Mitzi, my . . . uh, my, the woman who arranges these things, says no one needs to know that. We need to protect ourselves, too. By the way, I don't know your full name yet."

"I'll get there. Mitzi. Yes." She walked to the balcony doors, then turned. "She's the business end of this. Your pimp, so to speak. Where and how did you team up with her?"

Relaying the made-up story was Stanley's weakest point, and he knew it. He pretended to study the outside view so he wouldn't look at her while he answered. "We've been acquaintances for years."

"Have you ever been married?"

"Yes. Once."

"Widowed? Divorced?"

"Doesn't matter. It's nobody's business."

"But you're all alone now."

"Yes."

"Please look at me."

He did, not enjoying this interview. None of the other women had grilled him, they only wanted him to do what they'd called him for.

"Your face is red," Von Cletan said.

"I don't like talking about what happened, and I don't see

why you'd care anyway."

She picked up a remote from the table nearest her, aimed it into the bedroom, and pressed a button. Soft jazz began to play. "I'm going to tell you this now, one time, on your first visit. Act like you're in love with me, every time you're with me. It's my fantasy. I want to be *romanced.* You will be well compensated if you can act the part. I've paid for company before, and it's been stilted. I felt cheap. I think your pretending is the only way I'll be able to really let go and experience the erotic pleasure I crave. Can you do that?"

Stanley stared at her, his initial reluctance ebbing. "Depends. Are you going to treat me like a potential criminal? I won't put up with that. I don't give a flying . . . uh, fig, how flipping rich you are. Not to mention you believing I'm pond scum isn't going to help me do my part."

"We're in agreement then. Please address me as Catherine when we're alone. If there is *ever* anyone else around, you will address me as Mrs. Von Cletan." She held out her hand to him. "I'd like you to dance with me."

He took her hand and rose. For a thousand dollars, he thought he could be a convincing actor. He put his arm around her bulk and began a slow dance.

"Hold me closer."

Tightening his embrace, he considered whether or not to tell Shirley about the romancing thing Catherine wanted.

She nestled her head into his chest, then gazed up at him. "Kiss me."

"I don't kiss my clients." Shirley had stressed that was an absolute no-no.

"I need a man who loves me. Even if it's a temporary charade. Do you understand? It's essential. I won't enjoy myself otherwise. If I don't enjoy myself, what's the point of you being here?"

Whatever squeals your wheels, lady, he thought. There was no way he'd tell Shirley any of it.

CHAPTER FIFTY-TWO

Catherine pulled her robe tighter, then crossed her arms while she watched Mack's car exit the driveway onto the road. The gate began its slow close, and she came in from the balcony. She felt as flustered as she had at seventeen. Butterflies whirled around her insides, and she couldn't decide whether to lie down, go for a walk, sing a song, or take a shower. Her mind raced with excitement. Concentrating on anything for more than a few seconds was impossible.

What a man. No wonder Leticia raved so about him. Catherine decided a shower might bring some calm. She did a twirl on the way to the bathroom. "You make me feel so young," she sang, then hummed the rest of it.

She hung the robe on the hook by the shower and, for the first time in months—well, years—took a good look at herself in the mirror. Mack hadn't seemed to mind the extra pounds. She stroked her stomach and closed her eyes. Her hands migrated to her breasts, then to her face. She touched her swollen lips. The kissing felt awkward at first, but by going slowly, romantically—as she'd insisted—it had built, and built, until exploring each other's mouths became an overwhelming need. He smelled like a man. He tasted like a man. They became like animals. Grunting. Moaning. And when his manhood rose against her bare skin, she gloried in the sexual power she'd always wanted to wield. *She* caused that. Lingering in the memory, she went back to bed and laid against the pillows, conjuring the thrill of how his touch worked in the exact right ways. The excitement, the chemistry had brought her to quivering. Actual quivering. Had he experienced it, too? Or—was it all acting, as she'd requested?

Sighing, she stopped, sat, and returned to the bathroom. It was too bad he was so far down the social scale. Perhaps raised in the countryside to simple folks? He didn't have the breeding necessary for her world. But, oh—if he did. She might snatch him up. With the correct tutelage, could he learn to be a gentleman? He'd never pass muster with her friends, though.

The poor man was clearly tortured by the past. What happened to his wife? Was it a tragic death? Had she left him for another man? The sadness she thought she detected in his eyes tugged on her heartstrings. One of her worst faults was being too compassionate with the unfortunate. She knew that. It was why she put up a tough front—otherwise, the risks were too great. She had duties and responsibilities commensurate with her station in life. Melting into a puddle and throwing money at individuals in the underclass would bring ridicule, and everyone knew it was no solution, anyway. Such ham-handed tactics only served to de-motivate them, thus making them even *more* dependant. Why, it would do more harm than good, and she didn't want any part of making their plight worse.

Mack was different from those people, though. She could tell. Eying her reflection once more, she admitted she hadn't felt sexy when he arrived, but afterward? She felt she would explode with raw sexuality. "Imagine how you would feel," she told the woman wearing the smile in the mirror, "if you lost twenty pounds. Imagine Mack's reaction, too." If she were more shapely, he wouldn't need to act—she could have him wrapped up like a personal present.

Whether or not their arrangement became a relationship—and that relationship either remained hidden or they went public—one thing was certain. She wanted Mack. Going back to the nightstand beside the bed, she took her Daily Dan from the drawer and dropped it into the bathroom waste can. She knew she could have Mack. She turned and reached for the shower knob, hearing her daughter's nagging in her head. "Muffy, darling, I think I finally found the motivation I needed to lose weight."

***

Stanley blew out a large breath as he parked in the townhouse's carport. As usual, he stowed the magnetic signs and his tool belt in the car trunk at the convenience store before re-entering Silver Sago Village. But what to do with two-thousand dollars in cash? The snotty woman had done a one-eighty once he'd completed his job. She insisted he take it.

Should he tell Shirley or hide all but maybe six-hundred? The third-degree he was sure to get scared him. He'd broken the rules, but that particular rich broad could change things for Shirley and him. Catherine said she wanted to see him at least twice a week, and using some of the extra money, he was to stop and bring flowers each time—to help her fantasy. From the way the woman carried on when she had an orgasm though, he figured she didn't need any more help. She'd screamed, grunted, moaned, and afterward, broke down and sobbed a little. He had to admit, the kissing got things moving, and he found himself getting lost in what he was doing. He'd come to reason that since he had to make love to big women, he might as well psych himself into it. He chuckled to himself—any port in a storm. Many ports. One hell of a storm. His tips were larger, and the clients now fought for the available time slots.

He made up his mind. He'd give Shirley six-hundred and hide the rest. Any extra from Catherine he'd set aside, let it pile up, and surprise his wife one day by announcing they'd reached their goal sooner than expected. What he had done to earn it wouldn't matter then. It would all be in the past. He separated six bills from the rest and stowed them in another pocket.

The front door swung open. Shirley, hands on hips, approached the car with a questioning expression. He smiled, slid from the seat, and locked up.

"Hi, honey." He kissed her on the cheek.

"What's going on? You were sitting in the car for so long, I thought maybe you'd fallen asleep."

"Nah." He took her hand and led her into the house. "You're a genius, that's all." He dug for the six-hundred from his pocket and handed it over. "The five-hundred, plus a tip. She seemed to like that I was on time." He rolled his eyes, hoping she'd notice and start to dig on Catherine. "Guess in her world, that's a big deal?" He went to the fridge.

"Was *the Von Cletan* as nasty in person as she sounds on the phone?"

His head hidden by the refrigerator door, he clinked some bottles around, then grabbed a beer. "I almost left. Right in the beginning. She was so, jeez, what's the word . . . imperial?" He closed the door and looked at Shirley. "That's it. Imperial. Hadn't done a thing but step inside the house, and she just about called me a thief. Said she had cameras in every room, so don't even think about taking anything." He twisted the cap off and took a big swallow.

"How rude."

"I was insulted and would have walked out right then, but I thought you'd kill me. Her being the blah-blah-blah-richest-most-important person and all that."

"And then what?"

"Aw, come on. It's the same old shit every time with them. They're so desperate for a man, it doesn't take much. It was nothing out of the ordinary, 'cept maybe she's in the worst shape of all of them. Thank God for those blue pills. We'd be out of business." He thought Shirley would love that point. Grinning, he took a step forward, then gave her a lascivious stare. "Have I told you lately that you are not only beautiful, but very sexy?"

Her face flushed.

"Tomorrow is *our* day," he said. "Don't make any other plans. I need a Shirley fix. I need it bad." He winked, then turned for the stairs. "I'm headed into the shower."

***

Shirley watched him disappear up the stairs. She felt awful about making him go to that horrid Von Cletan woman. It sounded like she was even more unpleasant than Shirley imagined. Yet, somehow, he'd managed to have sex with her and come back with a hundred more than their new fee. She shuddered, thinking of how unpleasant it must have been for Stanley, touching that disgusting woman.

CHAPTER FIFTY-THREE

Nina left the bathroom and walked to the bed with tiny, even movements, the reverberation of every step making her chest hurt anew. Sitting first, she lifted her legs one at a time onto the mattress, then shifted her weight to settle into the pile of pillows behind her. Between the implants, the swelling, and the voluminous bandages, her chest looked and felt larger than Dolly Parton's. She rested her head and took a shallow breath. Deep ones hurt too much. The plastic surgeon had told her the first day would be the worst.

"Mom? You here?" Mary Ann peeked in from the hall.

"Where else would I be? I can hardly move." She tugged the sheet higher over the giant sized pajama top she wore over the bandages. "Come in."

Her daughter flounced into the room. "Dad just called my phone. Said you didn't pick up on yours."

"I was in the bathroom. You didn't tell him, did you?" Nina stared at Mary Ann. Something seemed off kilter.

"Nah. I said you were outside in the yard somewhere, and you'd call him back." Mary Ann sat at the end of the bed. "While you were sleeping, Mrs. Asbury dropped off a cheeseburger casserole for dinner. I'm glad you made up with her."

Nina grinned. "Why? Because she saved you from making a meal for you and your brother tonight?"

Mary Ann stood. "Yeah, that's part of it. But you're not as crabby when you have her to talk to."

The pain medication made her foggy-brained, and Mary Ann's teeny and too-tight white shorts finally clicked in her head. "What are you wearing? You haven't left the house in that today, have you? And what do you mean, not as crabby?"

An exaggerated eye roll, followed by a monster sigh, came from Mary Ann. "Jeez, Mom. They're just shorts. Chill out."

"One, they look painful. I can see everything. Have you ever heard of *camel-toe*? Two, it's too chilly out for shorts. And three, wear those anywhere but in this house, and you're grounded. You look like a hooker. In fact, I change my mind. Don't wear them in the house, either. I don't want your brother seeing you in those. He's overcurious as it is about the female anatomy."

"Yeah, like he hasn't bookmarked porn sites." Mary Ann whirled around and headed for the door.

"What?" Nina called after her, then winced from the strain on her incisions. "Get back here." The idea of her thirteen-year-old son having access to such filth upset her. "Your father said he put some kind of filter on Charles' computer."

Mary Ann froze. "Mom, it's cool. I was only kidding. The little doofus probably doesn't even know what porn is. Can I go now? Oh. I forgot." She stepped closer. "Can Dustin eat here and hang out tonight? His parents are going to some fancy dinner."

Straining to remember, Nina conjured the image of a brown-haired teenager. "Dustin? Is that the one I met when I picked you up from the party last Saturday?"

"Yes."

"Tall and skinny kid?"

"There you go again." Mary Ann put her hands on her hips. "I don't make fun of your friends. You know, you shouldn't judge everybody else."

Nina shook her head. "I'm not judging. I was attempting to see if I had the right person in mind. Stop being so defensive." Over the past year, talking to her daughter had become an ever-widening minefield.

"Well, can he, or not?"

"Yes. It's okay. Does Dustin have boyfriend potential? I'm getting the feeling you really like him."

Mary Ann's face reddened, then she pivoted and left the room. "I don't *like* him." Her voice faded as she walked away. "God. Why can't I just have a friend? I can't believe you."

Sean had never been that moody. Nina assumed it was a hormone-crazed girl thing. It was exhausting to be around. She counted to ten, and another ten, then picked up her phone and called George. It went to voice mail. She wanted to sound cheerful. "Hi. Mary Ann told me you called. Sorry I missed you. Please call me back."

She noticed a voice mail icon on the screen and hit the button to retrieve it.

"Nina, I've got to make this quick. I'm heading into another set of seminars. I'll try calling later, but I know from the past, it'll get hectic." There was a pause. "Anyway, I decided to stay a few extra days. There's a brokerage group I'd love to get into, and they're meeting separately after the convention. They asked me to join in. I think it's a good opportunity. I'll probably be home by Friday? I don't know."

George's message ended there. Nina stared at the phone, tossed it onto the bed, and shut her eyes. Maybe it was for the best. She'd be better healed by the end of the week, so George's first glimpse of her new breasts would be a more enticing surprise. She'd be able to wear something to show off her cleavage without the remaining bruises showing.

The back door slammed. Charles's voice channeled up the stairs. "I'm home. When are we eating?"

The pantry doors banged shut. Dishes clattered. The

doorbell rang.

"I'll get it!"

The familiar sounds of Mary Ann dashing down the hall and the stairs made Nina smile. She remembered the nervous excitement of liking a boy at sixteen.

More noises—shuffling and whispers—then silence. Until Charles apparently entered the foyer.

"Gross," he said. "Why don't you just suck her face off, dude?"

"Shut up, you dork," Mary Ann said.

Nina fought the urge to yell, knowing the pain it would cause, and counted to ten again. She wished she could fast forward. The next five years promised to be a rollicking challenge.

CHAPTER FIFTY-FOUR

Stanley emerged from Leticia Basslebrook's bathroom to find her standing in the bedroom door to the hall, arms crossed. She'd already put her clothes on. Most times, she languished in bed afterward, and he let himself out.

"I guess you've got somewhere to go," he said. She'd hurried him through the sex. They'd finished in fifteen minutes—unusual for her. Normally, it took her longer than that to declare she was ready. He wondered if he'd annoyed her in some way.

"No," she said, "not going out." A sly smile crept onto her face. "I have a surprise. Follow me."

Surprises in his new business were never good. He sighed and dipped for his tool belt by the bed. His hand came up empty, and he did a double take. Getting on hands and knees, he swept his arm under the bed and, finding nothing, lifted the dust ruffle and peered into the dimness. "I could swear I . . . Huh."

He stood, scratching his head.

"Mack?" Leticia's voice carried into the room. "Come on."

"Can't find my tool belt," he called back, walking to the door.

"I have it. Here, in the dining room, with me."

Why would Leticia have it? He'd seen the formal dining

room before, but hadn't ventured in. He cringed, thinking she had something for him to repair. One more thing he wouldn't tell his wife. Listening to the increasing wrath of Shirley wasn't high on his list.

As he crossed into the room, the scene sank in. An enormous crystal chandelier shone with soft light. Candles glowed from the table and sideboard. At the far end of the rectangular table sat two place settings. At each, a silver dome gleamed.

"You're having company?" he asked. "Well, whatever it is you want me to do, tell me. I'll do it and get out of here as fast as I can for you." He figured since she'd paid him, he ought to at least give her a full hour.

Leticia chuckled, then spread her arms a lá Vanna White. "*You* are my company. Sit, please."

"I don't understand."

"I know it's early, but I'd like you to have dinner with me. Sit."

"I can't." Shirley would have a fit if she found out.

"I paid you the whole amount, didn't I?"

"Yes, but—"

"So if I choose to spend that time with you this way, does it matter?"

She gave him a look that reminded him of a reprimand in grammar school. He checked his watch. It was four-fifteen. He wasn't due to pick Shirley up from Paulina's until quarter after five. The woman had a point. It was her money and the same amount of time—did it make a difference? He didn't think so, but he doubted Shirley would see it that way.

"I'm not giving you your things until you dine with me."

His keys were in a pocket of the tool belt.

"I think you'll like what I had the chef prepare." Leticia approached, placed one hand on his waist and the other on his arm, and led him to the chair. "I'll bet you've never had anything this delicious before. He used to run the best restaurant in New

York."

He shrugged. "Okay. It's your dime." He sat, then scooted the chair in.

Letting a tittering giggle escape, she pulled her seat out. "I love your pedestrian humor."

Pushing his chair away, he leapt to his feet and moved to help her get settled.

"Why, thank you." She turned and beamed at him. "How gallant of you."

I wasn't raised with monkeys, he thought. Although he'd been accused of it before.

As he re-sat, he studied her face in the soft lighting. She really wasn't a bad looking woman. That devilish grin of hers—the one she always greeted him with—was growing on him. It seemed she'd lost a few pounds since they'd started the every Wednesday schedule, too. He wondered if he should say something.

Leticia lifted the silver dome covering her plate, set it aside, and gestured for him to do the same.

The moment he did, an incredible aroma hit his nose. He recognized a grilled filet mignon covered in a dark sauce, asparagus, and a mound of mashed potatoes. "I didn't think I was the least bit hungry, but this smells amazing."

She smiled. "I suspected a man like you would enjoy prime beef. Would you do the honors?" Her right hand waved toward an open bottle of wine sitting within reach to his left in a silver bucket filled with ice.

"Certainly." He lifted the bottle. Water cascaded from it onto the tablecloth.

"Use the folded napkin there. Normally, my staff would attend to us, but under the circumstances . . . You know."

Stanley nodded as he wiped the remaining moisture from the bottle and poured some in her glass, surprised when he realized it was red. "I thought only white wines were supposed to be cold."

"I prefer this one chilled. Pour some for you."

"Um." He thought fast. "I shouldn't drink. Doesn't agree with me." He returned the bottle to the bucket.

"That's too bad." She lifted her glass. "To a healthy, long life."

He held his water goblet up and moved it forward to clink against hers, but she ignored the gesture and took a sip instead. He set it down. Taking the knife and fork in hand, he carved into the filet. When the meat hit his tongue, the herbs and smoke flavor sensation wowed him. He finished chewing that first tender bite, put his fork on the plate, and tilted his head back until it rested on the top of his chair.

Leticia giggled again. "You approve?"

"I think I've gone to steak heaven. That is the best thing I have ever tasted."

Her eyebrows angled, and that grin came back. "The way I figure it, since you make me come with better orgasms than I've dreamed of, maybe I could please you with an orgasm of another kind. It's a pleasure to see you respond to it."

***

At five-thirty, he pulled into the lot behind Paulina's and grimaced when he saw Shirley sitting on the bench with her arms crossed. He'd left Leticia's as soon as he could manage after their meal. Shirley's body language spelled trouble. He popped another breath mint into his mouth to mask the garlic from the potatoes.

"Why are you late?" she asked as she slid into the passenger side.

"I stopped to use the bathroom at the gas station when I took the signs off the car."

She gave him a sideways look.

"How was work today?" he asked. "Any more rich or famous women stop by? Boy, Paul and Lance really know how to bring 'em in, huh?"

The look developed into a glare. Perhaps silence was better.

They rode to Silver Sago Village in an uncomfortable shroud of quiet. As soon as they got home, Stanley went to shower and brush his teeth. When he went downstairs again, Shirley was breaking up a mound of hamburger in the frying pan. She'd changed into shorts and a T-shirt.

"Cheeseburger-noodle casserole for dinner," she said. "I'm too tired to make anything else."

He sidled up to her and kissed her on the cheek. "Sounds great." Without warning, a giant burp escaped him. "Jeez. Sorry." He retreated a few steps.

Spatula in hand, she faced him with a disgusted frown. "Yuck. I'm standing in a cloud of garlic now. What on earth did you eat for lunch? I hope you didn't smell like that at Leticia Basselbrook's. She'll cancel her appointments."

No, she won't, he thought. "Pizza," he lied. "At a new place. Guess they use more garlic in the sauce. I won't go there again." He moved to the living room and the safety of his recliner.

A half hour went by until Shirley announced dinner was ready. His stomach was bursting from the food at Leticia's, yet he couldn't tell Shirley about it. He didn't know how he'd fit another meal in. He sat at their dining room table.

She plunked an enormous plate full of cheesy pasta, hamburger bits, and chopped onions and peppers onto the plastic place mat in front of him, then put a much smaller portion in front of her.

"This looks wonderful," he said.

"It's the same quickie thing I always make," she said.

Fake compliments weren't going to fly. He intended to divert her attention talking about her day, then hopefully, distract her—somehow—and dump his dinner.

After the filet mignon, his first bite of the cheeseburger casserole tasted cheap, with a gamey taint to it. He washed it down with water.

"You seem a little on the burned-out side today," he said. "Why don't you tell me about work? Might help to talk about it."

She swallowed. "Same old thing. It's hard not to resent the women with so much money. They don't have any idea what normal people go through. They complain about their butlers, their maids, about their chauffeurs. It's obscene. I'm so tired of it already." She shoved another forkful in, chewed quickly, then continued. "On top of that, Lance and Paul are still arguing over that empty storefront they're trying to fill. Sometimes, they're as clueless as the clients."

He patted her hand. "I'm bringing in more than we thought. You were right. In a few years, we'll be able to go back to goofing off."

"I hate what you're doing."

"Well, so do I." Except he didn't hate it anymore. The women were becoming friendlier. Some of them were really nice. The sex was getting better with all of them.

"Why aren't you eating?"

"Huh?" He looked at his plate, then her. "I guess I was more involved in listening to you."

She lowered her fork and gave him a hard stare. "You're not telling me something. I always know when you do that."

Thank God you don't, he thought, but decided he should tell her about the meal. He braced himself. "Don't be mad. Leticia Basselbrook made me have a dinner with her."

"She *made* you? What? Are you twelve years old now? That's ridiculous."

"Actually, she hid my tool belt—where I put my car keys by the way—and wouldn't give it back unless I ate with her. What was I supposed to do?"

Her eyes drilled into him. Her lips began to move, as if to speak, then clamped shut.

"She purposely made the sex part go fast." Stanley inflated his lifeboat of a story. Tell only as much as needed, he thought.

Shirley cocked her head. "Really? What does that mean?"

He looked at his plate. "We agreed not to share details that might make you picture it in your head. That was a smart decision. Normally, Basslebrook needs time before I can do what I'm supposed to. Today, she didn't care. Wanted me to get it over with." He resumed eye contact. Her face hadn't softened. "She reasoned that she'd paid me for the hour, what difference did it make how I spent that time?"

"It makes a difference," Shirley said. "She's changing the rules. You should have said no."

His lifeboat was about to be shot full of holes. "Actually, honey, I thought she had a valid point. It's her money. Do we really care how we get it?"

Shaking her head, she stood. "She likes you enough to eat with you? That's not good. You're much too easy. Why can't you stick to the rules we set up? Letting them believe you're becoming friends, or whatever this is, is dangerous. It could spoil everything."

"I don't remember any rule about not cutting short the sex and eating instead."

"Well, it sure as hell is a rule now."

"And getting my keys and tool belt? Was I supposed to search her house? That would've caused a worse problem." He stood, picked up his plate, and deposited it in the sink. "I'm sorry, but things we can't predict are going to happen."

"Maybe so," she said. "But I will find a way to reign in these haughty, *I can do whatever I want* bitches."

Stanley's eyes widened. "You don't use that word."

"If the shrew fits . . ." Her mouth curled up on one side. "I think I have an idea."

CHAPTER FIFTY-FIVE

Fletcher found a guest spot in the lot near Agnes' townhouse. She lived in a different section of Silver Sago Village from his parents. Maddy's Mercedes sat about ten spaces down. Although he arrived five minutes early, she'd beat him there. No surprise. She'd been talking about this visit to Agnes' studio non-stop since the two met in the coffee store.

He thought it was kind of cool, though. Maddy, who always seemed so in control, lapsing into serious *fan girl* mode. Agnes' unit appeared to be the same as his folks', but the carport was on the opposite side. He wondered why someone like Agnes, who Maddy insisted *must* rake in plenty from selling paintings, chose to live in the older and dumpier retirement village. There were so many luxury adult-only communities in West Sago Beach.

Knocking on the door, he heard a faint laugh. It sounded like Maddy.

"Come in," Agnes yelled.

He did and studied the living room, amazed at how different it was from his parents' blah, average, and boring place. Lavender walls—what could be seen of them—had painted canvasses hanging everywhere. Stacks of more canvasses, both painted and not, leaned against the walls wherever a gap in the furniture occurred. A blue-flowered sofa and two huge, cobalt-blue side chairs surrounded a gleaming stainless-based coffee table. They looked expensive. An enormous white hand sculpture, mounted on the wall behind the sofa, reached toward him. The look was funky and sophisticated at the same time. He wished his parents could be a little more adventurous, but they resisted anything new or edgy.

"We're back here." Agnes' voice came from the doorway behind the living room, where bright light spilled into the hall and bounced from a shelf of crystal objects, causing tiny rainbows.

He hurried in. The room had to be Agnes' studio. More canvasses, purple walls, and directional work lights with chrome, cone-shaped surrounds aimed at a center table. A blue cloth draped the table, and on the blue cloth lay a nude Agnes. She faced away from the door and toward a shirtless young man holding a paintbrush next to a large canvas on a massive wood easel. A huge mirror leaning against the far wall reflected the scene. It all registered a half-second too late for Fletcher, and he couldn't muffle the *aaghhh* sound in time.

"Jesus," Fletcher said. "You're naked." He covered his eyes and turned, tempted to run back to his car screaming about his retinas burning.

Maddy's melodic laugh came from the corner. "Told you."

Agnes cackled. "Yep. You pegged him pretty good. I never would have figured you for a prude, Fletcher."

"I'm not a prude." I just don't want to see naked old people, he thought.

"Then open your eyes and turn around," Maddy said. "Your face is bright red. Come on. Sit down. There's room on this loveseat for both of us."

Swiveling to his right, he saw Maddy with a huge smile on her face. He sat beside her and whispered, "You could have sent me a warning text."

"Hell no," she whispered back. "This was way too much fun."

"I'm nearly finished with Agnes for today," the young man said.

"Oh, thank you," Agnes said. "It's hard to stay in one position this long."

The man laughed. "Serves you right. Paybacks are hell, aren't they?"

"I'm so grateful you let me watch you work," Maddy said. "I *love* being near creative forces."

"My pleasure, pretty lady," the man said. "I am happy to be in the company of two such delightful beauties."

Fletcher wanted to know who he was, but couldn't stomach looking in that direction again. Instead, he surveyed the finished and unfinished canvasses hanging on the walls. Most were strange botanicals done in vibrant colors, but another caught his attention. A young man leaning against a stone column, gazing into a hilly distance while holding an apple. A young man who looked exactly like the guy now painting Agnes. A young man who was naked, and whose penis, shown at rest, was impressive enough to shame the best of the porn kings.

He dared a few furtive peeks at the guy for comparison to the painting. Sun-bleached blond hair to his shoulders, chiseled bone structure, dark-blue eyes, and a six-pack torso. It was him.

"Isn't that an amazing likeness?" Maddy said. "Agnes said she finished it last week."

"Where are my manners," Agnes said. "I'm sorry. Fletcher Nowack, this is Ronny Tate. He's here on a guest artist program from California. He's staying with me for a month." She gestured to her body. "This was his idea—doing the portraits of each other. But I have to say, I'm rather liking it."

"Nice to meet you, Fletcher," Ronny said. "The girls have been telling me about you."

And one of them, no doubt, making comparisons. Fletcher flinched.

"I have got to sit up," Agnes said. "Sorry, kiddo, we'll have to continue tomorrow."

Studying his fingernails, Fletcher heard the table creak.

"You're safe now," Agnes said. "All covered up."

Maddy elbowed him. "Stop that. Be polite."

He looked at Agnes, who had donned a fuzzy pink robe.

She smiled at him, then shook her head. "With some things, even when the apple rolls down the hill a bit, it's still not far from the tree, huh?"

"What's that supposed to mean? I'm nothing like my folks." He hated the mere suggestion that he fell into their hyper-conventional mode. "Because I'm not comfortable seeing women my mom's age in the nude?"

"Why thank you for the compliment." Agnes stood by the table and crossed her arms. "You know I've got at least fifteen years on your mother."

Ronny paused from wiping a thin brush. "A healthy body is beautiful in all its stages. Someday, you'll be older. I imagine you'll want whoever you're with at that time to think so."

Bite me, Fletcher thought as he watched Maddy's face light up with admiration.

"You have such well-developed sensibility," she said to Ronny. "If you don't mind my asking, how old are you?"

"Twenty-four." Ronny dipped a thick brush into a jar of mineral spirits and swirled it around.

"He's been selling his portraits since middle-school," Agnes said. "A real prodigy. When I found out he wanted to study with me, I was thrilled. Nothing like some young blood to add vigor, I say."

Fletcher cringed, his mind jumping into a deep and filthy gutter.

"I've always wanted my portrait done," Maddy said. "My way. My mother attempted to make me sit for a couple when I was a kid, but gave up. I wanted nothing to do with posing in a party dress. Your portrait of Ronny up there is remarkable, Agnes. I love the setting. Very reminiscent of Flandrin. The colors and skin tone are lovely."

“I thought the same.” Ronny moved from behind the easel and sat on the table.

“Who?” Fletcher wanted to punch Ronny-the-suck-up.

“That’s what I had in mind.” Agnes grinned. “How’d you know about Hippolyte Flandrin?”

“I minored in Art History,” Maddy said. “I saw a gorgeous work of his in the Louvre. It was titled *Young Man by the Sea,* if I remember right.”

“When were you there?” Ronny’s voice grew animated. “I went last spring. “Spent three days at the Louvre. Fantastic. Did you see Michelangelo’s *The Dying Slave*? Gave me chills.”

Maddy’s eyes widened. “Yes. It made me cry.”

Fletcher grew more wary and needed to steer the conversation away from common ground between Maddy and Ronny. “Agnes. What does Jerome think of you painting Ronny this way? Doesn’t it bother him?”

Agnes snorted with laughter. “Lord, no. He got a kick out of it. Says we need to hang it on his living room wall, on account of the fact he says it’s *exactly* what he looked like in his twenties.”

Maddy laughed. She seemed to be in heaven. Fletcher caught Ronny staring at her.

“I told him,” Agnes said, “you go on believing whatever makes you happy, slim. I’m not sure Jerome ever possessed a muscle in his life, but don’t tell him I said that.”

Ronny and Maddy chuckled. Crap, Fletcher thought, their bonding continues.

“Would you consider painting me, Agnes?” Maddy asked. “I’d pay you, of course.”

“I usually don't do people, dear," Agnes said. "Not my thing. But Ronny here, as you can see, makes even my old carcass look decent. With his talent and your beauty, he'll turn you into a goddess. He's here for two more weeks. I'd grab him."

Maddy stared at Ronny. "Would you? What would you charge?"

"I'm not sure that's such a good idea," Fletcher said.

"Why not?" Maddy's eyes drilled into him.

"Yes. Why not?" Agnes said.

Fletcher wasn't prepared with a reason. He couldn't say he didn't want Maddy anywhere near the boy with the wonder-dick. "I . . . I think you should look for a local artist. Because of the time. The time limit."

"Nonsense," Agnes said. "He'll have finished mine in six days total."

"Maybe seven," Ronny said.

"It'll be fine. You worry too much, Fletcher." Agnes sent him a pointed glare.

"We'd have to start soon," Ronny said.

"You'll do it?" Maddy stood, clasped her hands together, and beamed.

The boy wonder's brow furrowed. He stroked the stubby, sparse blond whiskers on his chin. "You do realize . . . I only do nudes."

Relief flooded Fletcher. He stood to join Maddy. "Well, I guess that's that, then. Too bad—"

"That's fine," Maddy said. "It's what I wanted anyway."

Fletcher gaped at her. "It is?"

Rolling her eyes, she sighed. "Always have." She winked at Agnes. "Maybe I'll give it to my mother as a birthday gift."

"No," Fletcher said. "No effing way you're sitting naked in front of junior here."

All three stared at him.

"Excuse me?" Maddy's face was dark pink and turning red in a hurry.

"He's jealous," Ronny said. "I've seen it before. Dude, I've painted so many naked babes. I don't sleep with them."

"I can attest to that." Agnes snickered.

"The whole idea is . . . It's . . . I mean, where did this come from?" Fletcher knew he had no argument. Blood rushed to his head, and he felt the veins by his temples begin to throb. "You should stop and think about it."

"Fletcher," Agnes said, "you're driving at night with no headlights."

"I'm a pro," Ronny said. "Besides, you're showing your lady you don't trust her. Be cool, man."

"Is that the problem?" Maddy asked in a terse voice. "You don't trust me enough not to fool around with an artist?" Her tone got angrier. "I see and talk to men every day. Gorgeous men. South Florida is choking with them. Yet somehow I've managed to not throw myself at them in fit of lust. Why aren't you worried about them?"

"Shit. I do worry. Every day." Fletcher gripped his head in both hands. "It's not that I don't trust you. I don't trust them." He pointed at Ronny. "He's not different. He's just saying what you and Agnes want to hear. He's a guy like the rest of us. And you're unbelievably beautiful. Trust me—he wants you."

"Pardon me," Ronny said. "Not to get in the middle of your lovers' spat, but don't speak for me. You don't know jack about me."

"Shut up." Fletcher fixated on Maddy. "I won't let you pose naked in front of him."

"Don't go there," Agnes said.

"Won't *let* me?" Maddy raised her voice. "Who are you? My father? I'm a grown woman. I make my own decisions."

"When you're in a hole," Agnes said, "stop digging."

"Not about this," Fletcher said to Maddy, ignoring Agnes. "This involves both of us."

"Like hell it does." She stared at him with hardened eyes. "*You* have nothing to do with it."

Agnes took Ronny by the arm and led him to the door. "We'll just be in the living room."

"Maddy," Fletcher said, "any guy would feel the same way. No one could stand the idea of his girlfriend laying naked, *naked,* in front of that phony for one minute, one hour, one day—much less a week." He grasped her hands. "C'mon, have some mercy on me."

"Don't project your weaknesses onto me. I think you're getting crazy about this because if our roles were reversed, you'd be tempted to play with the woman. Admit it."

He paused a second too long. "Not true."

"You are a colossal fool." She whipped her hands out of his. "I have zero interest in a man who doesn't trust me." Leaning toward the loveseat, she looped the strap of her purse onto her arm, then stormed from the room.

Fletcher followed.

Stopping in front of Agnes, Maddy gave her a quick hug and kiss on the cheek. "Thank you so much." She turned to Ronny. "Can we start tomorrow?"

A wide grin filled his golden-tanned face. "Sure."

"Great. I'll be here at nine." Maddy walked to the entry, opened the door, and exited.

"Wait." Fletcher hustled to catch up with her. "Please. Maddy, I—"

"Tell it to the door." Maddy closed it in his face.

"I tried to warn you," Agnes said.

Fletcher stared at the door, not quite comprehending how things went so wrong so fast. He glanced at Ronny.

The kid wore an obnoxious grin. He let out a long, low whistle.

"I knew I liked that girl," Agnes said.

"Me, too," Ronny said.

"Okay, asshole." Fletcher strode to the jerk and threw a punch. Expecting to connect with the kid's face, he didn't register an incoming blur fast enough. A crushing impact to his jaw, then pain, shocked him.

CHAPTER FIFTY-SIX

Shirley waved goodbye to Stanley as she opened the back door to Paulina's and entered.

"Shirley?" Lance stood in the hall wearing a puzzled expression while holding a doughnut on a napkin and a mug in the other hand. "You're an hour early, sweetie. Did you misread the time?" His face froze in alarm. "Unless. Oh, shit. It's not time to switch the clocks, is it? Dear God, please tell me I didn't screw that up *again.*"

"No." Paul's voice came from the office. "That's only in October and March. Hi, Shirley."

"Hi, Paul." Shirley smiled at Lance. "Didn't mean to kerfuffle you." She'd taken to using his quirky words when talking to him.

Lance sighed, took a sip from his drink, then a bite of his doughnut.

"I came early in hopes I could ask you two something," she said.

"Come in," Paul said. "Have a sit."

"Thanks." She went into the office. Placing her purse on the floor, she sat on the sofa opposite Paul's desk.

Lance plopped beside her. "This sounds mysterious."

Paul tossed aside the morning paper and looked at her

"What's up?"

Taking a deep breath, she began the speech she'd rehearsed. "It's in regards to the empty store you own across town. Please don't think I'm nosy, but you've been arguing about it in front of all of us."

Shrugging, Paul gestured her on.

"I thought up an idea that might help us both. You can't find a tenant who'll take the place as is, correct?"

"Yes," Lance said. "Because it's not in the most prosperous section of Sago Beach, they think they can dictate all sorts of things. Like they're doing us a favor by filling it up."

Encouraged, Shirley felt her anxiety lessen. "You know Stanley and I got ourselves in a pretty deep hole. And I am forever grateful to you for hiring me. It's been a godsend."

"Oh my stars and bars," Lance said, appearing horrified. "You're quitting."

"No." She put up her hands. "No. Well . . . maybe. Hear me out. My idea is to open a baby boutique. It's in the category of stores that people will seek out—when they're searching for a special shower gift or something different for a grandchild. A store that's a destination, not a *happen-by*, as you term them, Paul. There are a zillion old women in the Sago Beach area, let alone Palm Beach County, and what do they care most about?" Besides getting laid and plastic surgery. "Their grandbabies. Plus here, it's a one-upmanship thing. Price is rarely an object."

Lance set his mug and doughnut on the coffee table and cocked his head toward Paul.

Paul stared at her for a moment, then at Lance. "You know, it might not be a bad idea. You and Stanley would own your own business and rent from us."

"My thought," Shirley said, "was we'd be able to recover faster than if we keep working at regular jobs. We're in good physical shape, but personally, I don't want to work into my nineties."

"How much do you think you could pay in rent?" Lance

asked.

"Well, whatever we have would be needed for inventory. As for fixing the place up, I drove by and peeked in the windows. It wouldn't take much to make it look like a baby store, a lot of paint, really, and Stanley can pretty much do anything. He's a retired electrician, you know."

"You're saying you can't pay rent." Paul leaned back in his chair and formed a steeple with his fingers.

"Unfortunately—"

"Wait." Paul put up a silencing finger. "Maybe we can work something out. Give me a little time to think."

Lance grabbed his mug and stood. "Come on, let's let him stew it around. I need a refill anyway." He took her hand and helped her rise.

***

It was eleven-thirty. During the morning, Shirley tried to ignore two things. One, Paul hadn't responded about the store. She hadn't figured he'd jump right on it, but what if it took him weeks to decide? She *had* to rectify their out-of-control-women problem—and fast. Which brought her to number two. Stanley's second *appointment* with Von Cletan was scheduled at one o'clock. She tried to run around Shirley's rules from the get-go.

On her way to the stock room, Lance emerged from the office and closed the door behind him. He waggled his eyebrows, then gave her a thumbs up. "I think," he whispered, "he's going to go for it." He hustled to the retail area. "Vera? Got a question, hon."

Shirley's stomach did a flip-flop. What had she started? Disastrous ways for everything to careen down the toilet began a relentless parade through her head. It wasn't too late. Yes, it was. Sweat broke out on her forehead. With both hands, she braced herself against the wall and took a deep breath. "Don't dwell on it," she muttered. "It'll work."

Fifteen minutes later, Paul summoned her to the office.

"Shut the door, please," he said as she crossed the threshold.

She did, then turned. Had she detected an impatient tone in his voice?

He waved a hand at the sofa, and she sat, frightened that Lance had it wrong.

"You okay?" Paul asked. "You look like you're about to jump out of a plane."

"I'm fine." She manufactured a small laugh. "Don't be silly."

Paul picked up a couple papers from his desk and leaned forward to hand them to her. "Some notes I made."

Glancing at the top sheet, Shirley realized the typewritten bullet-point list outlined details. She glanced at him and smiled.

"We'll go through it point by point," he said. "But before we bother, see if you agree with the basics. You get free rent for one year. We examine the success and profit, if any, of your first year, then re-evaluate any rental fees. I know it takes some time to become profitable, so don't panic. I get a twenty-percent stake of the net profit. I'm not worried about you and Stanley, but lord knows what an accountant might do on your behalf. Therefore, my accountant gets to see everything."

"Um." She chuckled to cover her concern over hiding Stanley's illegal income. A big part of her plan involved finding a way to legitimize it. "You might recall, the last guy we trusted took our money to the Caymans. Can't we just use your guy from the beginning?"

"Sure. We'll work that out. If the business takes off, and you and Stanley make enough to retire again, then I get the first option to buy the business. Most importantly, do you understand that it may very well take years to turn it into a viable business?"

"Yes. But I think we've got a better shot at making up our losses by being store owners than by being hourly wage employees."

"I know you do."

Lance came in, shut the door, then sat on the sofa arm.

"One thing that I know won't be on this list," Shirley said. "It's kind of an unusual request. I heard you say in the past that the shop has a huge storage area? More than what's needed? That was what all the potential renters wanted—convert half that space to retail area?"

"You expect us to do that for you?" Paul's expression grew leery.

"No. Absolutely not. What I'd like to do is have Stanley add a wall back there and we'll make half of it his space."

"For?"

She snickered. "You're going to laugh. Stanley and I, we're weary of spending so much time apart. He'll help me in the store, of course, but we both get tired. Sometimes, elderly people just need a nap. We'll insulate the walls—my husband snores loud enough to vibrate the house—and he can rest up when he needs to. Or I can. We won't be able to afford employees, so between the two of us, we'll cover the hours that way." She gave him her best innocent doe-eyed expression. "Would that be okay with you?"

"Or maybe you and your gorgeous hubby could have a nooner." Lance's eyebrows rose, then his lids lowered. "When the moods hits."

Shirley laughed to camouflage her alarm. "Lance." She patted his arm and used her best *grandma* voice. "Of all things. Goodness. You are *so* funny. You're giving us old folks way too much credit. Just wait until you're in your seventies." Her face was flushing. "For heaven's sake."

"You've embarrassed her," Paul said. "Apologize."

CHAPTER FIFTY-SEVEN

Stanley put the Buick into park and grabbed the flowers. He'd gone to a real shop, not the Publix supermarket floral department, and bought the biggest bouquet of fussy-looking flowers they had. Huge, white blooms with strange pale-green, long, leafy things were peeking from a thick cone of lavender tissue paper. He hoped they would be all right.

As Catherine had instructed him, he didn't ring the bell, but let himself in the service door. The house seemed abandoned, like the last time. He walked past the warren of china and silver rooms on his way to the stairs, not daring a head turn. Her spy cameras wouldn't catch him so much as glancing into other rooms.

Mounting the stairs, he shifted the flowers so they'd be the first thing she saw. As he approached her private enclave, he heard music playing—Frank Sinatra. He knocked on the open French doors.

Catherine came into the sitting area from the bedroom with a big smile. She wore a wispy, low-cut, flowing dress. "Darling Mack." She glanced at the flowers and appeared surprised. "For me? Oh. They're lovely. Really lovely. How thoughtful of you."

She accepted the bundle and sniffed them. "Heaven." She placed them on the side table.

Not sure what to do next for acting his part, Stanley tried to recall how he courted Shirley so many years before. He opened his arms wide.

A huge smile erupted on Catherine's face, and she bounded into his arms. He enclosed her tight, and she sighed.

"Tell me how you've missed me," she whispered.

"I . . ." The words caught in his throat. He coughed to cover his hesitance, then forced himself. "I've been counting the hours until I would see you again." And not in a good way.

She put her head on his shoulder, facing him, and made a purring sound. "More. Tell me more."

"You smell really good." That was true. The soft powdery scent of her perfume was nice. He liked it better than the thick stuff from the first appointment.

"I bought it for you." Her left hand reached to his face, and her fingers stroked his cheek. "Dance with me?"

Frank had begun singing *I've Got You Under My Skin.* Stanley took her left hand, and they danced around the sitting room. She nestled in, pressing close, then grinding against him. Because of the blue pill, Stanley Junior responded to her body touching his right on schedule.

"Why Mack," she said, "is all that for little old me?" She gently pushed him back and batted her eyelashes. "Gracious."

Not knowing how much of her Scarlett O'Hara act he could take, he danced her to the bed, grateful that he wouldn't have to keep the flow of baloney talk going.

***

Fletcher put his laptop case on the granite counter and opened the fridge to get a beer. He picked an amber ale, opened it, and drank half in one go.

The doorbell sounded.

Setting the bottle down, he walked to the door and checked the peephole. Maddy stood there with a wide grin. Since his disastrous visit to Agnes' two days earlier, he'd called her and left messages. But only one per day. He was capable of learning from his mistakes, and that pleased him. She wore a loose, yellow, sleeveless dress. He shook his head, not eager for her to see his face.

"I know you're in there," she said. "I heard you get home."

He opened the door, swung it to the wall, and pointed to his jaw.

"Ooh," she said. "Quite a bruise. Love the green and purple colors."

"Told everyone at work that I fought off a carjacker. Thought the standard *ran into a door* wouldn't work. By the way, I'm sorry. Eight-thousand times sorry."

"So you said. May I come in?"

"I can't believe you want to."

She sauntered into the kitchen, stole a sip of his beer, and laughed. "Ronny's gay, you know."

"Yeah. Once they revived me, he and Agnes howled over that one. Guess I've got some insecurities to deal with." He came to stand in front of her.

"You think? Let me take a closer look." She traced a finger over his jaw. "Must've hurt, huh?" Her eyes flicked into his eyes for a second, then darted back to his bruise.

"Like a mother. Still does. The little show-off's a boxer, too? Figures. How's the portrait coming along?"

"Too early to see much detail, but I love the composition."

"That's nice. What's it feel like to pose naked?"

"Similar to skinny-dipping. Very free. At times, a bit chilly. If you hadn't made such a fuss, I might have talked him into doing the two of us together."

"Ah, no."

She kissed him on the tip of his nose. "Agnes is right. You're more like your parents than you realize."

"You've never met them. Believe me, I am not."

"From the descriptions you give, it sounds accurate."

"Trust me. They are the blandest people you'll ever meet. The only interesting thing about my mom is she's ambidextrous."

"See? That's different. And they named you Fletcher. Bland would have dictated a common Bob or Jim. I'm betting there's more to them than you know. Otherwise, your personality doesn't make sense. You're conservative in some ways—as you say they are, an example being embarrassed to be seen naked. Want to know something?"

"Sure."

"The penis on Ronny's portrait? It's an exaggeration. He swears he's normal, not that I care. Agnes super-sized it for him for fun. Ronny's having the canvas sent to Santa Barbara. He's going to hang it in his living room and watch people's reactions. He said after seeing the blow-up it caused between us, he can't wait." She put her palm on Fletcher's chest.

The kid was a sick son of a bitch, he thought, but said nothing. He felt her bare arms. "Speaking of chilly, you've got goose bumps. I'll go raise the temperature."

Taking his hands in hers, she said, "No."

She brought his palms up and placed them on the gauzy fabric over her breasts. Her nipples were stiff and protruding. His breath caught, and a stirring began. "Why, no wonder you're cold, miss. You forgot to wear your bra."

"What? Again? I wonder what else I've forgotten." With a seductive smile and lowered eyes, she put her arms around his waist.

Gliding his hands down her back, he brought them under her dress and cupped her soft and lovely bare bottom. He gently nipped at her neck, mindful of his bruise. "No knickers, either. My God, two days of going native, and you're a girl gone wild. You've got some nerve. You came here to seduce me."

"I figure I owe you."

While moving his jaw as little as possible, he teased her nipples through the fabric with his teeth and tongue.

She shuddered. "Wait. Doesn't that hurt?"

"Not enough to stop me. I'll manage. Now, why do you *owe* me?"

"I knew before you got to Agnes' that Ronny was gay."

He sucked on her left nipple through the thin fabric while sliding his fingers into the silky cleft between her legs. Slippery warmth greeted him.

"Unnnhhh." Her body quivered. "I didn't plan on withholding the info." Her words came between raspy breaths. "But you started the possessive rant—which you'll have to promise to never do again—" A moan escaped her. "I never dreamed you'd be Mr. Alpha Male and try to deck him. I'm sorry."

"You *do* owe me, then." The tightening of his pants became unbearable. "I'm running out of room here." He lifted her. "Come on. You can help me with a severe problem I have while I warm you up."

"Two birds. One extremely hard stone." She giggled.

CHAPTER FIFTY-EIGHT

Three weeks later, the bells on the new *baby* shop door jingled. Shirley looked up from her inventory list on the counter and smiled when she recognized Chad, the young UPS delivery guy, coming through the door with a big package.

"Morning, Ms. Shirley. The place is chilling fast," Chad said. "Got another one for you. Where do you want it?"

"On the floor in front of the register here is fine. How are you today, dear?"

"Super busy. Slammed." He set the box down, then approached her with his tablet.

Shirley signed on the window area, then studied the signature. "Huh. I'm getting better at this. Now it looks like I'm in the second grade instead of first."

He chuckled. "It's better than most of 'em." He headed for the door, then waved. "Guess I'll see you tomorrow."

"Probably." She looked at the return address on the box. It was from Cute Quilts. "Stanley?"

"What?" His voice carried from the storage room.

She crossed the sales floor and went through an arch in the rear wall that led to the former private rooms of the converted bungalow. The front store area occupied the former living and dining rooms. It was the perfect size for her purposes. Big enough to look like a real store, yet small enough that a minimum inventory made it appear fully stocked.

The kitchen, with still-functioning appliances, served as the office. Previous retail tenants made one large storage room from the original two bedrooms. In a fantastic stroke of luck, there were two bathrooms, one accessed from the hall, and the other would be completely private to Stanley's room. All she and Stanley had done to make Mack's lair was reconstruct the wall between the bedrooms—and insulate all of the walls. She hoped it would be enough to mask any sounds from the activities. A feeling of dread came over her, and she shuddered. The growing realization that Stanley would perform behind that wall with other women *while* she waited on customers, pretending everything was ducky-peachy, made her nauseous, and at the same time—angry.

She forced those emotions aside and went down the hall, stopping in the newly created doorway. Stanley's designated room was almost finished. In the middle of painting the last wall, he stooped with the roller to cover the bottom section in front of him.

"Ahem."

He turned and looked at her. "Yes, my dear?"

"You've outdone yourself. Good thing. The bed's being delivered by five."

"Great. I can take a nap after that. I'm pooped."

"Uh-uh. Those quilts I ordered came in. I need you to hang them for me." Bells jangled. "I'd better go see who that is. Let me know as soon as you finish with the paint." She hurried toward the retail area.

"Yoo-hoo. Hello?"

Recognizing Lance's voice, she answered, "Here I am." When she emerged from the back and saw him and Paul, she smiled.

Lance held a potted white orchid tied with a green organza bow. His eyes scanned all four walls, then landed on her.

"Here." He handed her the orchid. "I cannot believe how quick you and Stanley were able to whip this place into shape."

"What a beautiful orchid. My gracious. Thank you." She accepted the plant and placed it on the register counter. "It's like I told you. We're making do by using the racks and shelves left behind by the last tenant. Paint makes everything different. And keeping the sales floor this size helps our meager inventory look like more."

Paul nodded. "I love the baby colors on the walls." Pointing to the unadorned pale blue rear wall, the one shared by Stanley's *napping* room, he raised his eyebrows in a question. "Kind of bare over there, though, isn't it?"

"Funny you should say that. See what came in?" She grabbed a box cutter from the counter and opened the carton. "I predict these will sell like crazy. They'll be displayed on that blue wall." She took one of the blankets out and unfolded it.

"They are precious." Paul walked to the wall opposite the counter, where a floor-to-ceiling shelving unit held stuffed animals. He ran his hand along the edge of a shelf. "This is the same nasty old piece?" He whistled. "Hard to believe."

"Stanley did have to sand it first."

Right on cue, a muffled thump came from the back.

"Crap," Stanley's voice boomed.

"Our Stanley is here?" Lance's face lit up. "I'll go see if he's okay."

"I'm sure he's fine," Shirley said, but Lance was already through the arch. She stared after him.

Paul returned to where she stood and tilted his head. "You look concerned."

She hesitated, not knowing how to explain the bizarre thought that had hit her. "You don't think . . . I mean, is it possible . . . No. Never mind."

"What?"

"I'm being silly. Lance adores you. I had a ridiculous thought that perhaps Lance might have a little crush on Stanley."

Paul laughed. "Nah. That's not it. Yes, Lance is a notorious flirt, and he does think your husband is *gorgeous.*" He imitated Lance's inflection on the word, then rubbed his chin. "I am beginning to think he may have some unresolved daddy issues, though."

"Thank God. That's a relief."

He gave her a confused look, but before she could clarify what she meant, the bells jangled again.

Twisting to see who-the-hell-else was *just dropping by,* Shirley froze when she saw it was a uniformed Sago Beach policeman.

"Good," Paul said. "Right on time. Come on over here."

The cop nodded. "Hey, Paul." He had a deep and gruff voice. "Can't believe you finally got someone in here. I'm tired of checking on an empty building." He shook hands with Paul, then looked at Shirley. "You must be the new shop owner."

"Shirley, this is Jim. This is his beat. I've asked him to be especially thorough when he drives through the neighborhood."

Swallowing what felt like rising bile, Shirley gave him a tepid smile. "How wonderful." Jim was in his mid-fifties, had bushy black eyebrows with random wiry gray hairs protruding, a huge nose, and a no-nonsense expression. He didn't seem the kind of guy to overlook an indiscretion—or a *teensy* violation of the city's vice laws.

"You need to meet Stanley, too." Paul gestured toward the arch.

Jim started that way, and Paul followed him while giving Shirley a grin and a thumbs up.

Her fake smile dropped the instant they disappeared through the doorway. "I feel sick," she muttered. Her mind zoomed into hysterical panic mode. A cop paying close attention to their store was not what they needed. How could they discourage him from being too concerned with them? She and Stanley had to convince him that overdoing his vigilance could jeopardize the other businesses that needed him so much more—like the two quickie food marts. It would be smart to devise a signal system to let Stanley know if trouble approached. Maybe he could install a warning buzzer.

The sound of affable male voices roused her from the thick cloud of worrisome threats circling her head. The men were talking football and moving from Stanley's room. She prepared her phony pleasant face, but they went past the arch and into the kitchen. She recognized the whoosh of the refrigerator door opening.

"Okay," Stanley said. "I've got Bud, Coors, and one of those fancy ales my son keeps buying me."

"I'll take the fancy ale," Lance said.

"I'm shocked," Jim said, with sarcasm. "Got any of those frou-frou parasols to put in his?"

Lance laughed. "Not since you hogged them all at the last Christmas party."

"His team did win the umbrellas versus swizzle sticks war," Paul said.

"I claim Stanley for our team," Lance said in a rush. "For next year."

"Not fair," Jim said. "A clear violation of the team selection rules."

"We don't have any rules," Lance said.

"We do now. My shift's over. Give me a Bud."

Oh, no, no, no, Shirley thought. Stanley's making friends with the cop. She shook her head in disgust. How thick could he be?

CHAPTER FIFTY-NINE

Early Friday evening, Nina admired her new breasts in the bathroom mirror. They were gorgeous. Perky. And bigger than she thought they'd be, but not anywhere near as ridiculous as Fletcher's ex-girlfriend's. Although the bruising healed within the first ten days, they'd stayed painful much longer. George still didn't know about them. It worked out well that he'd returned from his Las Vegas trip a week later than planned because he missed seeing her in bandages. She'd worn baggy sweatshirts since then. His not noticing anything different fed her simmering discontent, but she knew that would change soon, and it worked for her ultimate goal. When she presented her enhanced look to him, she wanted it to be a surprise—and to take full advantage of it. That meant the pain had to be completely gone. And it now was. Fantasies about a romantic night of ravenous lust between them kept invading her mind.

Mary Ann's and Charles' silence on the matter cost her new smart phones for them. Both kids were spending the night with friends. Nina had dinner made, the table set for two with candles, and new black silk and lace lingerie. The anticipation made her antsy. She checked the time. Six-fifteen. George said he'd be home by seven. It was time to get dressed and perfect her make-up.

She put on the bra and panties, then inspected herself from all angles in the mirror. "Surrender, George, because I am one hot mama." Picking up a bottle of Chanel, she dabbed the perfume behind her ears, on her wrists, and slathered a triple-dose between her breasts. The perfect black dress waited on its hanger on the back of the door. She slipped it over her head, shimmied into it, and zipped the back. Her new cleavage looked amazing in the low-cut V-neckline.

Finishing with a touch of Outrageous Red lip stain, she decided she was ready. Defying her, a nervous knot of doubt formed in her stomach. What if George didn't respond the way she hoped? With an authoritarian air, she knocked that thought out of existence, refusing to allow the possibility, and went downstairs to the kitchen.

She heard the garage door open while lighting the candles. Running into the kitchen, she tossed the box of matches onto the counter and took her practiced stance several feet from the back door.

The trundling sound of metal told her George had hit the overhead door button. Any second, he'd be turning the knob and walking in. She bit her lip, then stopped and licked it instead.

The brushed stainless knob turned. The door opened. George appeared, his tie off and bunched in his hand.

"Hey there, handsome." Nina used the sexy voice she'd practiced. She lowered her eyelids halfway and stared out from under them. "Feeling adventurous?"

"What?" George seemed dazed. It took him a moment to study her, then his mouth formed a weird grin as his eyes targeted her cleavage. "Got yourself a push-up bra, huh? You're not looking too bad, Nina. What's the occasion?" He blanched. "Crap. It's not our anniversary, is it? I'm sorry. I've been so busy that—"

"No," she snapped. "It's not." She calmed the instant annoyance she felt. "I made your favorite—stroganoff. There's a bottle of good red aerating, and dessert . . ." She gestured to her chest. "Is me. What do you think? Big difference, huh?"

He seemed confused. "Yeah, I said you look nice. But, I have to go out later," he glanced at his watch. "In a couple hours, actually. We're checking out a building for a night club. Need to see what kind of clientele gathers around that area on weekend nights. You understand. Food smells great." He set his briefcase down and made his way toward the stairs.

"No." Nina pivoted and followed him into the front hall. "I *don't* understand, and neither do you." She stopped, unzipped her dress, then pulled the top part to her waist. "Look at me," she yelled.

He swiveled, with impatience on his face. A second later, his expression changed to wonder. "That's one hell of a bra."

Finally. She had his attention. "It's *not* the bra." She unclasped the front-closure and pulled it away from her breasts, dropping it on the floor and enjoying the huge gasp that came from him.

"What the hell?" He stepped closer. "When did you do this?"

"While you were in Vegas. I wanted it to be a surprise. You like them?"

Reaching to touch her, he shook his head. "They're spectacular. I'm flabbergasted." Using both hands, he caressed them.

A shudder of excitement coursed through her.

He rolled her nipples between his fingers. "They feel real."

"Good." She shivered. "Very good. Keep going." Her downtown pulsated with her pounding heart.

"Damn, Nina, this *is* a surprise. I like it." Panic flashed through his eyes. "Shit. Where are the kids?"

"Spending the night elsewhere."

"Excellent." Putting his hands on her shoulders, he gently pushed her onto the carpet.

She gasped. "Here? In the front hall?" They'd never done it anywhere but the bedroom.

"You said you wanted adventure."

"But the carpet—"

"Who cares? You'll have it cleaned for the millionth time, only this time—it'll be dirty."

***

Nina awoke and sensed it was past her normal six-thirty wake-up time. She reached for George beside her—and felt empty sheets. Maybe he was making coffee. Her brain kicked into gear.

George had gone out after their lovemaking, taking a couple bites of stroganoff on his way out the door. He promised he'd get back as early as he could. Now Nina wondered how she'd slept through his return *and* getting up that morning.

She felt wonderful. Sexy. Happy. Horny as hell, too. More. She wanted more. "Honey?" she called, hoping he'd hear her downstairs. "Forget the coffee. Come back to bed." Closing her eyes, she rekindled a vision of the best sex she'd had in years. It worked. The boob job worked. Fletcher's whore of a girlfriend was right. Big boobs were a power trip. George had practically whimpered.

Where was he? "George? I really need you to take care of . . . of a *problem* I seem to be having."

Hearing nothing, she began to push into a sitting position, realizing something felt strange. Her chest felt off-balance. She touched her breasts, glanced down, then screamed. Her left breast was now flat, its skin hanging like a deflated balloon beside her ultra-inflated right one.

She screamed again. "George. Christ almighty. George!" She bolted to the bathroom mirror. The left one looked like an empty wrinkled sack, its nipple bent and sagging against it like a dead flower stem. Grabbing her robe off the hook, she put in on as she dashed downstairs.

"George?" She went through the kitchen to the garage. His car wasn't there. Squeezing her eyes shut in fear and frustration, she slammed the door. "Okay. Calm down." She opened her eyes, walked to the table where her purse sat, and found her phone.

George's voicemail picked up. "It's me. Where are you? Call me immediately. I need you. Now. Right now." Tears dropped onto her cheeks as she placed the phone on the table, then fished for her wallet. Her plastic surgeon's card was right where she'd left it, behind the Visa card she'd used to buy the expensive lingerie.

It was Saturday morning, so as she expected, she got the answering service. When she explained what happened, the operator repeated what she'd said at the beginning of the call—she was part of the service, not part of the doctor's staff. "Well, it's a goddamn emergency," Nina shouted, "and I don't care where the hell the damn doctor is. You get a hold of him and have him call me ASAP, or I will sue his ass."

She took a deep breath and dialed George again. Still the voicemail. "Jesus, George, call me. It's an emergency. Call me!"

Putting the phone on the table, she dropped her head into her hands and let the tears flow. Where the hell was he? Their magnificent night together now seemed so distant. Actually, it wasn't a night together at all, was it? It was a few hours. Then he went out. Was it really work-related this time? Since his job did entail entertaining clients at night—and always had—she couldn't be sure. Her hopes for a new beginning began to crumble away. An utterance he'd made during the sex came back to her. Something about Mary Ann? It was at the height of things, while crazed with her rising orgasm, but she'd heard it nonetheless. Was he worried about their daughter? Such an odd time to be bothered by the kids. Maybe she'd heard wrong. Maybe he said *marry*, not Mary. Marry something? Did that mean he said he was happy he married her?

She lifted her head and dialed. Voicemail. Again. She disconnected. Then dialed and disconnected. She'd repeated the action several times. In the midst of waiting until the third ring to end one more call, the phone rang and startled her. It was George.

"What is the matter with you?" he said in an impatient voice. "I'm here at the office with a client."

"Oh, George." She couldn't stop the sobbing. "It's awful. I woke up and my left breast is gone."

"What?"

"My breast. It's not there. It's like all the saline drained out of it."

"That's ridiculous. Can't happen. You took a stupid sleeping pill again, didn't you? Have some coffee and wake up a little."

"I'm telling you, it's disappeared. And I didn't take anything. I didn't need to, you wore me out, remember? When I woke up and you weren't there—"

"Yeah," his voice lowered. "I'm sorry about that. I, uh, fell asleep in my car. Drank too much with the buyers. Decided I'd sleep for a bit before driving home, then next thing I know, it's freaking morning, and I had an appointment at nine. So here I am."

"You need to come home and help me."

"Help you do what? I can't do anything about it. Call the doctor who effed up."

"I did. His service is supposed to be finding him."

"Great. So you're covered. Look, I've got to go. There are people waiting for me in the conference room. I'll call you later."

She stared at her phone. He hadn't even come home. After that wild sex? She exploded into a crying jag.

CHAPTER SIXTY

"I simply won't go." Catherine, in a ivory silk bathrobe, crossed her arms and glared at Stanley. "The very idea of having to travel to you is preposterous. To some tawdry, disease-infected bedroom in the back of a store? As though I were common trash, skulking around? And it's a *baby* store? That's ludicrous. Horrible. We'll have to end our alliance."

"If that's the way you feel," Stanley said, "there isn't much else I can say."

"You said you liked that I was thinner now. You called me voluptuous."

Cringing, he recalled saying something like that. She *had* lost weight. He pocketed the six-hundred and headed for the bedroom suite doorway. It was their sixth appointment pretending *Mack* was courting her, and the first time she'd given him less than a thousand. "It's been a pleasure, Mrs. Von Cletan."

The use of her formal name seemed to startle her. "Mack." Her voice sounded shaky.

He turned.

Uncrossing her arms, she held them out to him. "Tell me you feel something. That you aren't just acting. I *know* we've connected on a deeper level. I can sense it. The past six weeks have brought such a passionate awakening—for both of us."

Not wanting to hurt her, he nodded. What difference would it make at that point? Their playacting was over. Let her believe what she wanted. A white lie wouldn't do any harm. "I'm sorry we won't see each other anymore."

"That bitch," Catherine said. "Mitzi. What is the hold she has over you? Why does she care if you make one little exception for me?"

"Whoa." Angered, Stanley held up a hand. "Do not call her names." Realizing his words came out too strong, he softened the next ones. "I owe her a lot. Without her, I wouldn't be able to make this work." Thinking fast, he added, "In fact, without her, I'd have never met you."

Catherine smiled. "You *do* care. I thought as much." She approached him.

"I'd better be going." He proceeded through the hall, past the fancy rooms to the back service staircase. Behind him, he heard her padded footsteps on the thick carpet.

"Mack."

He increased his speed. "It's best if we don't talk anymore."

"Wait." She kept up with him. "Wait, please."

Stopping, he twisted to see her halt a foot away from him. She looked like she'd cry any moment. Christ, he thought, what the hell?

"This is difficult for me." She reached for his tool belt and unbuckled it, laying it on the floor beside them, then unzipped his jeans, glancing up at him with glistening eyes. "I don't like to be the aggressor."

"What are you doing?" he asked.

"Something I should have done a long time ago." She fondled his crotch, then pulled his underwear out of the way. "Something to remember."

In a mild state of shock, Stanley's brain went numb.

Catherine got on her knees and put her mouth on Stanley Junior.

"Jeezus," he said. "I'm seventy-four, woman. I don't think that's going to do what you seem to want it to. Twice in an afternoon? I mean, I'm flattered, but . . . "

Truth was, more than flattered. Other than verbally complaining, he didn't want to stop her. He couldn't remember the last time he'd received a blowjob.

"We'll see what happens," she said and went back to work.

The apprehension soon turned to amazement as he felt himself rising again.

***

"So," Shirley said. "Is the Von Cletan going to conform to our rules or not?"

"I doubt it. She sure wasn't happy about it." Stanley shoveled another bite of his dinner into his mouth. The less he said, the better. Catherine's second act not only worked, but it rocked him. She'd claimed she never done it before, but he had to doubt that, and her enthusiasm made it exciting. Very exciting. Hidden talent.

"With or without her, we'll have enough clients." Shirley shook her head. "I'll be glad in a way, if she won't go to the shop. She's been a pain-in-the-neck and word about you is spreading. It won't make any difference. Such an unpleasant person. I really do feel bad making you see her. It must be awful for you."

Better to say nothing. He nodded, chewing and remembering.

"Your face is flushing," she said. "You feel all right?"

He almost spit out his food. "Fine." He swallowed, then cleared his throat. "Fine."

"I think Fletcher has a new girlfriend," she said.

"Oh?" The change of subject was a huge relief.

"Edna thinks she saw him with a pretty blonde at the movie theater last Saturday. I asked him, but he won't discuss it. I sure hope it isn't some young bimbo again."

"Edna could be wrong. She often is." Stanley finished his meal and pushed his plate away. His naked left ring finger caught his attention.

"True. And she needs new glasses. Still, I want him to go back to Janice. It would be so much better for the children. I know I say this too much, but thank the lord Nina's marriage is so stable. Our daughter is a bit on the controlling side, but at least she uses it to manage her own family."

"A bit?"

"All right. A lot."

He murmured vague agreements while she chattered on, his mind preoccupied with the bizarre turn of events in his life. And Catherine's surprising ability. And how in blazes was Shirley able to act like everything was normal? To gloss right over the giant polka-dotted rhinestone elephant in the room every day. He admired her for that. He studied her face, her mouth, as she spoke. She seemed to be thinner, almost too thin.

"Why are you staring at me like that?"

"Huh?" He realized she'd stopped her chatting.

"You're looking at me in a funny way."

He thought fast, then grinned. "You're beautiful."

A huge smile formed on her face. "You know, I needed that. I get so worried sometimes."

"I love you, Shirl." He reached for her hand and caressed her fingers.

"I love you, too. I'm looking forward to *my* appointment day." She pulled her hand away, piled his plate on top of hers, and shoved her chair back. "We won't talk business then." She stood and carried the plates into the kitchen. "Right now, we have to. With the store opening tomorrow, there's a ton to go over tonight."

"I'm not really understanding why we're not having a grand opening or telling the kids and our friends about the store. They're going to find out eventually anyway."

"Yes, I know they will. Keeping it quiet for now gives me more time to refine our story. Work out the kinks. Lance and Paul think it's because we're starting on a shoestring—no money for advertising, parties, etc."

"That part is true. We're less broke, but nowhere near where we were." He brushed aside the vision of the stack of hundreds from Catherine's overpayments. It was seven-thousand above what he'd handed over to Shirley.

"I want to see how getting your appointments in and out without raising suspicions works before we draw any added attention to ourselves. Don't forget, I have to wear my wig and answer to Mitzi while I'm there. Your clients think that's who I am. I'm afraid my cover story for that isn't good enough yet to fool Lance and Paul, and your new buddy—Jim-the-cop, much less our family and friends. How would we handle it if Dora, Agnes, or God forbid—Edna—decided to start dropping by on a regular basis? We've got to be prepared for that."

"I'm beginning to think the store is a mistake."

"No, it's not. Those horrible women make it impossible otherwise. Hiding your keys and tool belt until you had dinner with her? That was beyond manipulative. Making you fix things? Wanting to take you shopping for clothes? To Vegas? It's crazy."

Stanley blanched at the last reference. That was the wackiest of his clients, Drucilla Lavender. Insisted that he needed a new wardrobe, and if he went shopping with her, she'd take him to Vegas for a weekend. That earned her a stern warning from Mitzi that Mack would no longer be available to her. Women.

Returning to the table with a plate of chocolate cookies, Shirley placed them in front of him. Stanley grabbed one and popped the whole thing into his mouth.

"There's something else I want to ask you," she said.

He couldn't respond, so he eye-gestured for her to continue.

"I did reserve one spot a week for Von Cletan, but I'll have someone else penciled in there by tomorrow. You know I can't stand that woman. I have one appointment every weekday for you at the store for the next three weeks. We're full up. That's twenty-five hundred a week. We're now getting calls wanting to be on a wait list. A wait list. Can you believe it?"

"I'm not doing it on weekends," he said. "No way."

"I don't want you to. That's my time. But . . . is there any way you could do two appointments in a day? Maybe two or three days a week?"

Staring at her—stunned—he thought. Some of the women were fun in bed, but with most of them, it was a job. Keep stroking and poking until they'd had enough. Pretending he was as excited as they were? The idea of having to do that twice a day?

"Stanley?"

"I'm considering. I don't think, even with my blue pills, that it can happen. Remember when we tried it? Nothing."

"But . . ." She frowned. "You said that was because you'd actually had an orgasm that day. That it wasn't usual."

"We're going into that weird territory we said we wouldn't talk about."

"I know. I know. I need to understand this, though. Are you saying you have orgasms now with all of them?"

He knew how he phrased his answer would affect everything. "As I explained before, even though I do think of it as an acting job, I would rather not be doing what I'm doing—in my head, mind you. I *do* have a healthy male body. And my healthy male body, once things get going, doesn't understand that logic. I can't fight eons of evolutionary human behavior."

Raising her eyebrows, she smirked. "You're saying they all get a squirt now?"

Locking eyes with her, he dared a chuckle. "You're making light of this?"

"I'm resigning myself to believing you're human." She lifted a cookie from the plate, stared at it, then snapped it in two.

"Honey, I swear, it does not happen every time. When it

does, it surprises the hell out of me. What I'm saying is, it's not a predictable thing. A second appointment on a given day could be a total washout."

"Hmmm . . ." She bit into a cookie half. "I've been doing some research."

"Uh-oh."

"There's a pump-ring thingie. With it, you can make an erection any time you want. Doesn't matter if you're not interested. Doesn't matter if you've already done it once. You could stop taking the pills—which are not good for your eyes or your heart. We need to go back to the urologist to get you the pump thing."

CHAPTER SIXTY-ONE

"You know—I've kissed way more than my share of toads."

Fletcher, emerging from Maddy's bathroom, stopped. She lay on her back, her head propped by several down pillows in ivory silk cases, and that shining blonde hair fanned out behind her. Tan lines revealed how tiny the bikini she'd worn to the beach that morning actually was. She was exquisite.

"Did you hear me?" she asked.

"What? No princes?" He sat beside her, caressed her face, then leaned in to plant a gentle kiss on those perfect lips.

"Only a couple."

"I don't care." She may very well have kissed royalty. It wouldn't surprise him.

"You say that now."

He picked up her left hand and ran a finger from the tip of her ring finger to her elbow and back. "I'll say it forever. If you'll let me."

Her eyes widened.

"I love you, Maddy. You're everything I've ever wanted. Smart. Beautiful. Won't take a moment of shit from me, either. Maybe that's what I've needed all along. Just didn't know it."

A teardrop welled, then dropped from her right eye, and she smiled. "I love you, too."

He moved to the other side of the bed and nestled beside her. "You know my track record. It isn't very good. But in my defense, I did believe I loved my exes."

"What makes you think this is different?"

Her voice was calm, not challenging. He felt he could be honest. "The way you asked that, for starters. You don't sound upset or jealous." He kissed her neck. "While I was with Lauren, Janice . . . and assorted others, if I saw a hot woman giving me *the look*, I'd feel some serious lust. It was hard *not* to find a way to get away from who I was with. Like it was a contest. Could I get her number and hook up with her later? I mean, it was kind of crazy. All I could think of was nailing her. I—"

"Stop." Maddy placed her hand over his mouth. "Enough. I get the idea."

He took her hand away and held it. "See, but you don't. This is the most amazing thing. Now that I'm with you, when somebody hot shows me she's interested, the first thought I have is—*yeah, in your dreams. I'm with her.* Meaning you. Mentally pointing at you."

"Really. You're not attracted to these other women?"

"I didn't say that. I'm still a guy who appreciates a good-looking woman. But that driving need . . . I guess it was a challenge? It isn't there. I'm happy. I only want you. For your mind and your body. There's something about the way we *fit* together. You're my own custom-made landing place. Warm and soft and wet and hugging me perfectly. I'm consumed with desire for you. You're all I want."

She giggled. "What's that I feel against my thigh?"

"Uh-huh." He pulled her on top of him.

***

"I don't believe it, Mother," Maddy said several hours later. "You've lost weight."

Catherine couldn't stop her broad smile. "You noticed."

She motioned for Maddy to enter her downstairs study.

"How could I not? Has it been that long since I saw you? Stand up. Let me see."

Rising from behind her desk, Catherine walked toward her daughter.

"Turn around once."

Catherine complied, feeling beyond pleased.

"How much have you lost?"

"Almost twenty-five pounds. I have a ways to go, yet, though."

Maddy plopped into the down loveseat. "Maybe we shouldn't go to lunch today. I don't want you to blow your diet."

"I won't." Catherine turned off the laptop on her desk and reached for her purse. "I'm motivated, don't you worry. Come on."

They headed for the main foyer, their footsteps echoing on the marble.

"What's made this time different?" Maddy asked. "What's got you motivated finally?"

Trying to control the flush she felt rising, Catherine thought about how to respond. She decided there was no harm in this lie. "You know what they say, Muffin. The love of a good man . . ."

"You're in love? With whom?"

"I didn't say *I was in love,* but he very well may be. I, on the other hand, am quite interested." They approached the front door, where Lucinda stood waiting to open it. Catherine whispered, "The uh, *bedroom* activities are most satisfying."

"Mother, please." Maddy nodded to Lucinda as she opened the massive etched-glass and mahogany door for them. "Thank you."

Catherine followed her to the portico, then remembering, turned. "Lucinda. I don't believe I told Andre that the Mintons will be joining me for dinner this evening. Tell him to have fresh shrimp at the ready and plenty of caviar. It's Mrs. Minton's favorite."

"Yes, ma'am." Lucinda closed the door.

"Where is Hector?" Catherine crossed her arms. "What on earth takes that man so long just to pull the car around?"

"I heard the engine start up," Maddy said. "He's coming. Tell me who your new flame is. How did you meet him? How long have you been seeing him?"

Holding a hand up, Catherine grinned. "No. No. I'm not about to jinx it. Let's see where it goes first." She felt devilish. "But I will tell you, I never knew what people were talking about before. The excitement. There are moments I feel I'm going to burst."

Maddy's eyebrows rose. "You've never had an orgasm before? Tell me you're joking."

The car pulled up to the steps. Hector got out of the driver's seat, and Maddy ran to hug him.

"Hey, Hector," Maddy kissed him on the cheek. "I've missed you."

A crooked smile came across his face. "Thank you, Miss Madelaine." His eyes flicked toward Catherine, and she sent him a shake of her head.

After they settled in, Catherine raised the glass divider between the front and back seats.

Maddy rolled her eyes.

Ignoring that reaction, Catherine returned to thinking about Mack. She didn't dare bring the subject up again. It made her too giddy. Her plan to please him had worked—exceptionally well. She wished she had someone to talk to about the way she felt. Because of the way they'd met, mentioning Mack to anyone else was too risky. Her friends would never understand, especially since several of them were utilizing his services as well. That had to stop. She wanted him for herself only. The thought of him touching the others the way he touched her? She dismissed that idea. There was no way he'd be that intimate with anyone else. With the others, it was probably, in, out, and done. With her, she *knew*, she could *feel* it—he reveled in the pleasure they gave each other. The only reason he saw the others was the poor man needed the money. She could fix that. How to fix it without hurting his pride? Offending him would break the magical spell they were under.

"Mother?" Maddy's voice broke into her thoughts.

"What, dear?"

"I asked you a question."

"Sorry. Lost in my thoughts."

"I'll say. You've got it bad. I think you're in love with this man."

Catherine harrumphed. "Don't be ridiculous. It's too soon. I've only known him a couple months. Let's change the subject. Tell me about your dating life. Still seeing the same gentleman?"

"Yes." Maddy laughed. "Aren't we a pair? You won't tell me, and I won't tell you. Much."

"There's a glimmer of hope? Any chance I'll have a grandchild in my lifetime?"

"That's a definite maybe."

Catherine hoped it was someone suitable. "Can't you give me a hint of who his people are? What industry are they in?"

"I'll tell you this much. He's older than me—"

"That can be a plus, depending on—"

"and he's very handsome."

"If we're going to have a wedding at The Breakers up in Palm Beach, you'd better let me know well in advance."

"Not to worry. *We* are not having a wedding at The Breakers."

"It's a possibility then? A wedding?" Catherine jumped for joy inside.

"I didn't say that. Calm down." A low beeping sound came from Maddy's purse. She retrieved her phone, spent a moment reading something, then texted back, and put it away. "Your turn. Tell me two things about your new man."

"Let me see. He is also very handsome. He looks a bit like that man who played the agent guy in that movie . . ."

"James Bond? You mean Sean Connery?"

"No, no. The other movie. He also played the president. On a plane. I know. Harrison Ford. That's who he looks like."

"Really? Somebody like that moves in your social circle? And he's not married? Or dating a thirty-year-old? Or gay?" Maddy clucked. "Hard to believe. What else?"

"He . . ." Catherine felt a blush coming on. "He makes me feel things I've never felt before."

CHAPTER SIXTY-TWO

On the Monday after *Plum—The Baby Store*'s opening, Shirley stood behind the counter, concentrating on what she hoped would change their illegal cash into register sales. The real Cute Quilts invoice was on the right. Using her left hand to disguise her writing, she hand-printed the information onto the three-part carbonless generic invoice in front of her. She'd need to fool Paul's accountant with it. A flash of movement on the porch got her attention. Paul was about to enter. She hit the warning buzzer hidden under the counter once—the code for Paul, Lance, or any of their friends and family entering the store. Hitting it twice meant a client had arrived, and three times was the alarm for Jim-the-cop. It could only be heard in Stanley's room.

"So," Paul said, as he closed the shop door, "how was your *soft* opening on Friday?" He grinned when he looked at Shirley behind the register and pointed to her head. "What the hoo-hah is that for?"

She straightened the papers she'd been working on, stashed them on a shelf by her knees, and touched her wig hair. "Do you like it? Makes me look a little younger, more cosmopolitan. Customers won't think they're shopping in an old age home."

"I doubt anyone would think that. But whatever makes you

more confident as a shop keeper. As requested, Lance and I stayed away Friday and Saturday. I'm dying of curiosity, and Lance is beside himself with questions. Did you make any sales?" He walked to her.

"A few. Nothing big." Shirley took the thin stack of paper-clipped sales slips from their first two days of business off another shelf and waved it in the air. "I guess the *We're Open* banner was enough to make people curious. I'm glad we didn't have an opening event. On Friday, while ringing up the first sale, I was so nervous, my hands shook." She laughed. "Don't know why."

"Once you get over the beginner's jitters, you need to throw a grand opening party. Get the word out."

No time soon, she thought.

Stanley, holding a wrench, came through the archway. "Good morning, Paul."

"Hey, Stanley. What are you working on now?"

"Drippy faucet in the second bathroom. I have to run to the hardware store. Either of you need anything?"

Glancing at her watch, Shirley noted that Stanley's first official appointment in the store was in two hours—at three o'clock. She knew Paul wouldn't stay long, but there were things she wanted squared away before then. "No. But don't take too long. We have a lot more that needs doing."

"I'm aware of that." Stanley waved on his way out the door.

"It must be so handy to have a man like him around," Paul said. "It seems he can do anything. Lance and I can barely change the light bulbs without screwing it up."

"I'm sure if you had to, you'd learn pretty quick." She smiled at him although she felt another twinge of resentment. "Luckily for you, that's not a worry, is it?"

Paul picked up the sales slips she'd put down. He clucked while flipping through them. "Six sales. Looks like about four-hundred dollars. Don't worry, it'll increase as people realize you're here."

Through the window, Shirley saw their old Buick leave the driveway. Was Stanley as uneasy as she about performing his duties while only a wall separated them?

"I wish you'd reconsider the point-of-sale system I recommended," Paul said. "Writing sales by hand? If you use the other system, then all your accounting is automatically updated."

"Yes, I understand," she said. It wasn't possible to write up fake sales with that system. "But this register is really all we need to start with." She patted the side of it. "I don't mind a bit writing up a sales slip, and until we get much busier, the basic bookkeeping is going to be easy. That fancy thing you wanted me to get was eight-hundred dollars. I was so excited to find such a bargain. This little machine cost us eighty. It had been hardly used at all."

He sighed as though having a conversation with a stubborn grandparent, and Shirley smiled inside. Being a senior citizen was paying off in ways she hadn't considered. Another flash at the window made her turn.

"Hey, look." Paul gestured to the black car parking in front of the building. "A customer."

A chauffeur opened the rear door of the sedan, and an older woman wearing enormous sunglasses emerged. She wore an expensive-looking suit and low heels. She seemed familiar.

"My God," Paul said. "That's Catherine Von Cletan. Good grief, how'd she know about this place already?"

Stunned, Shirley composed a blank face. "Who?" She studied the woman making her way up the three front steps to the porch. Von Cletan was fat. This woman was overweight, but not like Von Cletan.

"She's the richest woman in Sago Beach, maybe all of Palm Beach County." He gave her shoulder a gentle bump with his fist. "Good for you."

She managed a weak smile, as panic coursed through her. Maybe the battle-axe had a sister.

The door opened, and the tiny bells attached to it jingled. The woman stepped inside and removed her sunglasses. If it wasn't Von Cletan, then she had a twin for sure. Seeming to examine the shop, she took her time walking around the store.

The scent of a powerful, flowery perfume hit Shirley's nose. She remembered it from the day Dora and she window-shopped in Sago Beach. Her stomach sank.

"Go ask her if you can be of assistance," Paul whispered. "Don't be shy."

Shirley needed to get Paul out of the store. "I'm not shy. I'm nervous with you watching me like a mother hen. I appreciate it, but . . . don't you have some underwear to sell?"

"Gotcha. I understand." He headed for the door. "Call me later."

Waiting until Paul was outside, Shirley turned toward Von Cletan.

"Where's Mack?" Von Cletan's voice from across the room was demanding and impatient.

There was no question, it was indeed Catherine Von Cletan. A thinner one. One who almost looked shapely. Shirley boiled inside. "Excuse me? Who?" As far as she knew, Von Cletan didn't know what Mitzi looked like. The nasty shrew didn't have an appointment, said she wouldn't make any, so Shirley didn't care what she told her. She tried to disguise her voice by pretending to have a sore throat, making it raspy. She coughed for good measure.

"Who are you?" Von Cletan approached her. "Where is that Mitzi woman? Is that you?"

Coughing again, Shirley reached for a tissue and blew her nose. "I'm sorry. I don't know those people. Are you sure you're in the right shop?"

"But Mack told me this was the place."

"Who told you what? What place?"

"He said his room was in the back. I'll go see for myself. He's probably there now."

"Excuse me. The storage area is not open to customers. No one is in there. I need to get something from the stockroom anyway, so if it will make you feel any better, I'll double-check." Shirley scooted from behind the counter, darted through the archway and down the hall to the storage room, fumbling for her keys in her pocket.

Heels echoing off the tile floor were slow, but approaching the archway. "What is going on here?"

She rushed through to the rear of the storage area. They'd located the door to Stanley's bedroom so it couldn't be seen behind the shelves occupying the middle of the room. Not having much stock, they'd placed huge empty boxes as blockage. She locked his door, hurried to the furthest set of shelves, and positioned herself by a stack of bib boxes. She pretended to be reading the label when Von Cletan poked her head into the stock room, then looked at her with a careful innocence. "See? Nobody's here. Perhaps you misunderstood. Found it." She grabbed a box and headed to the retail area. "Maybe your friends played a practical joke on you. I'm sure they'll call soon, and you'll all laugh. Is there something I can help you with before you leave, ma'am?"

Footsteps followed her. Good. Shirley set the carton on the counter, then went to a round display table with piles of onesies near the front.

Von Cletan came around to face her. She looked angry.

"Well, as long as you're here—did you see how cute these are?" Shirley held up a pink one. "Anyone in your life having a baby?"

Von Cletan's eyes narrowed and a deep frown formed. "I don't know about any of this. Something's not right."

Several issues swirled around Shirley's mind, not the least of which was Stanley could return soon. She felt a strange sensation—her instincts telling her not to let Stanley near Von Cletan again. She grabbed a flowered diaper bag from a different rack. "How about one of these? Aren't the things they make for babies so much nicer now than when we were young?" Offering it to Von Cletan, she pointed across the room. "I have a book of special order items. You can request a stroller or carriage with this same sweet little pattern on it. Isn't it darling?"

Shaking her head, Von Cletan walked to the door, opened it, exited, then slammed it behind her.

Left holding the bag, Shirley watched the chauffeur jump from the driver's seat and open the car door for her. Even the vehicle seemed to leave in a huff. She slumped to the floor and buried her head in her hands. There was definitely something off about that woman.

CHAPTER SIXTY-THREE

"Of course I told her where it was." Stanley threw his hands up. "I explained it to all of them. Just like you wanted."

"But you said she was not going to come here." Shirley wiped a tear. He'd shown up five minutes after Von Cletan left. "Do you have any idea how upset I was? What did she want to see you about with no appointment?"

"How the hell should I know?"

"What if she comes back?"

"Then she comes back. So what? You said it yourself. A woman in her social position isn't going to do anything to cause a scandal. You've never actually been introduced to her, right? If she sees me here, then tell her you are indeed Mitzi and you played dumb before because you didn't realize who she was. You had to pretend innocence. She'll get it."

"Why didn't she call me and make an appointment? She's a loose cannon. It think she's not all there. She's . . . weird. Sneaky. Crazy, maybe."

"They're all effing nuts. I told you that the first day with the creepy cat and dog lady." He grabbed the plastic bag from the hardware store. "This was *your* brainstorm, remember?"

"One more thing. Why didn't you tell me she'd lost so much weight?"

He cocked his head and looked puzzled.

"She used to be fat," Shirley said. "Now she's, she's thinner." She couldn't bring herself to say *attractive.* Truth was, without being so heavy, she'd been almost appealing.

"Now you want me to report on their personal lives? If they change their hair color? Gain or lose a few pounds? I don't care about any of that." He glanced at his watch. "Lily Wentworth is due in less than an hour, and I've got to fix that faucet before she gets here. Otherwise, she'll have to use the bathroom in the hall. Your customers might get a clue." He took a few steps, then came back to her. He reached as though to touch her face, then stopped. "Let's concentrate on getting through today, okay?"

***

A few minutes before three, Lily Wentworth arrived. A Versace silk scarf covered her head, and she wore dark sunglasses. She couldn't have looked any more like the cliché of a cheating housewife. Except Lily was divorced. And thankfully, still on the hefty side.

As Lily approached her at the counter, Shirley pressed the buzzer twice.

"Mitzi, hi," Lily whispered. "I have an appointment at three."

"Yes. Before I take you to Mack, I'd like to discuss this a little." She gestured to the empty shop. "It's not a problem at the moment, but if you're ever arriving or leaving while there is *anyone* else present, we have to be more careful."

"Certainly."

"For starters, don't use our names in front of others. Second, don't wear the disguise. You look like you belong in a bad B movie. Pretend to shop a little, then approach me and ask to use the restroom. I'll take you to Mack. If someone's here on your way out, thank me for letting you use the facilities, then buy something—so it looks like buying a gift was your reason for coming in."

"That's very good." She seemed relieved. "Okay. I still pay Mack?"

"Pay him for . . ." Shirley's insides twisted. She cleared her throat. "Pay him for his services. Anything you buy out front here, you pay me here at the register. Like a normal store." She walked toward the archway. "Follow me."

"It's so hidden away," Lily said when they got to Mack's door. "I like that." She snickered. "Almost like we *are* in a movie, isn't it? It makes it more exciting. I feel so dangerous."

And Shirley felt literally nauseous. Lily seemed giddy with the situation. It was nothing more than entertainment to her. Shirley's resentment of rich people was becoming a hatred. "Go ahead in. He's expecting you." She turned and fast-walked away so she wouldn't hear Stanley and Lily greet each other.

***

The volume on the radio was set as loud as she could stand it. The seconds dragged like sludge slowed by a time warp. Shirley repositioned the oversized teddy bear that sat on the solid top of the closest rack. His eyes were huge, painted magnetic buttons that children could change out. He wore a flowered shirt and held a mini-surfboard. Shirley checked the time. Three-fifty. It had to be the longest hour of her life.

A young brunette entered the store and smiled in Shirley's direction.

Relieved for *anything* to distract her, Shirley lowered the volume. "Good afternoon."

"Hi." The woman walked to a rack of infant dresses. "When did you open? I pass by this way all the time."

"Friday." Shirley took a few steps toward her. "I'm so glad you came in. Are you looking for something specific?"

Ten minutes later, while Shirley was ringing up the woman's

purchases, Lily emerged from the archway.

Her customer looked up from her wallet and seemed confused.

Lily's eyes betrayed a momentary panic. She smoothed her hair and smiled. "Thank you so much for allowing me to use your bathroom." She wandered toward the shelf of stuffed animals.

"Why is she shouting at you?" The customer asked, handing Shirley her debit card.

"She must be a bit deaf." Shirley accepted the card, ran it through, and completed the sale. Lily's acting ability left a lot to be desired. She'd sounded like a scared second-grader doing a stiff recitation of her lines in the school play.

The bells jingled, and another woman entered the store. Pleased to see it was no one she knew, Shirley waved. "Good afternoon."

The woman nodded at her and began to peruse the merchandise.

Lily grabbed a stuffed lamb and headed for the register.

Shirley finished with the brunette, who left with a promise to spread the word about the store, and Lily handed her two twenties for the toy.

"You know," Lily whispered, "I thought I wouldn't like this having to come to the store thing, but it made it better." She gave Shirley a knowing look with an eyebrow raise. "If you know what I mean."

Queasy, Shirley did her best blank face. "Great. Good." She handed Lily her change.

"Plus, I don't have worry about my staff catching on. They are *so* nosy. You have no idea how hard it is to get any privacy." She headed for the door.

Yes, my heart is aching for you, Shirley thought. Rich bitch.

CHAPTER SIXTY-FOUR

"I've never felt so happy," Fletcher said. "You are a miracle in my life. Exactly what I needed, exactly when I needed it."

The bespectacled, white-haired, and paunchy Justice of the Peace turned to Maddy. "And your statement?"

"Being with you, I found a piece of me I didn't know was missing."

Her smile was sublime, like the Mona Lisa. Fletcher's whole body seemed more alive.

"With the power vested in me, I now pronounce you man and wife. You may kiss your bride."

As he kissed her, their witness, Mrs. Holmes, applauded. She worked the tiny chapel's front desk.

"Congratulations," the Justice said.

"May you have many years of happiness," Mrs. Holmes said.

"Thank you," Fletcher said. "You've been terrific."

"I'll send the pictures to the email you gave me. Have a wonderful weekend."

He offered his arm to Maddy. "Shall we?"

She placed her left hand on his arm, and they walked toward the chapel entrance.

Outside, he opened the door of the Mercedes convertible they'd rented, helped her in, and sat in the driver's seat. He studied her and basked in the love enveloping them. "Best Saturday morning of my life. This is the smartest thing I have ever done."

She laughed. "It sounds so strange, but considering how my mother would take over everything to do with a traditional wedding, eloping to Vegas *was* smart." Touching his cheek, she gave him a seductive look. "Plus I feel so reckless. Adventurous. Wild. Lusty. Take us back to the hotel, Hubby. Now."

"Right now?" He shot her a sly wink. "But I *really* wanted to see Hoover Dam next."

***

Nina paced in the kitchen. Her deflation disaster was fixed. She was fully inflated again. The doctor was almost too solicitous—in his efforts to avoid a lawsuit, no doubt—and the bruising and pain were much less than the original surgery.

George seemed more distant than ever. He'd taken to sleeping at the office several nights a week. She drove there a couple of times to see if his car was in the lot, and it had been. So, the problem was what? Why didn't he want to come home? Sleep in his own bed?

She glanced at the clock, then went to the foot of the stairs. "Mary Ann. It's now nine o'clock. Get down here. Allison's mom will be here any minute to pick you up."

Mary Ann, Allison, and two other friends were going into New York City for the day. Shopping, dinner, then a Broadway show. All a sixteenth birthday gift for Allison from her parents.

The sound of a door opening stopped Nina from yelling again. Thudding footsteps came closer. Mary Ann appeared at the top of the stairs, still looking sleepy. She wore a turtleneck, tight jeans, and boots. She had a jacket and a backpack in her arms.

"Why aren't you ready? It's rude to make them wait for you."

"Relax." Mary Ann started down the steps. "I'm putting on my make-up in the car. It'll be fine." She shifted her backpack onto one shoulder.

Nina stared at her chest, and it made her question when she last took a close look at her daughter. "Honey, is that a push-up bra, or are your breasts finally starting to grow?"

"Jesus, Mom. Stop." She walked past Nina into the kitchen, set her things on a chair, grabbed a travel mug from an upper cabinet, and poured the last of the coffee into it.

"I made you a bagel with cream cheese. You can take it with you."

She shook her head, took a sip from the mug, and shuddered. "No, thanks. Eating breakfast makes me sick."

"Since when?"

"Since *ever*." She pointed out the window over the sink. "They're here. Bye." She gathered her coat and pack and headed for the garage door.

Watching her get into the back seat of the SUV, Nina saw Allison's mom wave to her. She waved back, wondering if Allison was as prickly with her mother. Sean had never been so testy as a teenager. Was it a girl thing? She wished she had someone to confide in. Evelyn Asbury was her closest friend, but she only had two boys, and besides, Nina didn't feel comfortable having her know even more about how her *perfect* life really wasn't. It was bad enough that Evelyn now knew all about George's affairs. She prayed Evelyn had kept her promise and not told anyone else. To be gossiped about behind her back? Enduring the further humiliation and stress of more people knowing gave her insomnia. That was probably why, she reasoned, she didn't want others to know her business. You just couldn't trust most people.

Feeling her burden gain another ton, she sat at the kitchen table. How much more could she take?

***

With a few minutes to spare before leaving for work, Shirley dialed Dora's number. They hadn't talked in over a week, and Dora had left a curt message on Shirley's home answering machine. Both guilt and dread surfaced. None of their family or friends knew about the store yet.

Dora picked up on the third ring. "Well, there you are, stranger."

Forcing herself to sound cheerful, Shirley fiddled with the tangled phone cord—she was using the old wall phone in the kitchen. "I know. I'm so sorry I haven't returned your calls. It's only that work has been so busy. The *season* has begun. Everything in Sago Beach is hopping."

"I take it the ooh-la-la underwear business is booming, too?"

Shirley laughed. "Always. I think some of those women toss their dainties after wearing them once, they buy so often."

"Are you working today?"

"Afraid so. Until five."

"Any chance you and Stanley want to play cards with us tonight at my place?"

"Sounds great. I'll ask him and call you back."

Dora and Tim had been inseparable in the three months since they met. In a way, it was a blessing because hiding what she and Stanley were doing from Dora would've failed otherwise. Tim kept Dora very busy. He'd even taken her away for a weekend to St. Thomas. Why was everyone else's life so easy? "All I want is our money back, God. Please?"

***

In her downstairs office, Catherine picked up the phone for the fifth time. She dialed Mitzi's number, then pressed *end* instead of *send*. She hadn't seen Mack in over a week. Being treated like an ordinary client infuriated her, but she supposed there was no way

Mack had told Mitzi about their love affair. He couldn't, she reasoned. He needed the money from Mitzi's client list. Was he missing her as much as she missed him?

Feeling wretched from lack of sleep—her desire and loneliness kept her awake the night before—she tried to clear her mind and think about what to do. Should she make a damned appointment? Maybe then she'd get the right address. They needed to talk. To hell with what anybody thought, Mack and she were meant to be together. After a lifetime of not understanding the electric wonder of such love, she now wanted to live with the man of her dreams. Although she wouldn't advertise the fact to her friends. She planned to take him to Europe.

No. She was sure she'd heard him right. 'Plum,' he'd said. 'It's a baby store.'

What if she made sure none of the other women wanted to sleep with him?. She could call the ones she knew and tell them a lie or two. But Mack would find out. And she would reduce her standing among her peers by stooping to gossip about a male prostitute.

She thought a minute longer, and an idea bloomed. What if she destroyed their business so Mack would have little choice but to accept her offer? Walking to the bar, she determined a different phone call and another trip to the shop were necessary. Pouring a hefty shot of Scotch, she downed it, slammed the glass on the bar, and steeled herself.

CHAPTER SIXTY-FIVE

Later that Saturday morning, Shirley was in Plum's kitchen pouring another cup of coffee when the bells jingled. Carrying her mug, she prepared a big smile for the first customer of the day, walked through the arch, then stopped short.

"Hell's bells," Agnes said. "You're wearing your bedroom-games wig."

Shirley knew her shock had to be obvious and tried to compose a normal expression. Her brain wasn't in gear. Several possible things to say came to mind. None seemed right. She stared at Agnes' outfit—a starched, man's white shirt and a flouncy denim skirt over black high-tops.

"You okay, Shirley?" Agnes took a couple steps toward her.

"Fine." The word croaked out. "I'm . . . I'm surprised to see you. Here."

"Well, imagine *my* surprise a little while ago when I asked for you at Paulina's and that cute young man, Lance, told me you'd up and quit and opened your own dang store. Plum—The Baby Store. I like the name."

Noticing a slight tremor in her hands, Shirley walked to the register counter and put the coffee down. She swallowed hard and took a deep breath. "Stanley and I didn't tell anyone. Not even the kids. I've been so nervous about it all. It's my fault. I wanted to wait until we had a few weeks experience. Please don't be angry."

"Angry?" Agnes shook her head. "I'm not angry. Flabbergasted is more like it. How did this come about? You told me you two were having hard times."

Shirley gave her the quick version of the proposal she'd approached Paul with.

Agnes rubbed her chin. "It's a risk. All retail is. But it could work." She nodded, as if deciding on something. "Good for you."

A loud bang made them both look out the front window. A black Mercedes backed away from the mailbox—which now leaned forty-five degrees to the left—by the driveway and parked on the street about three feet from the curb.

Shirley clamped her mouth shut to hold in curse words. The car looked like the one the Von Cletan arrived in that past Monday. Sure enough, the pushy woman emerged—but from the driver's seat this time. No chauffeur. She straightened her dress and huge sunglasses, closed the door, and gazed toward the front door. The sunlight sent rays of flashing sparkles from her requisite diamond jewelry.

"Think she's drunk?" Agnes asked.

"I don't know," Shirley said. "I do think she's a lunatic."

"You know her? Who is she?"

"Some la-dee-da snob here on the island." Shirley waved her hand in dismissal. "She came in on Monday asking for people—friends of hers maybe? She wasn't making any sense." Her heart raced, hoping Von Cletan wouldn't say anything about Mack.

Heels clacked on the porch, and the door opened. Von Cletan entered, scanning the retail area. She frowned in their direction.

"She looks kind of familiar," Agnes whispered. "Quite the sour puss, though."

Von Cletan approached Shirley and gave Agnes a

disapproving once-over.

Agnes stared at her, expressionless.

Doing a slight eye roll, Von Cletan cleared her throat and stared back at Agnes. "Do you mind?"

"Do I mind what?" Agnes grinned.

Taking a dramatic moment to close her eyes and do an audible exhale, Von Cletan then adopted an obvious phony smile. "I would like to talk to the shop clerk alone."

"Oh. Sure." Agnes winked at Shirley and wandered to the other side of the store.

"Where is Mack?" Von Cletan whispered. "You know more than you're telling me, and I'm losing patience. I need to speak with him."

Then call Mitzi's number just like everyone else, Shirley thought. But at that point, *Mitzi* had no intention of letting her see Mack again. She kept her voice steady and pleasant. "Ma'am, as I told you the other day, I don't know who that is. Someone gave you the wrong information."

"I've lost the number to get in contact with him."

Shirley suspected that was a lie, but she needed to get rid of the pest. Stanley had dropped her off so he could run errands, and he could return at any time. "Give me your number. If someone by that name comes in, I will tell him to call you."

Von Cletan glared at her. "You know what I think?"

Returning her mean look, Shirley said nothing.

"I think that—*you* are Mitzi. If I find out that's true, well . . ." She stepped away, sent another scathing look toward Agnes, and strolled out of the shop while taking a phone from her purse.

Not realizing she'd been holding her breath, Shirley gasped for air.

"Not a bad-looking woman." Agnes came back to Shirley. "Nice blue eyes. Good cheekbones. It's a shame she's a bitch. I'll bet that's why this Mack guy, whoever he is, gave her the run around."

"You *heard* that?"

Agnes gave her an enigmatic smile. "Not a thing wrong with my ears."

"Boy, I'll say."

"That, plus I *might* have edged a little closer behind her back. Why does she think your name is Mitzi?"

"Oh, God." Shirley braced herself with both hands on the counter. "Please, Agnes. Don't ask any more questions. I'm begging you."

Nodding, Agnes screwed up one side of her face. "All rightie. Guess I know what the wig is for, but the why is eluding me." She patted Shirley's hand. "Don't worry. Whatever's really going on here isn't any of my concern. Except you're my friend. When you need help, I'm here. Okay?"

Eight days. The store had been open for eight days and already someone was suspicious. "Thank you." Shirley knew Agnes wouldn't take long to figure it out. It was all the nasty Von Cletan's fault. Why the hell couldn't she have called and made an appointment like the others? Or better yet, just go away. "These wealthy women are the nastiest. They think they own us."

"You might want to tamp it down—your resentment. It's seeping out like a radiation leak and bringing you bad energy. Changing your aura. There are lots of wonderful people with money, too. Nice or not, the rich people aren't the ones who caused your problems."

"Paul and Lance. That's it. Two rich people I know who are nice."

"I think a change of subject is in order." Agnes stretched her arms wide, then made large circles. "Try this. Helps to get rid of the funk."

Shirley did it to humor her.

"Have you talked to your son lately?" Agnes asked.

"Last week," Shirley said. "Why?"

"Might want to call him."

Concern of a different kind filled her. "What do you know

that I don't?"

"I'm sworn to secrecy."

"Why would you know and not me? Is it bad?"

"No, I think it's good news. He didn't tell me. A mutual friend did."

Relief flooded in. "I could sure use some good news. Wonder why he hasn't called us?" Unless. "It has to do with a woman, doesn't it?"

Agnes kept a poker face.

"That's got to be it. He's convinced Stanley will never approve of his love life, no matter what he does." What a joke that was now. She and Stanley had zero moral high-ground anymore. "I understand why he'd want to keep a new relationship hidden from us. This must be a serious affair. Edna said she thought she saw him out with a blonde at the movies." Her curiosity would have to wait. She couldn't call Fletcher from the cell or the shop, because he'd want to know where the new number was from, and she wasn't ready to explain.

***

At eleven, Nina returned from dropping Charles at a friend's house, feeling reassured. George's office was on Nina's way home, so she dropped in to see him. He showed her all the current deals at play, including one with buyers in Europe, which was the reason for spending so many nights sleeping on the pull-out sofa in his office. The negotiation entailed lots of phone calls in the middle of the night. Then he hugged her, said not to worry, and promised to be home for dinner.

He'd explained the absences before, but seeing the pending contract files made her believe him. Opening the fridge, she took out chicken breasts. Chicken cacciatore was one of his favorites. She wanted to have as much of the prep and clean up finished beforehand so they could relax afterward. The night promised a good chance of another bout of floor tango. Maybe this time, they'd make it upstairs first.

The doorbell chimed as she set the package by the sink. Wiping her hands with a towel, she went to the front door and checked the peep hole. A tall brunette stood there. Her hair fell in controlled waves past her shoulders. She wore jeans, a plunging V-neck black T-shirt, and a light-weight blue jacket. Expensive sunglasses hid her eyes.

Nina opened the door. "May I help you?"

"You're Nina? George's wife?"

"Yes. Who are you?" Her suspicion flags cranked up.

"I'm Maryanne Genova. We need to talk." The woman glanced up and down the street. "Inside would be better."

An inkling of recognition dawned. "You wouldn't happen to live on Mason Drive, would you?"

"How'd you know?"

Nina sighed. "Come in." She was the woman George was fooling around with the night she followed him and played the tuna trick. The fact she shared a name with their daughter was weird. Had George finally dumped her? It could mean he *was* satisfied now that his wife fulfilled his desires. She closed the door, crossed her arms, and gave Maryanne a stern face.

Taking off her sunglasses, Maryanne revealed big brown eyes with enormous false lashes—and a nasty purplish bruise under her left eye. "Maybe we should sit down."

"Maybe not. You're not going to tell me George hit you. I won't believe it."

"No. Look, I got a story to tell you, and you're not going to like it."

"Make it a short one. I really don't have time to indulge you. I'm sorry if you thought he was in love with you, but you shouldn't have been with him to begin with. He dumped you, right? Get over it."

She rolled her eyes with great exaggeration. "Hey, Cleopatra—wanna pull your head out of denial? You are blind. I came here because I feel sorry for you, and you should know what he's doing."

"What do you mean?" Nina's insides did a sharp twist.

"I broke it off with him over a month ago. He didn't take it well. Kept calling me and crying. Said he knew he'd made a mistake and would I please forgive him? Wanna know why I did it?"

Nina stared at her. "I take it—not because of your guilty conscience?"

"Because he was cheating on me. Isn't that a kicker?"

Feeling woozy, Nina leaned against the hallway wall for support. She *had* heard him correctly that night—moaning the word Maryanne. "Okay. Let's sit in the kitchen."

Maryanne followed her in, plopped her large black purse on the table, and sat across from Nina.

Elbows on the table and rubbing her temples, Nina braced for disaster. She took a deep breath, straightened, and locked eyes with her husband's mistress. "How long had you been screwing my husband?"

"Almost three years." Maryanne fiddled with one stem of her sunglasses. "He is a pathological liar. I believed him. Two years ago, I left my marriage for him. Promised he'd leave you, too. But he kept putting it off, making excuses."

The news hit Nina like a giant judge's gavel—decreeing her hope dead forever.

"George told me you were frigid and had no interest in sex for over ten years. He said it was so hard on him. He'd taken all he could stand, and if it wasn't for your kids, he'd have been gone a long time before he met me. Actually cried that first night we did it. I felt so sorry for him. I can't believe I fell for that load of shit."

"He can be very convincing." Nina's hostility toward her softened—a little. "For the record, I'm not frigid. I love sex. He usually turns me down. Guess he had to save up his energy—for you."

"Not anymore—for the slut he's been running around with

for the last six months. His excuses for not seeing me weren't adding up, so I hired a PI." She reached into her purse, produced a manila envelope, and placed it front of Nina. "Better than an apology. But I owe you one of those, too."

Nina stared at it.

"Open it. It's better if you see for yourself."

Sliding the contents out, the photo on top made her brain short circuit. George and a curvy, huge-bosomed, over-bleached blonde were embracing on a beach. Palms trees and stunning blue water served as their backdrop. They were naked. A stabbing pain hit Nina in the gut. "I don't understand. When? Where? How?"

"It's a clothing-optional resort on a private island near St. John," Maryanne said. "They spent four days there. Third week of September."

"That's when he was in Vegas. For the annual real-estate convention." Nina stopped to recollect. "I know he was there."

Maryanne nodded. "Did you get the same story I did? He had a great opportunity to meet with some huge, important commercial brokers? Had to stay on for another week?" She pointed to the blonde in the picture. "She does have huge brokers. Even without clothes, she looks cheap. She's a suicide blonde with a matching carpet, but check out her nipple. It's dark. Can't fake that."

"Suicide? What?"

"Dyed by her own hand? She bleaches that haystack at home."

Turning the picture over, Nina wanted to vomit. "But, how? He couldn't have paid for it. I see his paychecks, pay all the bills. Is she rich?"

Patting the stack of papers, Maryanne said, "The PI has a tech guy. Can tap into just about anything. It's all right here. George has some commissions going to a fake business he set up. He's got separate accounts, credit cards, the whole works."

"Un-flipping-believable." Nina bristled. "How old is she?"

"Thirty-one. I figured you'd need all of this for the divorce. I hope you take his ass to hell."

"Divorce." Drowning in her rising despair, Nina realized things would never, ever get better. Reality was screaming at her, waking her up. She'd been living in a delusion. "I have to get divorced now?" It was meant more for herself than Maryanne.

"Well, yeah. Don't tell me you still want the asshole. Wait 'til you hear the latest part."

"There's more?"

"The slut—her name is Milla. Milla Jenkins. She's pregnant. We don't know if it's his, but we're almost certain she hasn't told him yet. She's in for a rude shock. He'll cut out the second he hears that news flash."

Nina thought about the gorgeous woman with a centerfold body hugging her husband, one hand on his butt. Both of them with sappy, stupid smiles. She'd been such a fool. She felt older. Dumpier. And mostly—tired. Tired of it all. Tired of hoping and praying. Tears formed, and she let them drip. It was over. Maryanne's hand holding a tissue came into view. She accepted it and dabbed at her eyes.

"He's not worth it."

"I know that now." Nina focused on Maryanne's bruise. "Mind if I ask how you did get that shiner?"

"My ex. Donnie. He wants me back. I told him I'd have to think about it. He didn't like that answer. We had a fight. Not a chance I'd be with him again. Not after that."

"Good for you."

"By the way, he wants to personally castrate George."

"Tell him to get in line."

Maryanne laughed. It eased the tension.

"I have to go. Are you going to be all right?" Maryanne asked.

"As if you give a shit."

"Actually, I do. Now. Having met you, you seem like a good person. Not the control-freak bitch he said you were. If your divorce goes to trial, I'll testify for you."

"He used those words? Control-freak bitch?"

She nodded. "All the time. Said you had to run everything. Drove him crazy."

CHAPTER SIXTY-SIX

Shirley imagined her stare laser-drilling holes into Stanley as he entered the store.

"Whew. Next time, maybe you should run the errands." He held up a white plastic bag. "I never know the right kind of—" He froze when his eyes met hers. "What?"

"The Empress Von Cletan came back. She said she thinks I'm Mitzi."

"You are. Did you admit it to her?"

"No. Agnes was here."

"Agnes?"

She explained. "Look. She hit the mailbox."

"Who, Agnes?"

"No. Von Cletan. The Entitled One. We have to stop her."

"How?" He deposited the bag on the counter. "You want me to go to her house and try to talk to her again?"

"No." Shirley picked up her cell phone and stared at it. "Maybe Mitzi should give her a call."

"I don't think that's a good idea."

"She acts like the world revolves around her and owns everyone in it. It's maddening. She's going to ruin everything. We *have* to do something."

"Honey, she figured out Mitzi is the woman who works here. There's enough friction between you two. Dial her number and hand it to me. I'll try and convince her that she needs to either make an appointment or stop dropping by."

Not knowing what else to do, she found her purse-sized notebook containing their client info and schedule, found the number, punched it in, then gave the cell to Stanley.

He listened, said, "Voice mail," and listened a moment longer. "Catherine, it's Mack. Mitzi tells me you've come by the store. Call this number, and I'll answer it." He hung up and set it aside.

She studied him, not thrilled with how familiar he sounded with Von Cletan. "Why did you call her Catherine?"

"That's her name." He shook his head. "Damn it, I call Lily and Leticia and all the rest of them by their first names, too. It would seem pretty strange not to, don't you think?"

She crossed her arms and looked out the window. "I don't know what to think anymore."

"Well, neither do I."

Not liking the testy tone he used, she quashed the impulse to point it out. The cell rang, startling her. Checking the incoming number, she said, "It's her."

He picked it up. "Catherine. Thank you for returning the call." His tone changed to kind.

Shirley leaned closer to him, heard a squawkish voice, but couldn't decipher words. "What's she saying?" she whispered.

Stanley waved her away, then walked a few steps in the other direction. "I'm sorry, I didn't hear the last part." His forehead furrowed as he listened. "I understand that. But the only way is to make an appointment. Unexpected visits could cause me all kinds of trouble. You don't want me to be arrested, do you?"

He nodded. "I didn't think so. I know I'm booked all through this next week, but let me talk to Mitzi and see if we can't change something around just this once. I'll call you right back." Clicking off, he tilted his head at her.

"You want me to bump somebody for *her majesty*?" Shirley clenched her fists. "I don't want her to see you at all. Let her wait for an opening."

"A few choice words from her with the other clients she knows, and our little enterprise goes *kaboom*. The sooner I unruffle her feathers, the better."

"Is that what we're calling it now?"

"Hey, you created this monster."

Ticked by the truth, she grabbed the notebook and double-checked her memory. "Drucilla Lavender on Tuesday. I'll tell her you got a sudden toothache and had to go to the dentist."

***

At five, they closed the store, and went home.

"Dora said for us to come over at seven," Shirley said. "I'm not in the mood for cards right now." She should've been happy for Dora but the new-found love depressed her.

"I'd like to see Tim. And Dora," Stanley said. "It's been a while." He went toward the stairs.

"Fine." What Agnes said earlier charged into her brain. "Wait."

Halfway up, he turned. "What now?"

"I forgot. Agnes said a friend told her some good news about Fletcher."

"Great. What is it?"

"Said she promised not to spoil it. We need to call him." She hurried to the handset they kept by the sofa and dialed his number. His voice mail picked up. "This is Mom. We want to know what's happened with you. Call us."

"I think it's time we told him about the shop," Stanley said. "If Agnes stumbled into it, it won't be long before somebody else in Silver Sago Village does, too."

"With our luck, it'll be Edna."

***

By the time they walked to Dora's, Shirley's negative mood had ebbed. "I'm sorry, Stanley. You know what nobody ever talks about? How difficult it is to stay positive when life is beating you into pulp." She rang Dora's bell.

He smiled. "It's been a weird week. Let's hope it was a fluke."

Tim answered the door with an open beer for Stanley. "Welcome."

Shirley, seeing Dora in the kitchen, realized how much she did miss her friend.

Dora, a bottle of white wine in hand, thrust it out toward her. "It's chardonnay. I assume you want some." She poured two glasses without waiting for the answer.

They brought their drinks to the dining table where decks of cards and cut-glass bowls of candies awaited.

Shirley took her usual seat and gulped half the wine.

"Tough day at work, was it?" Dora chuckled and retrieved the bottle, topping Shirley's glass.

"You have no idea," Shirley said. "Some of the women on that island are cuckoo."

"I'll say," Stanley said.

Tim and Dora both gave him a funny look. Shirley glared at him.

"Uh, from what Shirley tells me about Paulina's."

"I imagine spending your days buying fancy frillies, getting manicures, then digging on each other at lunch would make anybody crabby," Dora said. "Poor things don't know anything else, do they? That kind of useless life has to lead to boredom."

"Yes. The *poor* things," Shirley said. "I tell myself that all day long."

Dora laughed. "It's a good thing I don't work there. I'd be so tempted to play practical jokes on them. I'd have been fired the first week."

"Practical jokes?" A part of Shirley's brain lit up. "Like what?"

"Are you joking? You've never thought about it?" Dora patted Shirley's hand. "My dear friend, you are without a doubt much too good. Who's the worst of the lot?"

"There's one in particular." Shirley caught Stanley's warning glance. "But I can't name names."

"There is such a thing as itching powder, you know." Dora waved that thought away. "Although, you'd have to be more clever so you don't get canned. Do something that seems like just a quirk—would've happened all on its own."

Tim put up a hand. "Darling, stop. You are diabolical. I love that about you." He gestured to Shirley and Stanley. "These are innocent, nice people. They don't possess the necessary evil genius gene."

Wanna bet? Shirley thought.

"What about you and a new job, Stanley?" Tim asked. "Still probing?"

Sputtering though a mouth full of beer, Stanley raised a forefinger.

"No," Shirley said. "We decided he should stop looking. He wasn't having any luck. So, now he's my cleaning man. At my beck and call. Aren't you, dear?" She sent him a beatific smile.

"And the kids and grandkids?" Dora said. "Everybody good?"

"As I'm sure you've heard, Edna saw Fletcher with a new one," Shirley said. "Don't know a thing about it yet. And Nina—thank God for Nina." She clasped her hands in mock prayer. "Stabile as the rock of Gibraltar. She's great. Her kids are great. Their life is blessedly normal."

They played a few hands of spades, and Shirley fell into a wonderful lull, listening to Dora's updates—Morty moved in with Edna, Elinor did get the downstairs unit old Mr. Peters had to vacate, and Betty's *boyfriend,* Jeff-the-pool-boy, moved to California.

Shirley enjoyed the easy friendship between the two couples and pretended nothing had changed. She'd arrived at the mental oasis of believing it when, after another hand, Tim stood, went to the fridge and extracted a bottle of Perrier-Jouet Champagne.

"Whoa," Stanley said. "That looks pretty fancy. Are we celebrating?"

Tim grinned. "Yes. Dora has agreed to marry me."

"Marry?" Shocked, Shirley stopped herself from voicing the questions jumping into her head. Why bother at their ages? Wasn't it a little too quick?

"Congratulations." Stanley stood, gave Dora a kiss on the cheek, then shook Tim's hand. "I'm sure happy you two found each other."

Recovering, Shirley gave them both hugs.

"We'd like for you two to stand with us," Dora said. "Best man and matron of honor. Will you?"

"Of course," Shirley said. "When?"

"We want to right away." Tim beamed toward Dora. "But we'll wait until next month, because we need time to plan the honeymoon."

"We're doing two weeks in Paris, then two weeks in Hawaii." Dora did a mock hula. "Can you believe it?"

CHAPTER SIXTY-SEVEN

"You don't seem very happy for them." Stanley unlocked the front door and stepped aside to allow Shirley in first.

"I am." She walked to the dinette and threw her purse on the table. "It's the honeymoon part that's killing me. Paris? That's always been *my* dream."

He thought about commenting, then decided it was safer not to. Shirley was on the edge of one of her moods. They were becoming a frequent obstacle course.

"*And* Hawaii? Really?"

"Look," Stanley said, "there's a message on the machine." He touched the play button.

"Hi, Mom. Hi, Dad." It was Fletcher. "Everything's fine. I went away for a few days, but I'll be back on Wednesday. Maybe we can have dinner one night this week?"

"Gee, that was informative," Shirley said.

"Doesn't sound like anything's different. Maybe Agnes' grapevine was wrong."

"Maybe." She rummaged in the pantry, took a box of crackers out, then put them back.

"Hungry? Me, too. I'll slice some cheese if you want."

"No. Eating because I'm upset won't do anything but make me gain weight."

"You can afford a few more pounds, honey. Go ahead and indulge, if you want."

She glared at him. "What is *that* supposed to mean?"

Deflect, he thought, deflect. "Nothing. I just . . . Never mind."

"I'm too thin for you now?"

"I didn't say that." He'd been thinking along those lines for a while, though. "I love you exactly as you are."

Putting her hands on her hips, she studied him. "You've really changed."

"So have you. This enterprise of yours has affected both of us. Be honest. You know it, too." He reached for her hand. "We're both unhappy with what we're doing. I feel ashamed—scared to death the secret will get out."

***

On Monday, Catherine had Hector take her into Sago Beach's shopping district. By practically starving herself the past few weeks, more weight had come off—for a total of forty pounds. She felt svelte and very, very sexy. Sexy and confident enough to stride into Paulina's Peignoirs. When she saw Mack on Tuesday, she wanted to make him insane with lust.

But she wouldn't give in. No. He couldn't have her until he agreed to her proposal.

She tried on several lacey and scanty things and selected a black lace corset-type of bra and matching panties. For a moment, she saw Mack turning her down. Shaking that negative scene away, she concentrated how she'd use her new-found power. There was no way he'd say no.

***

Leticia Basselbrook came out from the archway looking side to side.

"It's all right," Shirley said. "There's no one else here at the moment."

"Good." Leticia went straight to the door. "See you next week."

The sound of water rushing through the pipes signaled that Stanley stripped the bed sheets and started the washer—his new routine. When the client left he locked the door, threw in the dirty linens, made the bed with new sheets, sprayed room deodorizer, and hit the shower. He thought it was the best way to avoid disaster if Joe-the-cop or the boys came by. It was also easier on her. She never wanted to see or smell the aftermath of his encounters.

She interspersed three falsified sales slips into the pile of real sales so far from the day. The fakes had one sale of a Cute Quilt for three-hundred each. Checking the front window first—to be sure she was alone—she took the nine-hundred in cash from her purse and placed it into the register. "I've done my laundry for the day, too."

The week before, she wrote up one phony quilt sale a day. Now actual sales had picked up, and she felt it was safe to try to sneak in more. Her goal was to launder twelve-hundred dollars a day until she absorbed the pile of cash they'd acquired. Soon, she'd create another false invoice from the Cute Quilts company. Paul's accountant expected to see invoices for the inventory.

Stanley emerged about fifteen minutes later. "Everything good out here?"

She nodded. "Basselbrook didn't stick around to chat like she did last week. And there were no other customers, so she didn't have to buy anything for show, either."

"You don't like talking to her, anyway."

"I don't want to talk to any of them, but that wouldn't be good for business."

The front door bells jingled, and a young woman carrying a toddler entered.

"Hello." Shirley put on her customer service smile.

"I'll see if I can find a ballgame on the tube." Stanley disappeared into the hall.

***

That night, they ate in silence. Stanley avoided looking at her. Shirley had the strangest feeling something was wrong. More wrong than usual. She wondered if it was only apprehension about Von Cletan's appointment the next afternoon. Maybe Stanley dreaded it as much as she did.

"Thank you for dinner." Stanley put his silverware and napkin on his plate and took it to the kitchen.

"We need to clear the air. Are you worried about tomorrow?"

He turned on the faucet, rinsed his plate, and placed it in the dishwasher. "I'm worried about you."

"Me?"

Walking back, he nodded. "Yup. I'm afraid of what you'll say. Catherine—"

"Stop calling her that."

"Von Cletan—she is a client. Like the others. For some reason, she really gets under your skin. Her refusal to obey your rules maybe. But that is a woman who isn't used to following anybody's rules. She makes the rules. You knew that when you scheduled the first appointment with her. She could make our lives miserable."

"You're saying we're stuck with her."

"Sure seems like it. She likes having sex with Mack, this person you invented. So do the rest of them. Might as well make the best of it. Think of her the same way you think of Leticia. You were fine when *she* left, both last week and today. No drama there. Why doesn't Leticia upset you?"

"Von Cletan's different. Worse. I can't put my finger on why."

"She's not that bad. She's agreed to come to the store.

That's progress."

"You're sticking up for her?"

"What?" He looked puzzled. "No. I just don't want to go jail."

"She's repulsive." Shirley shivered. "I hate her."

He sat. "How about this—before she gets there, we put a sign on the door that says, *closed until four.* Then you can leave and not have to see her at all. I'll play lookout and let her in."

She had to admit, that was a good way to escape the stress Von Cletan caused her. "It's not a terrible idea. But knowing her, she'd demand we close the store for her every time. I don't want to set that precedent."

"Good point. Think of it this way. She's a lonely woman, so desperate for a man's attention, she'll put her reputation at risk to get it. She's got nothing on you."

"And she's got fat ankles. Fat everything," Shirley said. "Right?"

"I don't know. I don't think I've ever paid any attention to her ankles."

"What about the rest of her? She's gross."

He stood and went into the living room. "This isn't serving any purpose."

A wretched thought popped in. "Don't tell me you're actually attracted to her." She followed him, beginning to fume.

"I didn't say that."

"You're not denying it."

"Jeezus, Shirl. I know you want me to hate her, but I don't. She's not that bad when you get to know her."

Something snapped inside. "You like her?" she yelled. "How the hell can you like that woman? She's horrible to me. She's nasty and mean."

Stanley closed his eyes. "Stop shouting at me."

"You're supposed to be on my side." Her suppressed frustration and anger boiled, and she let her rage increase until she screamed her words. "How dare you defend her? She's a total bitch. It's your fault we're in this mess. You owe me, big time."

A wild look came across his face she'd never seen before. He screamed back. "Yeah? Well, we could've sold this damn townhouse instead. And maybe we'd be living in a crappy place, but at least we wouldn't be at each other's throats, would we? I'm a man, not Superman, for Christ's sake. I like women. Always have. And you conveniently keep forgetting that unless I feel *some* kind of attraction, even with the pills, ain't nothing going to happen. You threw me into bed with these women, you'll have to live with the consequences."

They glared at each other for a second.

Stanley shook his head and retreated to the spare bedroom office, slamming the door behind him.

CHAPTER SIXTY-EIGHT

Sunlight through the blinds woke Shirley. She'd cried herself to sleep. Sitting, she looked at Stanley's side of the bed. It was untouched.

In the bathroom, she splashed water on her face. Her eyes were swollen. The smell of coffee wafted in. She made her way downstairs.

"Stanley?" She peeked around the corner to the kitchen.

Leaning against the counter and holding the newspaper, he glanced up from it.

"Stanley, I'm sorry." She took a couple steps toward him. "It's all that woman's fault, she—"

"Stop." He put the paper on the counter. "No more. This won't get us anywhere." He frowned. "I will drop you off at the store this morning. At quarter to two, I'll show up for my two o'clock with Catherine. As soon as I've cleaned up, I'll leave again and return to pick you up at five." Taking his coffee with him, he left the room.

Shirley felt like she'd been punched. She went to a cabinet, pulled out a mug, then stopped. She didn't want coffee. Pacing between the kitchen and dining room, she became aware of every crumb her feet touched on the cold tile.

The phone rang. She grabbed the receiver from the wall

unit.

"Mom?"

Nina's voice sounded wobbly. "What's the matter? Everything okay?"

"No. Everything isn't even close to okay. I need your help. Can you ask Dad to get on the other phone?"

Panic coursed through her. "Just a sec." She set the phone on the counter and ran to the stairs. "Stanley? It's Nina. Something's wrong. Pick up the phone."

A moment later, he did. "What's the matter, sweetheart?" The soft tenderness in his voice for his daughter made Shirley realize she hadn't heard that tone in ages.

"You'd both better sit," Nina said. "I have a lot to tell you. Don't ask questions until I'm done. All right?"

They both agreed.

"First, nobody's dead. Or hurt. Well, not physically." There was a long pause. "I haven't been honest with you about George and me. He's been cheating on me for a very long time. A succession of girlfriends. I was too humiliated to tell anyone, and I kept hoping he'd come to his senses. On Saturday, I found out a few more things that made it impossible for me to hope any longer. I decided to divorce him."

Shirley gasped.

"I confided in my friend Evelyn. She said I'd better get to the bank on Monday, yesterday. She knew of cases where one spouse cleans out the accounts, then the other suffers until the courts make them give it back. If there's anything left at that point."

"George wouldn't do that," Shirley said.

"Mom, he did."

"What?" Stanley shouted.

"Let me finish, please. We have power-of-attorney for each other. Without my knowledge, he cleared out our investment accounts, our checking and savings, and re-mortgaged the house. He left me with two-thousand dollars. Total."

"But, how? I don't understand." Bewilderment filled Shirley.

"This is embarrassing enough. I'm not going to get through it if you interrupt. I didn't get any sleep last night. I was up thinking about what to do, thinking about what the lawyer told me yesterday afternoon, what were my best options. I had to give the lawyer a thousand to get things started. His fee will be much more by the end. I need to hire a forensic accountant, too. They're trying to schedule an emergency hearing in front of a judge to make George give me enough money to live on until all this is settled, but the soonest date so far is two months from now.

"I talked to Fletch last night. He's sending me five-thousand, but says he can't do more right now without liquidating something. God bless him, he said he'd do that, too, but I can't promise to repay him and don't want to take away from his kids. Then, this morning, a solution came to me. I know you two don't have much extra cash, and I don't expect you to jeopardize your finances, but I came up with a way you can really help."

"Anything," Stanley said.

"A real-estate agent that Evelyn knows said I could rent out the house almost immediately. The rents around here are expensive, so I'd have to move to a different area. That means different schools for the kids. If they're going to have the trauma of moving from their home and their school, I figure why not move to where I don't have to pay any rent? I could use that money for so many other needed things, including Sean's tuition. It's his last year of college, and having him quit now would be heart-breaking. Your way of helping is letting us move in with you for free. I can't imagine it would be longer than a year, tops."

"We'll have to—" Shirley said.

"Consider it done," Stanley said.

Shirley felt her stomach convulsing. She ran to the

downstairs bathroom.

***

The ride to the store was too quiet. Shirley felt like she was enveloped in a dense cloud of doom. Several times, she tried to initiate a conversation, but Stanley only grunted and wouldn't look at her.

He pulled up to the shop and stared out the windshield.

"We need to talk," Shirley said.

"Not now, we don't."

She sighed, got out, and closed the car door.

Stanley didn't waste any time driving away.

Trudging up the four steps to the shop door, she couldn't fathom why things had gone so haywire so fast. Von Cletan *did* set her nerves on edge. She was bossy and rude. But why did the woman inspire such hate, and yes, jealousy? And why couldn't Stanley see her for the bitch she was?

She unlocked the door, turned the sign around on its hook so it said, *Open*, and hustled to turn on lights and get settled. Nina's dilemma had hit like a tornado. Out of nowhere, the one person she *knew* she'd never have to worry about had collapsed. True to form, though, Nina took the reins and rose to the challenge. But how were she and Stanley going to hide their dirty secret? It was definitely time to tell the kids about their store. She wished she didn't feel so fatigued and defeated, because she had to hone their cover stories if they were to fool Nina and two teenagers.

Her dread grew worse every hour as two o'clock approached. It helped that there were a few customers to break the tension. She tried to eat her bagged lunch, but put it back in the fridge after a couple bites.

At one-thirty, she freshened her makeup, smiled at herself in the mirror, and turned on the radio. She'd be damned rather than let Von Cletan know she'd had any effect on her.

Stanley walked in at exactly one-forty-five. "Good afternoon, *Mitzi*." He breezed by her without making eye contact. She heard his door shut.

A few minutes before two, Von Cletan entered. She wore a black and white patterned dress, cinched in at the waist with a wide black belt. A pricey-looking, wide-brimmed, black hat with white and black feathers adorned her head. The big sunglasses hid her eyes. The dress stopped at the knee. The three-inch pumps showed off her ankles—which didn't look fat anymore. She walked to the counter as though she'd never been in the shop before. Shirley's heart sank further. Von Cletan had lost even more weight.

"Hello, *Mitzi*. I have an appointment," Von Cletan said.

Shirley wanted to smack the beast, but kept her composure. Stanley was already mad enough at her. He was right about Von Cletan. She could hurt them—probably would love to.

"Yes," Shirley said. "Follow me." She led her to the storage room and pointed. "Back there. You'll find the door."

Von Cletan's heavy floral perfume floated by as she passed Shirley.

She fled to the front and turned up the radio volume.

***

Stanley heard the knock at the door and crossed the room, opening it to see a more curvaceous woman than he expected. "Come in."

Catherine waltzed in and did a twirl. "What do you think?" She lowered her sunglasses and batted her blue eyes at him.

He stuck his head into the storage area, checked for any sign of Shirley, felt relief when he heard the radio playing louder, then locked the door. "You look beautiful." This time, he meant it. She did.

Taking off her hat, she put it, her purse and sunglasses on the dresser that held the TV. She scanned the room. "It's not as horrible as I thought it would be." She approached, putting her arms around him. She braced her chin on his chest and stared into his eyes. "Oh, Mack. I have missed you."

At first he was hesitant to embrace her, but the memory of what she'd done to him the last time came racing back, and he felt a stirring. What the hell, he thought, putting his hands on her waist, liking the feel of it. He bent his head to kiss her.

She responded with a tiny moan, and their kiss went deeper until she pulled away. "No. I'm not here for that." Fanning her face with one hand, she moved to the easy chair and sat.

Stanley Junior was already halfway there. "You're not?" He sat on the end of the bed.

The dress buttoned in the front, and she undid the top one. "No. I'm here to talk to you." She unbuttoned another. "I have a proposal. You must promise to hear me out. Do you promise?" The next button went. Black lace became visible.

"Sure." He had no idea what she was doing, but he liked it.

"It seems obvious the reason you are doing this is you need the money."

He nodded.

"It's also obvious that you and I have more than a little *electricity*." She undid the fourth button and pulled the dress halves to the sides, exposing some sort of old-fashioned corset thing. Her breasts were visible under the lace, and her nipples pressed against it. She lowered her eyelids and made a little come-hither type gesture.

She was still overweight, but truly voluptuous now. The way some movie stars used to be. Stanley found himself wanting to dive in.

As if reading his mind, she held up a forefinger. "No, no. You know I can't stand the idea of you being with those other women. And having to answer to that awful, scrawny Mitzi creature must be a nightmare for you."

Mitzi creature? Wait. His brain engaged. That was his wife. "Don't criticize her. I need her. I know you two don't like each other, but *I* like her. Please respect that."

"Fine. If it will make you happy." She undid her belt and two more buttons. "What if you didn't have to do this anymore?"

"I'd love to go back to being retired," he said. "But my circumstances aren't so good."

"Forgive me, I assumed so. What I'd like to do, but dear, dear Mack, please do not take offense—it's the last thing I want—I want to give you enough money that you'll never have to think about this tawdry set-up again. All I want in return is for us to be together. Think about how much fun it would be. I have a villa in Italy, flats in London and Paris. I go to Cannes every year. Wimbledon. We can go anywhere, do anything. I'd love to share it all with you."

Traipsing around the globe with Catherine? He shook his head. "I have children and grandchildren." Nina's situation reared to the forefront. "There are some in the family having pretty rough financial times. My daughter, especially." Not to mention a wife.

"I have a daughter, too. Did I ever tell you that?"

"No."

"I'm sure you will meet her. Now, how best to help your daughter? If I were to give you two million dollars, would it clear up everybody's issues?"

Stanley's jaw fell open. He stared at her. "Say that again?"

Leveling her gaze at him, she smiled. "Two million. I'll write the check right now. You can wipe clean your family's problems. You'll have enough left over, I'm sure, to be independent. Let's make it three. That way you'll have plenty of your own, so you won't feel I'm lording it over you. I don't want that. I only want you. Go back to Florida and visit as often as you like. But we'll be a couple."

Stunned, he tried to imagine it. The whole mess, his and Shirley's, Nina's, all whisked away like magic. He'd give Nina and Shirley a million each. No, there'd be taxes. And it wouldn't be fair to ignore Fletcher. His head buzzed with the calculations.

"You're considering it." She stood, removed the rest of her dress, and touched her breasts.

His mind whirled. What to do? Could he leave Shirley? He loved her, but was it out of habit? Their relationship was a disaster now. The ugly side she'd shown the night before haunted him. What were the chances of healing the two of them? Not good, as long as they had to keep up the prostitution. Which they'd have to for a few years at least. That would kill whatever they had left for each other. He could see that now. Either way, it seemed they were doomed.

Catherine approached him and unzipped his jeans.

He snapped back from his thoughts. Her hand caressed him, and the stirrings began again. "I need some time to think about it, Catherine."

"Understandable." She knelt in front of him.

His body's quick reaction surprised him. He abandoned the exhausting fight going on in his head and gave in to the pleasure.

***

At three, Shirley heard the telltale clacking of Von Cletan's heels headed her way. She busied herself with refolding tiny T-shirts on one of the front tables.

Von Cletan didn't look at her. She clattered her way across the tile wearing a smug smile and left the building.

There were two shoppers in the store when Stanley emerged. He walked straight to the door and outside without saying a word. Faking a smile for her customer while she handed her a credit receipt, Shirley's doom cloud dragged her in. She couldn't remember ever feeling so depressed. Instead of her own troubles, she switched to thinking about Nina's.

Stanley had had a second conversation with her while Shirley was in the shower. Nina would fit as much as she could into her minivan, have a storage facility pick up the rest of the valuable things from the house, and rent the house furnished. Their goal was to arrive in West Sago Beach in a week's time.

The bells jingled. It was too happy a sound. They had to go. Maybe replace them with dry bones and chicken feet. A little voodoo might spook the evil Von Cletan away.

Lance came in, his forehead etched with worry lines.

What now, she thought. What petty issue was wrinkling his perfect starched-shirt life? "Hello."

He pointed to the street, seeming to be tongue-tied and shaking his head. "I'm confused. I was at the gas station three blocks down and went inside to buy a soda. I have to sneak them, you know. Paul doesn't want me to have it. Says it's poison."

She forced a half-smile. "Probably is."

"Whatever." He screwed up one side of his mouth. "Is Stanley here?"

"No. He's picking me up at five. Why?"

Lance glanced toward the street again. "I think I just saw him getting into a black Mercedes. At the gas station. And your car is parked along the side."

Fear struck her. She felt paralyzed.

"Sweetie, what's going on?" Lance touched her shoulder. "You're white as an Englishman's bum in the winter."

She began to tremble. "I don't believe it."

"Here, let's sit you down." He took her arm and guided her toward the counter.

Her knees gave way, and she landed on her bottom, despite Lance's grip on her. He lost his balance and came close to tumbling on top of her.

"All rightie, then," he said. "I'll bring a chair from the kitchen."

"No," she said, getting up. "I'm going to be sick." She staggered into the bathroom, feeling both lightheaded and heavier than lead at the same time.

"Should I be calling an ambulance?"

"No," she yelled, bending and leaning on the bathroom door frame. "I'm fine." The urge to vomit passed, but everything inside her ached. She rinsed her face. When she looked in the mirror, words written in red lipstick greeted her. *Mack has STDs.* She yelped, snatched some tissues, and wiped them off. Von Cletan had to have done it. Why? Was it true? Was that why she insisted on talking to him? She made her way to the kitchen-office and sat.

Lance walked in, pulled the other chair close to hers, and lowered himself into it while reaching for her hands. "What's wrong?"

"Nothing." She stared at her lap. "I'll be okay. Didn't sleep last night. That's all. I don't want to keep you. You can go."

"Nuh-uh. Something is stinking like a dead skunk, and I am *not* going anywhere until you tell me what it is. Where was Stanley headed?"

"I have no idea."

"Look at me."

She shook her head. She couldn't face him. "Lance, you are a darling young man, and I appreciate your concern, but trust me, you don't want to know how complicated our lives are."

"Is he cheating on you? With the woman in the Mercedes? Is that it?"

Was that it? Had Stanley started a relationship on the side with Von Cletan? *Von Cletan?* It seemed inconceivable, but if true, explained so much. "What did she look like?"

"I only got a quick glimpse as he got in, but I think blonde hair, sunglasses, and wearing black and white?"

Stanley's betrayal sliced into her. The only way Von Cletan would know that Mack had a STD is if she gave it to him. Which meant he wasn't using condoms with her. Tears filled her eyes and splashed onto her khakis.

"This is how I met you." His voice was gentle. "Remember? You were crying on the bench outside our store."

She nodded. That day seemed like years before, not months. In retrospect, she'd swap the problems she had then with the current mangled mess. "You and Paul have been so good to me." She raised her head and looked at him. "You wouldn't understand. Go back to Paulina's. Pretend you never saw Stanley today."

Lance sat back and crossed his arms. "Not a chance. I've never seen anyone need a friend more. If you don't tell me, I'll sit here until Stanley gets here, and I'll confront him. Look what he's done to you. How dare he treat you like this?"

That would be worse than terrible. She needed to process the information. "If it's true, then as a wife, I want to decide how to approach my husband. It's my right."

Bells jingled, and Shirley cursed to herself. A customer right then was not what she wanted.

"Hello?" a female voice called.

Wiping away tears, Shirley rose from her chair.

"Mitzi? Are you here?"

She felt the blood drain out of her face again. "Who? I'll be right there." To Lance she said, "Stay here. She must be at the wrong place." Hustling to the retail area, she saw a look of recognition dawn on the woman's face. It was Hillary Uderbach, one of Mack's less frequent clients. Shirley did a warning wave, hoping Hillary would catch on to shut up.

"There you are," Hillary's voice seemed to boom. "I want an appointment with Mack."

Threatening her with her eyes, Shirley got up close to her. "Shhh," she whispered.

Hillary glanced around. "There's no one here."

"There's someone in the back room. Call me later."

"It will only take a moment. I'll make the appointment while I'm here," she whispered.

Grabbing the woman's shoulders, Shirley turned her around. "Go. Quickly."

With an exasperated sigh, Hillary left.

Shirley turned to find Lance, arms crossed with a glass of water in one hand, leaning against the side of the archway.

"Mitzi?"

"She *was* mixed up," she said. "Wrong store."

"She recognized you. Who's Mack?" He lifted the glass. "Thought you might need some water. Why are the words, *Don't trust Mack. He has STDs* written on the cabinet?"

"Damn her, that woman." Shirley glanced at the time. Four. She turned the *Open* sign around and locked the door. "I'll explain. Promise me you won't tell Paul anything about this, and you won't let Stanley know that you know. You have to be gone before he returns."

He wore a skeptical frown. "You want me to keep a secret from Paul? For how long?"

"Until I tell you otherwise. If you promise, I'll tell you everything. If you don't, you'll have to unearth the dirt on your own."

"There's dirt?" Lance's love for titillating gossip rivaled Dora's.

"Tons." Shirley went back to the kitchen and reclaimed her chair.

Lance followed her. Scratching his head, he stared at her for a moment, then nodded. "Okay. I promise. Don't make it for too long, though. Paul will get pissed as hell, but the longer I keep something from him, the less make-up sex I'll get."

"Don't worry. The wheels are coming off our lives so fast, it's frightening. The blonde in the Mercedes, from what you described, is Catherine Von Cletan."

Lance's jaw dropped. "No way. The Sago Beach maven? Stanley's fooling around with her? How'd he meet her? Oh, wait, you couldn't know that."

"I introduced them."

His eyes grew huge.

"Von Cletan is a client of Mack's. Stanley is Mack." She went back to the beginning of the sordid story and told him everything.

"Holy crap on a crusade." He looked at the glass of water, still clenched in his hand, like he had no idea where it came from. He downed it and set the empty glass on the desk. "And your daughter and two teenage grandkids are moving in with you next week?"

"Probably by Monday. We're all in deep, deep trouble. It was working fine. We were recovering the money. I thought if we could keep it going for a few years, we'd be back to where we were. The one thing I'd didn't figure on was how unpredictable people are. I thought the women would follow the rules. Now that stupid conniving bitch ruined everything."

"People do what they want, not what they're told. Especially rich people. I could have clued you in on that. But now—we don't know for sure what's happening between Von Cletan and Stanley, do we? You might be right, maybe he's not cheating with her, well, I mean . . . Cheating the regular way. Maybe she took him to a private doctor to get tested."

"It's all too much." She glanced at her watch. Four-thirty-five. "You need to get out of here. I need time to regroup before he comes back."

"What will you do?"

"Nothing until I know more."

CHAPTER SIXTY-NINE

Stanley didn't complain when Shirley didn't make dinner that night. He ordered a pizza and ate it in his recliner while watching television. Several times, she asked about his appointment with Catherine. He ignored her. He had to. Now, still in the recliner, he pretended to be dozing. There was a sports round-up show on, but his thoughts were on how to divvy up the money if he took it. Traveling the world in style tempted him. In the company of a woman who wasn't screaming at him every day sounded even better. He heard footsteps.

"Stanley, we do have to talk. You're mad at me. I'm furious with you. I haven't slept and can't keep any food down."

He opened his eyes. "It will lead to another fight."

"You are not telling me something very bad. I know it."

How in blazes did she know?

"Look, I know we're falling apart. But we can fix it."

"Seems doubtful. Do you see any way out of this mess? You're beyond jealous of a situation that you created. I'm in a no-win position."

She moved to the sofa. "I don't understand why you're siding with Von Cletan. It's killing me. What aren't you telling me?"

His wife seemed to have aged ten years in the last two

months. She looked haggard, and in her eyes, he saw a meanness that wasn't there before. He felt sorry for her, but no matter what he said, it would be wrong. "I'm not siding with anybody. Our lives now depend on my not pissing off some socialites. Honestly? I decided I should start sleeping at the store."

"Don't you dare. You're saying that so you can be with her."

That thought had not occurred to him. "With who?"

"Von Cletan." Her voice began to rise. "The lard-ass who thinks she owns you."

"Calling her a lard-ass isn't helping. And no, that's not why. It would be to escape the hounding you're giving me every day."

"So, you find her attractive."

"This sounds like a repeat of last night."

"Because you haven't answered me. Do you or do you not find that horrible, nasty woman attractive? I want the truth."

Standing, he counted to ten. "The truth?" His pent-up anger threatened to take over. It was time to retreat to the spare bedroom, but he didn't. "The *truth* is you set me up with big women. At first, no, I didn't like them. But a man gets used to new and different things, and I discovered some extra padding can be okay, kind of nice, actually. Mostly, I found out these women are lonely. They've been hurt. They're desperate for attention. They may be a little nutty, but they're people—longing for what we have. What we had. We were richer than all of them. We just didn't know it. They're not bitches at all, and I wish to hell you'd stop using that word. You never used to say it."

"You like them?" she yelled. "You find them sexy now? Including Von Cletan?"

"God damn it. Yes. Okay? Yes. Catherine is beautiful, and I find her *very* sexy. Is that what you wanted to hear? Are you happy now that you've destroyed us?"

"I knew it," she shouted. Tears dripped down her face. "I knew it. You are having an affair with her."

"Affair? You're insane. I'm having an affair with over twenty women right now. You arranged them. Didn't you think that maybe, just maybe, some of them would be appealing to me?"

"I'm talking about outside the shop. About how you got into her car this afternoon. Where did you go?"

He wasn't ready for that. "How do you know? You know what? I don't care how you know."

"She wrote two messages today for me to find. One on the bathroom mirror and one in the kitchen. They said you had sexually transmitted diseases. Do you? Did she give them to you? When were you going to tell me?"

Unbelieving, he processed that. He shook his head. "No, I don't. And Catherine? Stooping to the level of writing lies in a bathroom? I doubt it. If there really were messages, somebody else left them. Maybe someone whose friend Dora recently told her to play dirty tricks? Maybe someone whose jealousy is out of control? Someone who hoped Catherine would see it and never come back?"

He went upstairs, threw some essentials into a duffle bag, his hidden money stash, too, and clomped back down.

Shirley looked terrified. "Where are you going?"

He wanted to care about her at that moment, but didn't. "Somewhere you won't be at me constantly for the crime of being a man. Maybe if I can get some peace, I'll be better equipped to deal with this. We gotta do something, but I'll be damned if I know what the hell the right answer is." He charged out the front door and headed for the main entrance of the village, thinking he'd have the gate guard call him a cab.

***

Shirley's voice stopped working as Stanley stomped out the door, leaving it swinging behind him. Her brain was telling her too many things at once. *Stop him. Let him go. This is all Von Cletan's fault. It's his fault. It's my fault for letting her meet him. This isn't fair. Does he love her?*

Her tears streamed, and her eyes stung from all the crying she'd done. She felt so alone as she closed the door. Curling into a ball on the sofa, her head hammered.

The house phone rang. She ignored it. When the machine answered, Fletcher's voice came on. "Hey, Mom and Dad. It's nine o'clock, Tuesday night. I haven't heard back from you. I guess you're either in bed already or out having a wild night—you crazy kids. Call me back, okay? I still want to do dinner with you. How's Thursday night?"

It rang again. Clearing her throat, she picked it up. "Fletcher. Sorry, I couldn't get to the phone. I—"

"No. It's me," Nina said. "I'm so overwhelmed. I needed to talk to someone I trust."

Talk about terrible timing. Shirley tried to sound normal. "I know, dear. But when—"

"No. You don't know. You couldn't possibly. And now . . ." Nina's voice faltered. The next sentence came out in a crying whine. "Now—now my baby's pregnant. Mom, can you believe it? This is all that rat-bastard's fault."

Dazed, Shirley couldn't speak. A pregnant sixteen-year old coming to live with her? Her life was becoming *The Nightmare at Silver Sago Village.*

"Mom? Did you hear me?"

"Yes. I'm in shock, I think. And who is the *rat-bastard*?"

"George, of course. Aren't you listening?"

Dropping the phone, Shirley went into brain freeze.

"Mom? Mom?" Nina's voice wailed from the handset lying on the floor.

She picked it up. "I'm here. But I don't believe it. George got Mary Ann pregnant? Why haven't you had him arrested?"

"What?" Nina shrieked. "I didn't say that at all." She went on to explain about the young man who'd had his way with Mary Ann.

All Shirley could focus on was one more heavy straw on an overburdened camel.

When she finally got off the phone with Nina, wishing *she* could confide in someone, she thought about calling Lance. He'd be home with Paul, so that wouldn't work. A spark of hope scratched through her despair. She reached for the handset on the end table and dialed. "Agnes?"

***

Stanley tipped the cabbie and grabbed his duffel bag. He unlocked the shop's door and went in the back to his room where he sat on the bed for a while. His life had gone from an ordinary retirement to a complete disaster in less than six months. How did Shirley know he went anywhere with Catherine? What was lunacy was how Shirley went ballistic because he was spotted in Catherine's car, yet *knowing* something sexual had occurred with Catherine in another room was okay? What Catherine did to him while behind the wall separating his wife from his lovers would have sent Shirley into raging territory. In a bizarre twist, it was innocent enough in the car—a short drive around the island to talk more.

Shirley had looked so distraught. He felt horrible about that, but it wasn't *his* fault. Why hadn't he refused her stupid idea? The damage it caused looked like too raw a wound to ever heal in either of them. Would she be capable of returning to the trust and love she once had for him? No. Her suspicions would never stop. Also, he knew if, by some miracle, they did get past all their present problems, *he* would have a new issue. His attraction to her had all but gone dormant. Between the ugly side of her jealousy and resentments and her now too-thin-for-him body, he'd have trouble with it. Bigger, more womanly curves turned him on. He shook his head. Who would have foreseen that?

As far as why he went along with her plan, maybe there

were two reasons. Thinking back over the years, he realized that, just about every time they'd argued about anything of importance, he'd given in. Upsetting her never seemed worth pursuing it further. The second possible reason was hard to admit. After so many years of marriage, the prospect of bedding someone—anyone—new excited him. Being able to do it with his wife sanctioning it?

"And now here we are." His daughter was desperate for immediate help. He and Shirley were equally messed up. If he didn't take Catherine up on her offer, life would only get worse, much worse. If he did, at least his family wouldn't have to worry about money anymore. It was worth exploring.

Taking a piece of paper from his wallet, he walked to the register counter. He picked up the store's phone and dialed the number on the paper.

CHAPTER SEVENTY

At seven on Wednesday morning, Shirley ran to the door.

Agnes stood there holding her tiny dog, O'Keeffe.

"You look awful." Agnes put a hand on Shirley's shoulder. "Did you get any sleep?"

"A couple of hours. Thanks for coming. Let's go to the kitchen. I need coffee. Want some?"

"No." Agnes sat at the dinette table and put O'Keeffe on the floor. He sniffed around the floor, then settled at her feet. "Hope you don't mind my bringing him. He can be a great comfort. Let me make sure I understood you last night. Stanley left you? Good old, solid, reliable, dependable Stanley? You two are the last couple I ever expected to split up."

Shirley poured her coffee and brought it to the table, sitting in the other chair. "Hard to believe. As you can see, I'm a total wreck."

O'Keeffe's ears picked up, and he moved to Shirley's feet.

"He's smart."

"This has something to do with your wig at the store and the names Mack and Mitzi. Am I right?"

She nodded. "You've probably already guessed there's trouble. I need your help."

"You two are selling drugs, aren't you?"

"No." Shirley let out a sad chuckle. "That might have been a better idea, though. Remember when we talked a while ago about Stanley and I having money problems? Well, it was much worse than I let on."

"I kind of figured."

"An accountant took almost all we had left and fled to the Caribbean with it. Ours plus lots of other people's money. We never had tons to begin with, but that was devastating. We were going to have to sell this house and go live in some crappy rental in a dangerous neighborhood."

"People do move in with their children sometimes."

"Neither of us wanted to go to Jersey—Nina would drive us up a wall, and Fletcher had his hands full with alimony and child support payments. Stanley wouldn't consider it anyway. He's never told the kids a thing about our finances. He'd rather die than admit we screwed up so badly." She took a long sip, then reached down to stroke O'Keefe's head.

Agnes' face stayed neutral.

"So," Shirley said, "I came up with an idea that would make us a lot of money fast. Much faster than the dead-end jobs we were in. Neither of us could fathom how it happened we were going to have to work for the rest of our lives. Or until we dropped from exhaustion. It was so unfair." She paused, embarrassed.

"Your idea?"

Better to just spit it out. "We pimped out Stanley to those rich women on the island."

"What?" Agnes' eyes widened while her forehead shrank to an inch high, making her wrinkles bunch up like an accordion. "Stanley's a male prostitute?" She covered her mouth and began to laugh. "Are you kidding?" Instead of subsiding, her laughter got wilder, and she rocked sideways in her chair—until she shook out her arms and wiped tears from her eyes.

Shirley stared at her. "I have to say, I didn't expect this reaction."

"I'm sure you didn't. Oh, sweet Jesus, that's priceless. Hoo." She fanned herself with one hand.

"Somehow, I thought you'd be more help."

"I will be. I promise." She pulled a napkin from the holder in the center of the table, dabbed her eyes, then blew her nose into it. "Don't you see how ludicrous that sounds? Here you two are, the most normal, white-bread couple I've ever met, *anyone*'s ever met, and you're involved in prostitution?"

Shirley nodded. It was ridiculous. The whole thing. "Yeah. It's nuts." Agnes' residual laughing made Shirley start. It was the fatigue probably, but she erupted into full-blown laugh mode, which set Agnes off again.

When they'd calmed down, Shirley told her everything, including Nina's news.

"You're completely right," Agnes said when Shirley finished. "It's not funny at all."

"No. But that felt good. I can't remember the last time I laughed. It is absurd."

"What in blue blazes made you believe it wouldn't make you jealous?"

"I don't know. Now. I guess I was so desperate to save us, I convinced myself."

"Anybody else know?"

"Lance does. He promised not to say anything to Paul until I figure out what's happening. I called the shop this morning, but Stanley, if he's there, didn't answer. What if he went to Von Cletan's last night? By trying to fix our problems, I may have ruined our marriage."

"Maybe. Don't get ahead of yourself." Agnes picked up O'Keeffe, who'd fallen asleep. "What time is Stanley's appointment today?"

"Two. With Leticia Basselbrook."

"Think he'll show up for it?"

"Since it's our income at stake, I hope so."

Agnes seemed to study her. "Tell me, what do you want

most right now?"

"That's easy. I want this financial stress to go away. It's so hard, and it's what caused all this trouble between us to begin with."

Standing, Agnes gave her a hug. "Let me think a little. I'll stop by the store later, okay?"

***

Stanley had left the store early, not wanting to see Shirley when she arrived. He spent the morning sitting on a bench at the beach watching the gulls, the ocean, and thinking. As lunch time approached, he walked the four blocks to Alfred's. He checked his watch. Eleven-thirty. Right on time. In the ornate lobby, he gave his name to the maître d'.

"This way please, sir."

He followed him into the center room to a secluded booth behind a fountain.

The man dipped in a half bow and left.

Stanley sat on the booth bench opposite Catherine. "Hello."

She smiled and touched his hand. "I'm so happy you're considering this."

Observing her for a moment, he steeled himself for rejection. What he was about to say could upset the whole thing. Then no one would get any money, and his family would be in dire straits, *and* Catherine could purposely mess up their chances of making any more money if she wanted.

"Before we order lunch, or talk about anything else," he said, "I have to tell you something. I'm hoping you'll understand."

"Why, Mack, you sound so serious."

"I haven't been honest with you."

"Oh?" Her eyes narrowed.

He swallowed. "No. But not you alone. Everyone. I

mean, all the clients I've, uh, been with. I had to. To protect myself. Mack is not my real name."

"It's not?"

"My name is Stanley Nowack."

"I see. Well, I suppose that's understandable. After all, there are a lot of unhinged people running around these days."

"Exactly. But that's not all. I uh . . . I'm . . ." He felt his stomach drop. "I'm married. Estranged now. But married."

She stared at him. A slow smile crept onto her face. "Yes. I know."

"You do? How?" How long had she known the truth?

"I may be a woman in love, but I am not a fool. Before I decided to make you this offer, I hired an investigator to find out about you. He is very discreet."

The decision was made for him, then. He was back to nothing. Back to fighting with Shirley and having sex for money, causing more tension. How were they going to hide all of it from Nina when she arrived? He suddenly felt very tired. Sliding out of the booth, he said, "I'm sorry. I didn't want to lie to anybody. It seemed necessary."

"Where are you going? Please sit down. I don't want you to leave."

"You don't?"

"Of course not." With a small wave of her hand she summoned the waiter to the table. "Hamri, we'll have a bottle of Dom, please."

The waiter scurried away.

"Dom?" Stanley wasn't sure what was going on.

"Champagne." She gave him a broad smile this time. "You see, if you didn't tell me about your wife and your real name, I was prepared to walk away. But you did. You wanted our relationship to start with honesty. That means everything to me."

Nervous, he clasped his hands together to hold them still. He'd fessed up mostly because a big check had to be made out to Stanley Nowack, not a fictional name. "You should know I haven't one-hundred percent decided. It's a huge change. Although my wife and I don't get along any more, it's a big decision to leave her."

"I agree. You're an honorable man, so it makes sense. Your wife knows what you do for money now?"

"Yes. It was her idea. She's Mitzi. Her real name is Shirley. As your detective—I'm guessing—told you."

"Her idea? Interesting. Think about that. What sort of wife pushes her husband to sleep with other women? She can't possibly love you." She nodded. "Ah. That would be the estranged part. But even so, how could a woman arrange such a thing if she cared at any level? And, in my estimation, only a man who didn't love his wife would agree to it. So. There really isn't a relationship."

Hearing it stated so simply, Stanley had a difficult time thinking of a way to disagree. Maybe he and Shirley *had* stayed together for so many years out of habit. It was comfortable. Was. But not anymore. "I need a little more time."

"All right. I want an answer by tomorrow. I'm making two reservations for a flight to Rome tomorrow night."

"That seems kind of quick." Leave for Europe? He shook his head. "I don't have a passport."

"As for the quick part, I say, the quicker, the better. Like a Band Aid. Pull it off fast. It'll hurt less in the long run. Don't stay and drag out the inevitable dramatic scene."

That made sense to him, too.

"We'll go to New York first. Stay in the city for a few days while we get you a passport. Then we'll fly to Rome."

He hadn't expected things to happen so fast.

"And I haven't forgotten your money." She gave him a business card. "This is my accountant. When you decide, and it had better be soon, call him and he'll set up your account."

"I've never handled that much. How would I give some to my family?"

"If you provide him with their social security numbers, etc, he could set up separate ones for them, and you needn't be bothered with it."

The waiter returned with the champagne and poured it into two flutes. "Would you like to order your lunch now?"

Catherine ordered for both of them. She raised her glass. "To us."

He moved his forward to clink with hers, and she pulled hers away.

"Raise it toward me. Never touch them," she said.

"All right." He did and she returned the gesture. It occurred to him for the first time that she would have to coach him in the ways of being acceptable in her crowd. Or did she plan to keep him out of the public eye? A part of him felt cheap. Paid for. Get over it, he told himself, that ship was long over the horizon.

She pulled a cell phone from her purse and put it on the table in front of him. "Here. This is yours. We need a way to contact each other."

"I've never used one. Don't know how to turn it on."

"It's easy. Here, I'll show you."

CHAPTER SEVENTY-ONE

At the shop on Wednesday, to occupy her mind with something other than Stanley, Shirley practiced her lines and the happy voice she'd use when she called Fletcher to tell him about the baby store. Nina could wait to know about it until she arrived in West Sago Beach the next week. There was too much on her plate already. She saw motion on the porch. It was Agnes.

"Have you heard from him?" Agnes closed the door.

"No." Shirley tried to quash the disturbing feeling that something awful had happened. "The bed doesn't look slept in, but there was a damp towel hanging in the bathroom."

"Can I see your secret boom-boom room?"

"Why not." She came from behind the counter, led Agnes to it, and unlocked the door. "Nothing fancy. The walls are soundproofed. Stanley said they had to be. Some of the women get pretty loud." She shivered.

Agnes raised an eyebrow.

The merry jingle of bells sounded. "That's it. I'm taking those annoying things down right this second." Shirley headed for the front. "Close the door when you're done looking."

Expecting to see a customer, she pasted a smile on her face.

It was Lance. He wore an expression that asked the question, *do we know any more?*

She shook her head and walked to the blasted bells. "These sound much too happy. I can't stand it." Lifting them off their hook, she dropped them in the trash can by the register.

"I take it Stanley's not here?" Lance said.

"We had a huge fight last night," she said. "He packed a bag and left. I think he spent the night here, but I don't know for sure. He could have been with *her*."

Lance gasped and covered his mouth. "He wouldn't."

"I don't know what he would or wouldn't do."

Agnes came through the arch.

"I know you," Lance said. "You're the friend who came into Paulina's on Saturday."

"Lance, this is Agnes," Shirley said. "I told her everything I told you."

"I'm happy to see you. Our Shirley needs her friends right now." He tsked. "What are we going to do?"

"I know." Agnes swung an elbow to the side and back and stomped her foot. "We'll put on a *show*."

Shirley emoted a sad grin. "Thanks Micky. Or are you Judy?"

"What are you two talking about?" Lance scrunched one side of his face.

"Eh." Agnes sent him a dismissive wave. "From some old movies. You're too young to know." She turned to Shirley. "Stanley's got an appointment in an hour. Lance and I shouldn't be here when he comes in. Want me to come back later?"

The shop phone rang. Shirley clicked the handset on.

"It's me." Stanley sounded tired.

Her heart jumped. "Where are you? I was worried."

"Doesn't matter where I am. Cancel my appointments for the rest of the week. I can't deal with that right now."

"What about the money? We need it."

"Forget about money for a god damn minute, would you?"

"Will you come home? We should talk."

"No. I have to have some time alone. To think. I'll come

into the store tomorrow, near closing time. By then, I'll have things sorted out."

"Nina called." Shirley changed to a whisper. "Your granddaughter is pregnant."

"Damn. What the hell else can go wrong? I have to go."

"But Stanley—"

"Take care, Shirl. Get some rest." He hung up.

She stared at the phone.

"I take it he's not coming here today," Agnes said.

"No." Shaking, she put the handset back and wrapped her arms around herself.

"Aw, sweetie." Lance enveloped her in a huge hug. "You might be nuttier than a bag of squirrels, but I love you anyway."

"Thank you." Another crying jag threatened. She took a deep breath, trying to ward it off.

Agnes approached and threw her arms around them both. After a few seconds, she broke away. "Enough. What else did he say?"

"He'll be here tomorrow around five. I guess we'll talk after I close the store."

Stepping away from her, Lance grimaced. "I know one thing for sure. When he comes in, you'd better look a lot nicer than you do right now."

"He's correct," Agnes said. "You look like shit."

"Thank you both." Shirley walked to the hall bathroom and checked the mirror. An unrecognizable elderly woman with dark bags under her eyes and wearing a perky wig stared back. She pulled off the wig and went back to Agnes and Lance. "You're right. Now what do I do?"

"Can you give her a makeover?" Agnes said.

He gave her a *really?* expression. "Not all gay men know how to do that stuff."

"Can't blame a gal for hoping."

"I *do* know someone who could, though," Lance said. "I'll give her a call. Is it okay if I tell her to meet us here around three tomorrow?" He touched a finger under Shirley's chin and lifted it.

"Is that going to be enough time?" Agnes asked. "She's looking pretty rough."

***

"Huh." Fletcher hung up his phone and tossed it onto the bed. He removed the bag of dirty laundry from his open suitcase and threw it against the door, not seeing his wife approaching in time.

"Watch it." Maddy sidestepped the bag and sat in her bedroom side chair. "I just finished with that call from my mother. It was so hard not to say anything about us."

"Must be a mom-vibe thing happening. Mine phoned while you were talking to yours. I can't believe what she told me."

She gave him a quizzical look.

"They've opened a store. A baby store. In Sago Beach. It's very strange, don't you think? At their ages, all of a sudden they decide to get entrepreneurial?"

"I suppose I'd be a better judge of that if I'd met them." Maddy smiled. "It's not unheard of. Maybe it's their way of staying relevant in the world."

"I mentioned doing dinner tomorrow night. Mom said she'll let me know. That will be your Shirley and Stanley debut. I'm sure once they've recovered from the jolt of finding out we're married, they'll love you."

"Are you sure you can't tell them in advance?"

"Can you tell yours by phone?"

She laughed. "No. I'm her only child. She deserves to find out in person. Besides, having you with me will deflect the shock. She'll be so charmed by you, she'll forget to be angry with me. We have to see her soon, though. She told me she's leaving for New York tomorrow night, and a few days later, heading for Italy. She wasn't sure for how long."

CHAPTER SEVENTY-TWO

Despite her exhaustion, Shirley had another sleepless night. No matter how upset she was with Stanley, the house felt empty without him. She considered returning to the store at night to see if he was sleeping there, then realized how awful it would be to find out he wasn't. When she dragged herself out of bed on Thursday, it felt like she was pulling an anvil behind her.

While making coffee, she thought about her anger. No, it was outrage. Fury. How could he say he enjoyed sex with those women? Fueling her jealousy further. And admitting he found Von Cletan sexy—*sexy*? He might as well have slapped her. He had to know how much that would hurt. If he loved her, he would never have said it.

"So. There it is." She poured coffee into her mug and went to the shower. A stray inkling hit her—why would she want him back now anyway? After what he'd said and done? It was very possible that maybe she didn't.

***

Her day at the store went slow. Several customers came in, and she tried her best to be cheerful. A few minutes before three, Agnes came in. She wore a neon-pink Polo shirt, her standard blue-jean shorts, and the black high-tops.

"How are you today?" Agnes said. "Your eyes aren't as bloodshot, so that's good."

"Gosh, stop with the gratuitous compliments." Shirley hugged her. "Thank you for being here yesterday. I didn't realize how alone I've felt since Stanley and I began this venture. I thought about it all last night, and now I see it started to divide us almost from the start."

"Yes, it's not the kind of problem you share with most friends."

"And I realize it was because I was so panicked and stressed from our money problems that it seemed like an easy way to make money." She frowned.

Eyeing her up and down, Agnes stepped back and crossed her arms. "I hope you brought clothes to change into later. For when Stanley shows up. Because . . ." She pointed to Shirley's sweatpants and T-shirt. "This is not going to help."

Shirley resumed her seat behind the counter. "I haven't slept much in the last five days. I don't have the energy to fuss over what I'm wearing." Earlier, she'd set out a basket full of baby pacifiers. She picked up one and played with it. "Plus, I'm not sure I want him anymore."

"Defensive talk. Like when you tell someone they can't have something, and they tell you they didn't want it anyway."

"Here we are." Lance's voice came through the door before he did.

A tall and square-shouldered woman dressed in a tangerine velour jogging suit and carrying a silver hard-shell case followed him.

"This is Frankie," Lance said. "She's one of our best customers at the Fort Lauderdale store. She's amazing and will have you absolutely fabulous in no time."

Frowning, Frankie looked at Agnes, then Shirley. "Which one gets the makeover?" Her voice was deep and masculine.

Agnes pointed at Shirley. "That's her. She's trying to win

back her husband."

"Maybe not," Shirley said.

"Hush," Agnes hissed.

Frankie shot a dagger-eye at Lance. "It won't be *in no time.* Those are some serious dark circles. This is an emergency."

"Come on, let's set up in the kitchen." Lance led the way. "Shirley, get in here."

Leaning into Agnes on their way, Shirley whispered, "I think Frankie is a man."

"Well, no duh." Agnes chuckled. "It's nice to know you haven't lost *all* your innocent nature during this deranged episode."

***

"Almost done," Frankie said. "Hold still for another couple minutes. I want to try some false lashes on you."

"I don't want them." Shirley eyed the wall clock. It was almost four. "I've seen women with those things. They look like mutant caterpillars."

"Let Frankie do it," Lance said. "If you don't like them, she'll take them off."

Frankie glared at him.

"I've been in this chair for an hour. Why won't you let me see?"

"Relax," Agnes said. "You are ten times better off than you were this morning."

Lance nodded. "It's a miracle."

"No," Frankie said. "It's primer. Some of the girls come into work looking worse than tractor ruts on a cow pie. Primer is what makes the show go on."

"Frankie's from Indiana," Lance said.

"That's right." Frankie did a hula-hoop gyration of the hips. "I'm *Indiana* nice. With twice the spice."

"Are you in show business?" Shirley asked.

"Frankie's a drag queen," Lance said. "I thought you knew."

"Whoo-hoo?" A woman's voice called. "Agnes? Are you here?"

Shirley and Agnes exchanged surprised looks.

As Agnes rose to investigate, Edna appeared in the doorway.

"Hi." Edna waved. Her upper arm flap swung, and her flamingo earrings bobbled. "I *thought* that was your jeep. Then I saw Shirley's car, too, and I thought—isn't this fun? I'll go see what they're doing. I was next door at my dentist's office." She threw her arms up, causing dueling flaps. "Isn't this a coincidence? Are we having a makeover party? Can I get one?"

"Hello, Edna." Nearly speechless, Shirley's mind zoomed ahead on her newest problem. Getting Edna out of the shop as soon as possible.

"This is not a makeover party," Frankie said. "Maybe another time."

Edna stared at Frankie, then turned to Shirley. "Why are you doing this in a baby store? And did you know there's nobody working out there? Isn't that strange?"

***

At four-thirty, Maddy and Fletcher arrived at Catherine's. She pulled up to the front portico and parked.

Fletcher was in awe. "*This*—is your mother's house? It's huge. Did you grow up here?"

She laughed. "No. I grew up in many houses, but Mother didn't buy this one until I was a teenager. I spent those years away at boarding school, so this never felt like home to me."

He walked around and opened her door. "Now I'm more nervous than ever."

"Don't be." She took her keys and unlocked the front door. "Mother?" she called into the vast entry hall. "Mother?

Surprise."

A maid came scurrying down the front stairs. "Miss Madelaine. Hello. I'm afraid you've missed Ms. Catherine. She left not ten minutes ago."

"For the airport?" Maddy said. "She told me she'd be here packing until at least five."

"She left earlier than planned for some reason. I don't know why. All of a sudden, it was 'hurry, hurry, Lucinda.'"

Maddy chuckled. "This is Lucinda. One of the most patient people on earth. It's an unspoken job requirement if you work for my mother." She looked at Fletcher. "Darn. I really wanted to surprise her. And then have her leave. It would have been perfect."

He couldn't help staring at the surroundings. "This is quite a place."

"As long as we're here, I'll show you around," Maddy said.

"After that, I guess we'll head over to my parents' new store."

"Sure. Come on. I'll introduce you to Andre. He's the chef."

***

Stanley sat in his recliner, thinking about the previous few months. Shirley was at the shop, and the townhouse was quiet. His suitcase stood by the stairs.

He'd arrived there in the morning and watched a little TV. Then he steeled himself and ran the errands he needed to. Now on the dining room table were two dozen red roses in a cut crystal vase. He left a note leaning against it.

As his final moment to decide drew closer, he felt total confusion. He did not know any more what would be best for his family. Now Mary Ann—cute little Mary Ann—was having a baby? A teenage mom with no money, an incomplete education, and coming to live at his house. The stress exhausted him.

Hearing a car pull up, he rose from the chair and checked the front window. The cab he'd ordered was idling by the carport.

***

"Violá." Frankie handed Shirley a hand mirror. "Now you may see."

A somewhat familiar face greeted her. Her eyes were rimmed by dark liner, the lids were smoky, and she had refined eyebrows. The fake lashes weren't overly long and didn't resemble caterpillars. Her skin tone was even. "I don't look like me."

"That was the idea," Lance said. "You were haggard before. Stanley's been used to seeing you lately as tired and not the least bit glamorous."

"It feels like I'm in disguise."

"You are beautiful," Frankie said. "If you don't fuss with it, it should last until late tonight."

"Von Cletan can't come close to you," Lance said. "Now you're in contention, baby."

"Shhh." Shirley nodded her head in the direction of the retail area where Agnes was occupying Edna. "Why won't she take the hint?"

Frankie began to pack her cosmetics.

"You were very kind to come help me," Shirley said. "Thank you." She went to join Agnes and Edna. When she neared them, Edna clapped.

Agnes stood a little behind and to the side, rolling her eyes toward Edna.

"Great job. You could pass for ten years younger," Edna said. "Agnes told me this is your store. Aren't you the enterprising one? How come you didn't tell any of us? Now, what's the makeover for? You and Stanley having a big anniversary?"

"Something like that." Shirley touched her on the arm and attempted to lead her toward the door. "Agnes, didn't you say there was a great movie playing at the village tonight? It starts at a special early time, doesn't it? Oh, Edna. I'll bet that's something Morty would want to do."

"Nah," Edna said. "I made him move out a few days ago. He's cheap. I'm on the prowl for a better one. You know, while I'm here, I'll check out your merchandise. My oldest and his wife are expecting their second soon." She wriggled away from Shirley.

The woman had a better nose for gossip than any paparazzi working the Hollywood beat. She trailed Edna, fighting to find a way to get rid of her.

"Uh-oh," Agnes said. "Guess who's here."

Shirley whipped around to see Von Cletan entering. She had on a low-cut red dress with matching red espadrilles and a red alligator purse. No, no, no. What did *she* want? Stanley was due in soon, and the last person they needed there was that evil woman. Marshaling her courage, Shirley hustled to face down her rival. "Mack is not here," she said in a low voice.

Von Cletan leveled a hard glare at her. "I am looking for Stanley." She didn't regulate her voice. "He told me he'd be here this afternoon."

Confusion hit her. Shirley blinked. "Stanley?"

"Now, *Shirley,* don't pretend you don't know who he is." She walked around her and toward the back.

Frozen in place, Shirley began to tremble. He'd told her their real names?

"Just a minute there, Scarlett." Agnes' voice boomed.

Von Cletan turned. "Excuse me? Are you referring to me?"

"You bet." Agnes approached her. "What do you think you're doing?"

Giving her a scathing look, Von Cletan said, "I assure you, it's none of your business."

Lance and Frankie came from the kitchen and stopped in

the archway. Lance's mouth gaped.

"Nice espadrilles," Frankie said.

"Good grief." Von Cletan looked at Frankie. "Aren't you a picture. Move. I must speak with Stanley immediately. He'll want to know I'm here."

"Why?" Edna edged closer.

"You got a problem with me, *sweetheart*?" Frankie said.

"Dear Lord, what kind of pathetic menagerie is this?" Von Cletan made a shooing gesture toward Frankie and Lance. "Get out of my way. I don't have time for this stupidity. We'll miss our flight."

They stood firm.

"*Our* flight?" Shirley said. "You said *our* flight. Who is *our*?"

"Don't play dumb. I have won. You have lost. Muster a little graciousness."

Shirley stared at her, not understanding anything.

"I see," Von Cletan said. "Is it possible he hasn't told you yet? He said he would, but perhaps he thought it would be best to do so right before we leave." She raised her voice. "Stanley? Stanley, I'm waiting."

"The man is not here," Lance said. "Open your ears."

"Let me get this straight," Agnes said. "You think you and Stanley are going somewhere together?"

Edna gasped. "Oh, my God. Shirley, are you and Stanley breaking up?"

"Breaking up?" Von Cletan said. "Really. You make it sound as though there was something there. This is the best for everyone. Shirley and Stanley have been estranged for ages. Stanley is flying to New York with me tonight. Now, if you'll just let me tell him I'm—"

"He isn't here," Shirley said. "And no, he is not going anywhere. You're delusional. There's no way he'd leave, especially right now."

"Why would I believe you?" Von Cletan said. "Everything you've ever told me was a lie. And I have to say, what sort of creature pushes and nags and coerces her husband, however bad the relationship may be, into such a sordid business? You should be ashamed of the way you twisted that poor man around."

"You have no idea what you're talking about," Agnes said.

Anger steamed out of Shirley. "You—are a scheming bitch." She grabbed the giant teddy bear off the display on her right and swung it hard. The bear's head knocked into Von Cletan's.

"Ow. Oh." Von Cletan touched her forehead. "You're an animal." She reared her right hand clenching her purse strap backward, then launched it forward, smacking Shirley in the chest with the purse. "He's in love with *me*, you skinny old hag."

"Can I hit her?" Frankie said. "She's making me want to."

Von Cletan drew her hand back again, looking like she was about to whack Frankie, too.

"No." Agnes stepped in front of Frankie. "That's enough."

The red alligator purse got Agnes right in the nose.

Agnes staggered backward.

"That's it." Frankie grabbed the basket of pacifiers off the counter and began hurling them at Von Cletan—rapid-fire, pummeling her.

"Ow. Stop that." Von Cletan's hands moved like mini-shields in an attempt to deflect them.

"Can't hide," Frankie said, landing one in her cleavage. "I was the cow chip champion four years running."

"Lance, stop him," Agnes said.

"You think you own everyone," Shirley said. "You think you can do whatever you want to other people, including destroy them."

"Everybody stop. What the hell is going on?" a male voice boomed over the noise.

Shirley froze when she realized it was Fletcher. She turned to see him at the entry with a pretty blonde woman beside him.

Frankie dropped the basket. "I'm out of binkies, anyway."

"Mother?" the blonde said. "What are you doing here?"

"Muffin?" Von Cletan said. "Darling, help me. These people belong in a loony bin."

"From the porch, I saw you hit Agnes in the face. You were about to hit that tall . . . *woman*."

"Thank you," Frankie said.

"That was *after* she already hit Shirley." Lance stuck his tongue out at Von Cletan. "You must have missed that part."

"Wait a minute," Agnes said. "Maddy, did you just call the red menace here *mother*? Oh boy."

Catching up with Agnes, Shirley cringed and pointed to the blonde. "Catherine Von Cletan is your mother?" She looked at Fletcher. "And you two *know* each other?"

His face pure confusion, he took the blonde's left hand and lifted it to Shirley's eye level. A gold band gleamed on her ring finger. "Mom, I'd like you to meet my wife, Madelaine Forsyth."

"Mary, Mother of God." Von Cletan teetered, rested a hand against the wall, then slumped to the floor.

"I don't understand any of this," Edna said.

"Me, either, sugar," Frankie said. "Me, either."

CHAPTER SEVENTY-THREE

Shirley couldn't move. She could see and hear, but everything felt fuzzy, like a dream.

Maddy rushed to Von Cletan. She helped her sit and patted her face. "Fletch, can you get me a damp towel?"

He nodded.

"That way," Lance said, gesturing to the kitchen.

"Wow." Agnes rubbed her nose. "All right. Here's what we're going to do." She pointed to Lance. "Take care of Shirley. She looks like she's in shock. You, Frankie, and you, Edna. You're both dismissed."

"But I don't—" Edna said.

"You don't have a choice." Agnes escorted her to the door. "Go on. And for once in your life, do not tell every blooming person you know what happened. If I find out you told anyone, *anyone* at all, I will do something awful to you. Do you understand?"

Fletcher handed the towel to Maddy and, kicking pacifiers out of the way, returned to the kitchen.

"Muffin," Von Cletan said in a weak voice, "please tell me he signed a pre-nup."

"For God's sake, Mother," Maddy said. "Of course, he did. In fact, he brought it up first."

Frankie picked up her case. “I’m going to be late for work if I don’t get going. I’ll make sure Edna drives away safely.” She strong-armed Edna to the porch.

Carrying the two kitchen chairs, Fletcher placed one next to Von Cletan and one by the register counter near Shirley.

Lance put his arm around Shirley. “Come on, sweetie.” He helped her sit, then offered his hand toward Fletcher. “I’m Lance Tillman. Co-owner of Paulina’s, where Shirley used to work.”

Fletcher shook with him. “Fletcher Nowack.” He went to assist Maddy in getting Von Cletan into the chair.

“Great,” Agnes said. “Everybody’s settled.” She addressed Maddy and Fletcher, who stood on either side of Von Cletan. “Is she okay?”

“She’s fine,” Maddy said.

“Now somebody tell us,” Fletcher said, “why and how and when. I’m very confused.”

“Agnes,” Lance said, “you do it.”

“I’ll make this quick,” Agnes said. “Shirley and Catherine, both of you keep your mouths shut. I didn’t know anything about it until a few days ago. It all started, Fletcher, about six months ago. Your parents’ accountant ran off to some island with almost all their money.”

Shirley bent at the waist and placed her head in her hands as she listened to the rest of Agnes’ explanation. She heard the throaty sounds of disbelief from Fletcher, quiet gasps from Maddy, and an occasional *uh-huh* and *that’s right* from Lance. It was humiliating. At one point, she peeked from under her arm at Von Cletan. She sat rigid-straight, listening, and looking like she wanted to kill someone.

“That brings us to now,” Agnes said. “I don’t know—”

The door opened. “Crap.”

Shirley straightened at Stanley’s voice.

“Oh, mercy,” Lance said.

“Stanley.” Von Cletan bounded out of her seat, ran to him,

and gave him a hug. "You're not going to believe what's happened. You didn't tell her yet?"

"Catherine." He sounded artificially calm. He detached himself from her, then scanned the room, stopping at Shirley last. "Catherine, sit down, please."

"Tell her what?" Fletcher stood with a stern face and his arms crossed.

Von Cletan walked back to where she was, but didn't sit.

Stanley seemed stuck, tongue-tied. "I . . . don't know how to explain, and why are you all here? I was expecting to see Shirley alone." He glanced Maddy's way. "Who are you?"

"Maddy, your new daughter-in-law," Agnes said.

"And *my* daughter," Von Cletan said with a huff.

His eyes widened, and a dazed look came over him.

"I finished telling Maddy and Fletcher the whole ridiculous story not a minute before you came in," Agnes said. "You want to tell us what happens next? Your girlfriend over there," she indicated Von Cletan, "claims you two are going away together tonight."

"This is unbelievable," Stanley said. "It's like I'm facing a firing squad. I can't deal with it. I'm sorry." He walked to Shirley and squatted in front of her. "I'm really sorry. But I am doing what I think is best for all of us."

Horror filled her as she realized what he was saying. She started to tremble again.

He spoke softly and touched her cheek. "I left you a note at home. You'll see I made the right choice." He stood. "Let's go, Catherine."

Von Cletan secured her purse strap on her shoulder, stopped to kiss Maddy—who shrank away from her—and with a final glare at Shirley, marched outside.

"I'm so sorry," Stanley said as he left.

CHAPTER SEVENTY-FOUR

Fletcher stared at the door. The store was so quiet, he heard the hum of the refrigerator in the kitchen. He shook, then tilted, his head at Maddy. "My father just ran away with your mother?"

Maddy shrugged with a look of bewilderment.

Shirley erupted into tears.

"Aw, Mom." He stooped and cradled her in his arms. "It'll be okay. I'll make it okay for you."

"I think my head is exploding," Maddy said.

"I'm . . . going . . . to, uh, go." Lance gave Agnes a hug, then turned to Maddy and gave her one. "Shirley, honey?" He knelt by her chair and kissed the top of her head. "I promise I'll help, too." To Fletcher he said, "I'll get your number from Agnes."

Fletcher nodded. His mother's sobs tore at him. "Show us how to close up this place, and we'll take you home."

***

Half an hour later, Fletcher reached for Shirley's arm as she walked from the carport to the townhouse.

"No need," she said. "I'm much better now."

He ran ahead to unlock the door. As he swung it open, he

saw a huge bouquet of red roses in a vase on the dining room table. His father's note was there, as promised.

"Thank you," Shirley said. "Come on in, Maddy. The place isn't fancy like I'm sure you're used to, but it's home. Or it was. Guess I'll be selling it for certain."

"It's a nice home," Maddy said.

"I'll help you as much as I can," Fletcher said. "Maybe you won't have to sell."

"I know someone who can afford to pitch in," Maddy said.

"That's kind of you. But no. Anybody else need coffee?" Shirley went to rinse out the pot.

"I need something a lot stronger than that," Fletcher said. "I'm stuck in stun mode, I think." Indicating she should sit, he pulled out a chair for Maddy. "Mom? Did you happen to see the flowers on the way in?"

"I saw them. Big deal. Do me a favor, throw them out."

As he lifted the vase, Maddy put a hand on his. "Set them outside," she whispered, "she may change her mind."

He did, then went to the cabinet where his father kept the booze. He pulled out a bottle of Bushmill's. "Maddy?"

"Yes," she said. "I'm as stupefied as you. Might as well get a little stupid-er."

He poured two shots and carried them to the table. "Mom, I'll call Nina. You're in no shape to deal with her. She's going to go bat shit."

"Good idea." Shirley hit the coffeepot switch and joined them, taking the seat to the right of Fletcher. "That's his note?"

"Want us to take a walk so you can read it in private?"

"No." Shirley picked up the three by four inch blue envelope and tapped it on the wood. "No. If I'm going to get upset again, I'd rather have you here. I've been alone too much with my heartache in the last few days." Her forefinger traced the envelope's perimeter. "It's all my fault. I blamed him, but it was all my fault." She stared at him.

Her eyes were red and tired. He'd never seen her look so

ragged. "Mom, he left you. I know you're only trying to make me not hate him."

"I pushed him into it. If I'd agreed to sell this place . . ." She sighed. "Who am I kidding? It wouldn't have been enough. We were in deep trouble either way." She patted his hand. "The last thing I wanted was to be a burden to you or Nina." She tsked. "Now look. The whole family is depending on you. I'm sorry." She handed him the note. "You read it. Read it out loud."

"I shouldn't be intruding for this." Maddy rose.

"Nonsense." Shirley waved her down again. "You're family now. And there is nothing in that note that could possibly be more embarrassing than what you've already witnessed."

Fletcher exchanged looks with Maddy. They both nodded in agreement.

"Ain't that the truth," he said.

Shirley laughed.

He stared at her.

"Don't look at me like that," she said. "My life is so pathetic at this point, if I don't laugh, I'll cry more and die from dehydration." She pounded her fist on the table. "You know what? I'll have a shot of whiskey, too. Then you'll read what he has to say."

After pouring an additional shot glass full, he handed it to her. They clinked the tiny glasses.

"To a new life," Shirley said. She downed the shot in one gulp and shivered.

Maddy smiled and did the same.

"Well, I have to slam mine now." He swallowed it all, then opened the envelope. Pulling out a single sheet of folded blue paper, he un-creased it and recognized his father's handwriting covering one side of the page. After almost fifty years, the bastard didn't have much to say at all.

"My dearest Shirley," he read. "We had so many good years together, and I will always be grateful for your love and devotion during them. The events that tore us apart can't be undone. You will never trust me again, I know. And I will have a difficult time forgetting how my sweet and loving wife allowed our circumstances to change her. Our relationship was doomed from the moment I became Mack. That was my fault. I should never have agreed to it. I was scared that if I didn't agree, we'd fall apart from the financial stress. Truth is, I believe we would have been torn apart either way.

"Catherine and I made a deal. I told her about ours and Nina's problems, and she said she'd provide for that, if I left you and came with her. So, to be fair, I divided most of the money she gave me between you, Nina, and Fletcher. Listed below are the details, account numbers, and the name of the accountant who set them up. You each have seven-hundred-fifty-thousand. I know this doesn't make up for what I've done, but at least the financial stress will be gone from your lives. Much love, Stanley."

They sat in silence for a few minutes.

"That was the least she could do," Maddy said.

"Two-point-two-five million dollars?" Fletcher said.

"I think that just made your father the most expensive male prostitute in the history of the world," Shirley said. "I'm stunned. I can't accept it. Not from her." She looked at Maddy. "Sorry. Money or no money, I will never like that woman."

"I'll accept my share," Fletcher said. "I'm going to give half to you and half to Nina."

Maddy nodded. "I understand how you feel, Mrs. Nowack."

"Call me Shirley."

"All right. Consider this. That amount won't make her lose a second of sleep. It's nothing to her. Really. Nothing. She's thrown more than that away on silly indulgences. My mother is worth over four-hundred million, and her estate keeps growing. She'll probably earn at least twice that in dividends and interest this year. You'd be foolish not to let that money help you."

Fletcher felt his jaw drop. "What?"

Grinning, she shrugged. "Surprise?"

"Now I understand why, when she learned we were married, the first words out of her mouth were *pre-nup*."

CHAPTER SEVENTY-FIVE

That Saturday night, Stanley examined himself in the full-length mirror of the suite he and Catherine were staying in at The St. Regis. The charcoal suit he wore was finer than anything he knew existed before, yet Catherine said the custom ones they'd ordered would be even nicer. He couldn't imagine. If only Shirley could see him like this. It was a shame they were never able to travel in style. It was fun, but he missed her. Missed the Shirley she used to be. He'd snuck away to the lobby on Friday and called her. She hung up on him.

Catherine was dressing for dinner in the separate *hers* bathroom. Convinced he was spit-polished enough to pass her inspection, he sat in the ornate living room to wait and turned on the enormous flat screen television. He found a news channel, but drifted into daydreams.

Since Thursday evening when they'd arrived in New York City, he'd already experienced so many amazing things. Everywhere they went, the staff treated him like a king. They spent Friday morning at an attorney's office, who promised he could expedite the issuing of his passport, then they went shopping, and Catherine showed him landmarks he'd never seen. It had been almost twenty years since he and Shirley had visited the city.

He'd attempted to bring up the subject of Fletcher and Maddy several times, but Catherine refused to talk about it. Sooner or later, one of them would call. He was certain it would be Maddy calling her mother. Fletcher probably would never forgive him.

"Here I am." Catherine glided into the room and did a twirl. "How do I look?"

"Very beautiful." With all the weight she'd shed, she now resembled Catherine Deneuve, only with blue eyes. She wore a black lace dress that offered a tantalizing view of her cleavage.

With a saucy glint in her eye, she approached him, leaned closer, and shook her chest near his face.

He poked a finger into the cleft between her breasts. "You'd better be careful. Keep that up and you may never get your dinner."

She laughed and straightened. "Getting dolled up is so much more fun when you have a man who appreciates it. I believe it's time to go." She wiggled her hips. "We'll come home for dessert. Delicious dessert."

They left the suite, rode the private elevator to the lobby, and were met by the concierge who escorted them to their waiting limo.

"This is an exclusive supper club we're going to," Catherine said when they were on their way. "It was established by a dear friend of my late husband's. No one who doesn't belong there is allowed in. I know you'll love it."

"I'm sure I will."

She held his hands in hers and squeezed. "I'm so happy. For the first time in my life, I am truly in love. Tell me you love me."

"I love you." He kissed her cheek, careful not to muss her hair or make-up. The lying came easy to him now. He enjoyed the sex with her. A lot. The more he said he loved her, the better the sex.

The limo pulled to the front of a stone building with a grand arched door made of heavy wood. Expansive plate glass windows faced the street, but although it was already nighttime, no light from inside showed. There was no signage. Several tuxedoed men stood in attendance, and one hustled to open their door.

"The club is called The Penguin," she said. "See why? Old Geoffrey had such a sense of humor." She took the man's hand and allowed him to help her out.

The whoosh of a bus going by as he exited made him turn. It was a busy street. Bicycles, well-heeled pedestrians, and a continuous parade of cabs raced through. He hadn't paid any attention to the driver's route. "Where are we?"

"Greenwich Village."

"Catherine." A man practically ran to greet her inside the door. "It's been so long."

They exchanged air kisses.

Classical piano music floated in the background.

"This is Vincent, Geoffrey's son. And this, Vincent, is my Stanley." Her face lit up.

Vincent raised his eyebrows. "Ah, someone *special.* I see. Hello, Stanley. Your table is ready."

He showed them to a private booth against one of the front windows. From the inside, Stanley saw the action on the street under the outdoor lighting. He wondered what kind of new window tint made that possible, while no one outside could see in at the same time.

Catherine sat in front of the window, and he sat across from her. "Would you rather I sit beside you?" he asked. "On the same bench?"

"No. Not here. This is my favorite perch. I love this view of the club. See over there?" She indicated something behind him.

He twisted. There was a stage about forty feet away. The piano and its player were in the middle of it. "Very nice."

One of the waiters brought a bottle of champagne whose

label Stanley couldn't decipher. He assumed that meant it was expensive. It tasted good. While they were enjoying the bubbly, he studied the décor. It was dim inside, and it took some time for his eyes to adjust.

Bushy palms in fancy stone pots sat above them, on a ledge formed by the top of the window frame. There were four tables in their alcove section. All were filled with beautiful men and women conversing and laughing. The walls were a thick pumpkin-colored velvet.

"The same designer who did my East Hampton house recently supervised the renovation of this club," Catherine said. "I wonder if the budget was cut. It doesn't seem up to her standards. I'll need to have a word with Vincent about it."

"Looks pretty snazzy to me." Stanley paused. "I've been thinking."

"You probably shouldn't do much of that."

He winced.

"The way we met is strange," she said, "but best forgotten. I'll make up a story to tell people when they ask."

A red flag careened through his head. Making up cover stories had just caused a shit load of misery for his family. "No. I was thinking about Maddy and Fletcher. We haven't talked about that situation."

"Nor shall we." She downed the remainder of champagne in her flute.

The waiter hurried to the table, poured more with a serene smile, and left.

"I think we should," he said. "Talk about your weird coincidences."

"He signed a pre-nuptial agreement, which I'll have my lawyer review. I hope it's a good one, because the marriage won't last. Muffin will come to her senses. I'm sure your son is a wonderful person, but not the right one for her. There will be an annulment. So, you see. There is no point in discussing it and putting a damper on our lovely evening."

Stanley was curious how the kids had met, but dropped the subject. Catherine might be right. And she didn't know yet about Fletcher's track record. She seemed agitated, and he tried to put her back into her happy place. He reached for her hand and caressed it. "She's very pretty, your daughter. She looks like her mother."

That brought a lovely smile.

When the main waiter came, they ordered lobster bisque, a complicated salad he didn't recognize half the ingredients of, and Beef Wellington with seasonal vegetables. Other musicians joined the pianist, and they played standards from the forties and fifties. The music sounded great. Several couples got up to dance.

"Would you care to dance?" he asked.

"Love to."

When they made their way to the dance floor, Stanley noticed the club had filled since their arrival. Most the patrons were older, like them. While he led Catherine around the dance floor, he reflected on her incredible lifestyle. As much as he botched up his life, he'd landed in a damned nice sweet spot. He could really get used to it. The ancient city of Rome beckoned.

While eating one of the best meals of his life—every morsel a thrill for his poor deprived taste buds—the ongoing anthill-like frenzy of street and people traffic going past the window never ceased. He wondered about the folks he saw scurrying along, hauling bags, pushing carts. Did they have any idea what luxury lay hidden only a sheet of glass away?

He excused himself to use the restroom. Meandering toward the table again, he felt better than he had in months. He hummed along with the song the orchestra played, *There Will Never Be Another You.*

He was almost to their alcove section when out the window he noticed a bicycle rider had stopped in the street near the curb. It appeared his pant leg was caught in the chain. The man yanked and yanked at it, checking with nervous glances up the street.

As Stanley got closer, the man lost his balance and tumbled into the street. A cab swerved at the last second to miss him. "Move, you idiot." Stanley stopped about ten feet from his booth. "You'll get yourself killed."

"Who are you speaking to?" Catherine said.

"Out there." He nodded behind her.

She twisted in time to see one of the valets from The Penguin rushing to the man.

A bus appeared, headed their way. "Get him off the street." Stanley stood poised to run out there if needed.

"Shhh," Catherine said. "Lower your voice. He'll be fine. Look, another valet is going to help."

The second valet waved frantically at the bus. The driver hadn't seen him, because the bus stayed at the same speed in the same lane. Until it didn't. A second before what would have been a tragic accident, the bus veered to the side and plowed dead-on into a thick and tall green streetlamp post. The crash reverberated through the building.

"Crap." Stanley had been holding his breath. "Hope nobody's hurt on the bus."

Vincent came up to him. "Poor man. That was close." He laughed in the low nervous way of relief that occurred when disaster was narrowly avoided.

"Yes." Stanley turned toward him. "Would have been grisly." He saw Vincent's eyes widen and his mouth moving with no sound coming out. "What's the matter?"

He pivoted in time to see the lamp post falling—right toward the window. "Catherine."

She was facing the stage again and taking a sip from her Remy aperitif.

"Move," he yelled. He'd only taken two steps when the post hit the building with a thunderous bang. There was an unmistakable crack of glass coupled with severe rattling of the metal window frame. And motion higher up. One of the potted palms slid forward and fell. "Move! Duck!"

She wore a perplexed expression as the pot landed on her head. She and the pot fell to the side.

Stunned, he froze for a moment. "Catherine?"

CHAPTER SEVENTY-SIX

A knock rattled the jalousies. Shirley smoothed her hair, put on a bright smile, and opened the door. Seeing who it was, she walked away, leaving it open.

"May I come in?" Stanley said.

"I assume you came for more of your things? Go ahead." She did a double take and assessed the ritzy black suit he wore. "I heard you accompanied the body on the way down. How was the funeral?"

"Crowded. The church was overflowing."

"I thought nobody liked her. Except for you, of course."

"Apparently when somebody rich dies, especially a Sago Beach socialite, everybody comes to gawk and try to get on TV." He gestured to her outfit. "Wow. You look great. New clothes?"

"Thank you." Happy he noticed, she knew she presented a very different appearance than the last time he saw her. She'd gotten a ton of sleep. Stopping short of celebrating Von Cletan's demise, it sure didn't make her unhappy. She *did* feel horrible for her new daughter-in-law. Maddy was a great girl and impressed Shirley with how well she was handling the death, the scandalous behavior—everything. Bless her, she even called that morning to warn that Stanley planned to stop by the townhouse after the funeral in hopes of seeing her.

Shirley called Agnes, and they zoomed to the mall. Now her hair and makeup was perfect, and she wore a flared blue-silk dress that nipped in at her waist. She hoped Agnes was able to pull off the second part of her plan.

Picking up her coffee, she drank some. "If you could at least take everything of yours from the spare room closet, that would help a lot. The kids will need that space."

"Sure. Did you know Fletcher still won't speak to me?"

"*Still*? Why do you expect any different? Stanley, it's only been five days since you ran off with the circus."

He cracked a smile. "I didn't know if you would speak to me either, since you refuse to answer when I call. Maddy has been very fair. We've had to talk a few times concerning the accident and arrangements. She told me Fletcher said Nina would get here this afternoon. She didn't want to stay in Jersey now that she's got plenty of money?"

"No. She wants no chance of running into George. And once she found out about the choice you made, she wanted to be supportive. They're staying here until she finds a place she likes." She rolled her eyes. "God help me."

"I'm detecting a slight note of humor. Is it possible you're thawing toward me?"

"Having the money trouble go away makes a big difference, as much as I hate how it happened. We've been through a lot together. I can be civil to you. A good part of it was my fault." The fact Von Cletan was dead helped, too. Maddy had told Agnes the details of the accident, and Shirley nearly fell over laughing when Agnes shared how she'd died. Agnes said it was bad karma catching up with von Cletan. She warned Shirley not to gloat for the same reason. But it was hard to resist.

"Can I have some coffee? Sit for a spell?"

"Help yourself." She sat at the counter.

He went into the kitchen, poured some, and joined her. "Maddy's a doll."

"Yes. Nothing like her mother."

"Think it'll last?"

She shrugged. "Who the heck knows. Does it matter? Since our disaster, I figure that any amount of happiness two people find together is a good thing. However long it lasts. Celebrate what you've got when you've got it. That's my new motto."

"It's a good one. Want to know where I'm going to be living?"

"No." The last thing she wanted to hear about was Von Cletan's house.

"I rented an apartment about a mile from here. Didn't want to run into our friends from the village all the time."

"What, don't tell me the regal mansion lost its luster because your *beautiful* and *sexy* girlfriend isn't in it fawning all over you."

"That's not fair."

"Sure it is." She raised an eyebrow. "Her lawyers kick you out?"

"I was never in it. I spent the last few days in a hotel. I wasn't her husband. I wasn't her anything."

"You were *my* husband." She frowned.

He nodded. "Something we both chose to ignore."

"When I told Dora and the others we were divorcing, they were shocked. Dora actually cried. They don't know the real *why*. I said we were on each other's nerves all the time and were tired of it. You'd be safe if you wanted to visit Tim and your other friends. So far, it doesn't seem like our dirty little secret made it into the village gossip."

"That's a miracle. You really do look pretty." He reached for her hand.

She whipped it away. "What do you want, Stanley?"

"I think you and I should spend some time alone."

Shaking her head, she felt tears welling. "No. It's too soon." Her eyes locked into his. They projected sadness. Sorrow. Snap out of it, she told herself, he's sad because he watched his girlfriend die. Nothing to do with his wife at all. "I may never want that again. Besides, I thought I was too thin for you now. You like 'em curvier, you said."

His face reddened. "I was angry. I said a lot of things. I'd like to make it up to you. We can finally afford that trip to Paris you've always wanted. I'd love to take you. We can stay in separate rooms if you want."

Standing, she walked around him and sat on the sofa. When Agnes had asked, in the midst of the Von Cletan mess, what she wanted most, she'd answered *I want the financial stress to go away.* And it had. What did she want now? Seeing him in front of her again, she wanted her Stanley back. But Agnes was right. She shouldn't let him assume he could walk back in and pick up like nothing happened. He needed to win her back. And nothing made a man want his woman back more than another man taking her away.

The doorbell rang. She hurried to the front, put on her smile again, and opened the door.

Edna stood there. "Hi, Shirley." She poked her head in. "Oh. Hello, Stanley." She guffawed, then covered her mouth. "Am I interrupting something?"

"Yes," Stanley said.

"No," Shirley said. "Come on in. Stanley, why don't you pour Edna a glass of wine?"

"Thank you," Edna said, walking toward Stanley. "I thought you two were split up."

"Not for sure," Stanley said.

"Yes, we are," Shirley said.

He seemed to sag at that, but he went into the kitchen, took wine glasses from a cabinet, and found the chardonnay in the fridge. He poured two glasses. He handed one to Edna and walked to Shirley with the other.

"No, thank you," Shirley said. "You have it."

The jalousies rattled again. One more time, Shirley smiled like the sun and answered the door. Agnes, Jerome, and a tall, handsome man in his seventies stood there. Agnes had come through. They were dressed for the upscale restaurant they were headed to.

"I'm ready." Shirley gestured inside. "Look who stopped by."

"Oh, hi Stanley," Agnes said. "And Edna's here, too? Gosh, it's a party."

"Hi, Stanley. Edna." Jerome waved. He pointed at the other man. "This is Bob, my kid brother."

"How nice to meet you, Bob," Shirley said in her sweetest voice.

"Well, you *are* just as pretty as a picture," Bob said. "For once, my brother didn't lie."

Shirley stepped out, observing Stanley's reaction as she pulled the door shut behind her. Edna and Stanley stood next to each other holding their wine. Stanley looked shocked. This time, she assured herself, her plan was perfect.

THE END

ABOUT THE AUTHOR

Victoria Landis writes both fiction and non-fiction in multiple genres, including a monthly humor column for *The Parklander Magazine.*

Credits include her 2011 suspense novel, *Blinke It Away,* set on Oahu, chosen as a Reviewer's Pick on Bookrooster.com.

She has been a member of Mystery Writers of America since 2003. Victoria lives in South Florida. She is also an artist.

Please visit Victoria's blog at AuthorVictoriaLandis.wordpress.com.

CPSIA information can be obtained
at www.ICGtesting.com
Printed in the USA
LVHW110930230619
622070LV00001B/76/P

9 781492 907930